UNCTAD/DST/6

UNITED NATIONS CONFERENCE ON TRADE AND DEVELOPMENT
Geneva

Technological Capacity-building and Technology Partnership: Field Findings, Country Experiences and Programmes

Papers prepared for the
Workshop on Selected Cooperation Aspects for
Technological Capacity-building in Developing Countries

held in Geneva, on 10 and 11 April 1995, with the sponsorship of the Technology Partnership Initiative (TPI), Department of Trade and Industry (DTI), and the Overseas Development Administration (ODA), United Kingdom, and the Division for Science and Technology, UNCTAD

UNITED NATIONS
New York and Geneva, 1995

NOTE

The views expressed in this publication are those of the authors and do not necessarily reflect the views of the UNCTAD secretariat.

*
* *

Symbols of United Nations documents are composed of capital letters combined with figures. Mention of such a symbol indicates a reference to a United Nations document.

*
* *

The designations employed and the presentation of the material in this publication do not imply the expression of any opinion whatsoever on the part of the Secretariat of the United Nations concerning the legal status of any country, territory, city or area, or of its authorities, or concerning the delimitation of its frontiers or boundaries.

*
* *

Material in this publication may be freely quoted or reprinted, but acknowledgement is requested, together with a reference to the document symbol. A copy of the publication containing the quotation or reprint should be sent to the UNCTAD secretariat.

UNCTAD/DST/6

UNITED NATIONS PUBLICATION

Sales No. E.95.II.D.6

ISBN 92-1-112374-7

CONTENTS

---

[1]These contributions are concerned essentially with the analysis and description of experiences in technological capacity-building and partnership.

[2]This report was prepared under the project "Technological Capability-Building in Least Developed Countries" (INT/94/A43), funded by the Government of the Netherlands.

[3]*Idem.*

[4]These contributions deal primarily with action programmes and initiatives in technological capacity-building and partnership.

THE WORKSHOP ON SELECTED COOPERATION ASPECTS FOR TECHNOLOGICAL CAPACITY-BUILDING IN DEVELOPING COUNTRIES: INTRODUCTORY NOTE

Background

Rapid technological change has highlighted the growing importance of scientific and technological capacities in determining the economic performance and strength of nations. As suggested in the final report of UNCTAD's Ad Hoc Working Group on the Interrelationship between Investment and Technology Transfer, the process of acquiring such capacities, however, is not instantaneous, costless or automatic, even if the technology is well-diffused. Apart from physical inputs, it calls for various new skills, technical information and services, contract research facilities, interactions with other firms, equipment suppliers and standards' bodies. The setting up of this dense network of cooperation requires the development of special skills and a favourable economic, institutional and legal environment.[5]

To meet the challenge of an increasingly competitive international setting, innovative forms of technological cooperation have spread within the developed countries over the past decade. Such partnerships among firms as well as between firms and R&D institutions, blending capital, technology, know-how, marketing efforts and raw material resources, have contributed to technological capacity-building in the industrialized countries. The diffusion of partnership models has often been accompanied by supportive measures in the host countries, such as government policies, tax incentives and availability of new infrastructure.[6] Strategic alliances and technology partnerships are, however, still largely phenomena of the industrialized countries, and the use of such approaches in developing countries, particularly the least developed countries, has so far remained modest.

Over the past few years, UNCTAD has organized a series of events focusing on new approaches to technological diffusion and innovation, with emphasis on developing countries. These events included workshops on industrial districts (Geneva, 1992), university-enterprise cooperation in Latin America (Buenos Aires, 1993), the transfer and development of environmentally sound technologies (Oslo, 1993), technological dynamism and R&D in the exports of manufactures of developing countries (Colombo; Nyeri; and Guatemala City, 1994) and R&D community-enterprise cooperation and commercialization in the Asian region (New Delhi, 1994).[7] The Geneva Workshop on Selected Cooperation Aspects for Technological Capacity-Building in Developing Countries is the most recent in this series.

---

[5]Final Report of the Ad Hoc Working Group on the Interrelationship between Investment and Technology Transfer (TD/B/40(2)/17-TD/B/WG.5/12).

[6]Singapore's national biotechnology programme is a case in point. Among other elements, the programme incorporates a combination of policies targeting innovative foreign technology companies, created a venture capital pool, provided R&D incentives to companies, and set up a biotechnology research institute. These combined measures have enabled the country to fill certain gaps in national technological development and to leapfrog into biotechnology R&D.Sandor L. Boysen, "Biotechnology strategic alliances: A blending of capital, technology, marketing and raw material resources", *ATAS Bulletin No. 9, Biotechnology and Development*, New York, 1992, United Nations publication.

[7]The latter was organized together with UNCTAD's Division for Economic Cooperation among Developing Countries and Special Programmes (ECDC), in cooperation with the Asian and Pacific Centre for Transfer of Technology (APCTT).

The meeting and its actors

On 10 and 11 April 1995, the Technology Partnership Initiative of the Department of Trade and Industry, and the Overseas Development Administration (ODA) of the United Kingdom, together with UNCTAD's Division for Science and Technology, convened a workshop in Geneva to explore how new strategies for technological innovation could be used to effectively increase technological capacities in developing countries. The present publication was also financed through the same project (INT/94/A65) by the United Kingdom. The Government of the Netherlands provided special support for the preparation of reports on technological capacity-building in four least developed countries, namely Bangladesh, Ethiopia, Nepal and the United Republic of Tanzania.[8]

The Workshop was organized as a follow-up to recommendations made by the UNCTAD Ad Hoc Working Group on the Interrelationship between Investment and Technology Transfer.[9] The Workshop's main objectives were to: (a) examine and recommend specific modalities for follow-up action to foster the technological capacity-building of a selected number of least developed countries, and (b) identify and recommend ways and means for initiating technological partnerships between SMEs of developed and developing countries, with a view to defining proposals for their promotion. The Workshop's ultimate objective was to identify appropriate routes to technological capacity-building in developing countries, whether least developed or more technologically advanced.

Experts represented a broad range of actors engaged in technological innovation in developed and developing countries, including the enterprise sector, as well as institutions involved in bilateral and multilateral technological cooperation. In this context, the main questions addressed were: What specific measures were necessary to induce technological capacity-building in developing countries in general, and more specifically in least developed countries; how innovative strategies for technology development and diffusion such as strategic alliances and technology partnerships could be adapted to the needs of developing countries; and how such forms of cooperation could be used to promote a more effective dissemination of environmentally sound technologies.

Main features of the material presented

While technological capacity-building and partnership issues are closely interrelated, the contributions made to the Workshop have been divided into two groups in this volume: those concerned primarily with the analysis and description of experiences, and those emphasizing action programmes and initiatives.

From the field findings and experiences put forward it appears that a series of steps are necessary to ensure capacity-building in science and technology in the developing countries. These steps include the following: (a) establishing a policy and institutional framework for science and technology which is effectively integrated into the national economy and society. Such a framework would encompass, for example, the identification of clear developmental priorities, and specific measures for S&T policy implementation; the setting up of educational and training institutions adapted to current economic challenges, and of effective user-oriented R&D institutions; (b) the promotion of enterprise development by means of public-private sector consultation mechanisms (for example, through the creation of an enabling environment for entrepreneurship, networking among clusters of

---

[8]Project on Technological Capability-building in the Least Developed Countries (INT/94/A43).

[9]See Final Report of the Ad Hoc Working Group, *op. cit.*, section on Recommendations (TD/B/40(2)/17-TD/B/WG.5/12), para. 31 (a) and (c).

firms in specific critical areas, the provision of advisory services for technology acquisition); (c) establishing a special framework for technology cooperation in the area of environmentally sound technologies, e.g. tapping existing international programmes and facilities for training and financing, passing and enforcing environmental laws, and providing incentives for the utilization of environmentally sound technologies; and (d) reaching out across borders in seeking for diverse forms of technical cooperation on a regional or international level (access to international data banks and technology information services, identification and implementation of firm-level technology partnerships, provision of technical assistance).

In this context, the results of a pilot project carried out in Cape Verde, Jamaica, Pakistan, Togo, Uganda and Viet Nam on Technological Capacity-building in Least Developed and other Low-Income Countries were presented. The project, implemented under the guidance of the United Nations Development Programme and the United Nations Department for Development Support and Management Services, aimed at building an institutional decision-making mechanism that would be country- and demand-driven, at developing a portfolio of initiatives to address the institutional policy framework in each country and at mobilizing domestic and external resources.

From the contributions on Bangladesh, Ethiopia, Nepal and the United Republic of Tanzania several additional elements were drawn, which may also apply to other least developed countries. These included the need to review the present science and technology policies in these countries; the need for assistance in formulating comprehensive science and technology policies, closely integrated with other policies for such areas as trade, education and industry; the importance of identifying a new role for government in creating an appropriate environment for both scientific and technological capacity-building and entrepreneurship; and the recommendation that, in addressing technological capacity-building, the scientific and technological needs and priorities of farmers, small entrepreneurs, women and the poor should be identified.

The contributions made to the Workshop stress the fact that, for technological partnerships, the presence of basic scientific and technological capacities as well as of a cluster of small and medium-sized enterprises is essential. In this context, various papers described aspects related to technology partnership initiatives at the regional level, and interregionally, bilaterally and multilaterally. The experiences reviewed range from promoting, and providing incentives to, direct firm-to-firm partnerships, to training and to the need to focus on the adoption of environmentally sound technologies.

With regard to technology partnership, various recommendations addressed to governments, economic actors and the international community are contained in the contributions to the Workshop. It was considered critical, for example, that countries should formulate policies for strengthening human resource development and training possibilities, for creating an infrastructure and an environment conducive to entrepreneurs and small- and medium-sized enterprises as well as for establishing mechanisms to help in mobilizing financial resources. Foreign investors should be encouraged to engage in partnerships with enterprises from developing countries to increase their scientific and technological capacity. Support institutions for technical and information services are essential as well as programmes sponsored by the international community to strengthen entrepreneurship in developing countries.

With regard to partnerships involving environmentally sound technologies, additional obstacles to be overcome may be the relatively higher cost of such technologies (compared to conventional ones), a lack of financial resources on the part of developing country firms to carry out initial investments, and insufficient access to information on such new technologies or on possibilities for the adaptation of existing ones. The experiences of specific programmes providing training and concentrating on the sourcing of information were outlined as useful tools for promoting technology partnership in this domain.

The Workshop's interactions and outcome

The presentation of the papers at the Workshop and the exchange of experiences on different forms of technological development stimulated a constructive debate, and resulted in a number of recommendations and suggestions on ways to improve capacity-building measures in the developing countries, as well as on partnerships between firms from developed and developing countries.[10]

A number of conclusions and recommendations were formulated concerning technological capacity-building in the developing countries, with special emphasis on the LDCs. Thus, UNCTAD should undertake a programme to develop strategies for assisting interested LDCs in technological capacity-building. The programme would include elements such as: revisiting the changing role of the State and designing ways in which the donor community could best enhance the capacity to link macro-level policies to micro-level activities in S&T development and foster the activities of R&D institutions; projects to review the technology content of existing development assistance programmes concentrating on the private sector, with a view to broadening their scope for technological capacity-building; a pilot project to undertake S&T policy reviews in selected countries; a project to explore collaboration between firms in LDCs and in developed countries in the field of new and emerging technologies, with special emphasis on the possibilities of building on existing technological capabilities; a project to assist LDCs to implement the decisions of the Uruguay Round Agreement relating to science and technology.

With regard to the promotion of technology partnering between developed and developing country firms, the experts recommended that UNCTAD, in cooperation with other actors in the international community, should seek ways of deepening the concept and scope of technology partnership, of operationalizing the concept and of initiating policy-oriented pilot projects. The Workshop regarded partnerships as new forms of technology cooperation that were no longer "one-way", but involved longer-term mutual benefits for partners, as well as the "upgrading" of the technological capacity of firms from the developing countries (in terms of technological hardware as well as of "software" such as training). It was also felt to be crucial to draw the attention of the international community to the strategic role of such partnerships for increasing the technological capacities and competitiveness of developing countries.

---

[10] For the highlights of the discussion and the Workshop's full recommendations, see the Report of the Workshop on Selected Cooperation Aspects for Technological Capacity-building in Developing Countries (UNCTAD/DST/7).

PART ONE

FIELD FINDINGS AND EXPERIENCES

This part essentially reviews experiences related to technological capacity-building and partnership

FOSTERING TECHNOLOGICAL CAPACITY-BUILDING IN ETHIOPIA AND THE UNITED REPUBLIC OF TANZANIA

by
Samuel M. Wangwe
Executive Director, Economic and Social Research Foundation,
Dar es Salaam

INTRODUCTION

The purpose of this contribution is to facilitate discussion in the Workshop in examining and recommending specific modalities for follow-up action to foster the technological capacity-building of selected least developed countries. This paper covers two such countries: Ethiopia and the United Republic of Tanzania.

These two countries are among the poorest in the world with an income per capita of US$110 per annum in both cases. Even compared to other countries in Africa they rank among the poorest. Some development indicators are shown in the table below.

Some Development Indicators: Ethiopia and the United Republic of Tanzania

	Ethiopia	United Republic of Tanzania
GNP per capita in US dollars 1992	110	110
Population mid-1992	54.8 mill	25.9 mill
Annual growth of GNP per capita 1985-92	-2.0	1.9
Life expectancy at birth in 1992 (in years)	49	51
School enrolment (per cent) - primary (1990)	31	69
School enrolment (per cent) - secondary (1990)	13	5
Net ODA per capita 1992 (in US$)	22	52
Gross domestic investment as a percentage of GDP (1986-92)	13.3	34.6

Source: *African Development Indicators* 1994-95, World Bank: Washington, D.C., 1995.

Both countries have introduced policy reforms towards a market economy. The process of policy reform is directed towards improving resource mobilization and its efficient utilization with a view to enhancing growth performance and revitalizing development. The implementation of such reforms has become increasingly complex with a shift from narrow concerns with macroeconomic imbalances and stabilization towards more comprehensive institutional reforms. In this regard, the United Republic of Tanzania has gone further (since 1986) than Ethiopia, as the latter introduced policy reforms only in 1991-1992.

In both countries, deteriorating human well-being has been associated with difficulties in the deployment of resources to meet essential social needs, especially in the key areas of human resource development such as education and health. Yet growth and structural transformation call for higher levels of literacy and educational attainment and a healthy labour force.

In their efforts to implement policy reforms these countries have received assistance from the donor community. However, due to budgetary constraints in most donor countries there has been little improvement in the external resource inflow in recent years and the outlook continues to be uncertain. Over and above facilitating short-term stabilization and adjustment, the external resource inflow will need to be linked more closely to long-term development objectives. This will also call for improvements in aid coordination and aid quality to enhance aid effectiveness in adapting to special conditions of individual countries. Indeed in both countries strong concerns were expressed regarding the need to enhance the effectiveness of aid.

The policy reforms in both countries have made a turn around in the rate of economic growth. However, they have not succeeded as yet in promoting structural change and economic transformation. Supply constraints in the productive sectors have largely persisted. Productivity in agriculture, the dominant sector, remains low and dependent on weather, and sustainable diversification of their economies has largely remained elusive. Low productivity in agriculture poses a threat to the living standards of the majority of the population and threatens the competitiveness of exports which are predominantly agriculture-based products.

I. ETHIOPIA

A. The economy

The economy of Ethiopia was opened to the rest of the world after the Second World War, with coffee and hides and skins as the major exports. The infrastructure was geared to serving the export-import trade. In the early 1960s Ethiopia began to pursue an industrialization strategy based on import substitution with successively high tariffs being introduced to support the establishment and development of local industry.

Agriculture is the dominant sector in the economy. To date, however, the agricultural sector is still backward in the technology it uses and in the level of productivity. Industry has remained small and import dependent.

Early development efforts in Ethiopia were mainly devoted to putting in place social, economic and physical infrastructures. The economy grew at an average rate of 4.3 per cent per annum during 1960-1973.

Between 1974 and 1991, Ethiopia was basically a command economy, with the State attempting to determine resource allocation and distribution of output by administrative fiat. The decision-making freedom of private economic agents was curtailed during this period. From 1974 to 1990 the rate of growth of the economy decelerated to 1.5 per cent per annum. With population growing at 2.9 per cent this meant a decline of income per capita at the rate of 1:4 per annum. In particular, after 1988-1989 the economy faced a decline in output with real GDP falling by 1.6 per cent in 1989-1990, 0.3 per cent in 1990-1991 and 10 per cent in 1991-1992.[11] Income per capita during those years declined by 4.3 per cent, 3.2 per cent and 12.6 per cent respectively.

After 1991, Ethiopia decided to shift towards a market economy and promote private sector development. This also implies that the role of the State in economic management will need to change. The Government is

[11] *Survey of Current Economic Conditions in Ethiopia*, Inaugural Edition, vol. 1, No. 1. A publication of the Policy Analysis Unit, Ministry of Planning and Economic Development, Addis Ababa, Ethiopia, January 1993.

determined to work through the market rather than against it. In 1992-1993, GDP growth recovered to 7.6 per cent over the preceding year. Agriculture grew at 4.9 per cent while industry grew at 12.9 per cent. The industrial sector suffered a slight decline in 1993-1994 partly because of infrastructural constraints (e.g. power cuts), lack of demand, shortage of inputs and aging machinery. For instance, a road conditions survey of December 1992 showed that 60 per cent of the length surveyed needed periodic maintenance, rehabilitation or reconstruction (*Economic Reform Performance Impact Analysis*, Vol. 1, No. 4, May 1994).

The Ethiopian economy is dominated by agriculture, which accounts for over 45 per cent of GDP. During 1992-1993, the agricultural sector GDP increased by 4.9 per cent. The main factors behind this recovery were good weather, improved macroeconomic stability and liberalization of agricultural markets.

The industrial sector contributes 12 per cent to GDP of which one third comes from the handicrafts and small-scale industries. The sector absorbs 3 per cent of the total labour force, of which nearly half is accounted for by those industries.

The Investment Code was revised in May 1992 with a view to encouraging domestic and foreign private investment. This investment proclamation liberalized both local and foreign private investment. Foreign investors, in particular, are encouraged to invest or participate in areas that facilitate the transfer of technology and know-how (Tadesse, 1995).[12] By the end of 1994 over 1,200 projects had been licensed with a total capital of 8959.5 million birr (*Report on Macroeconomic Development in Ethiopia*, December 1994). However, the rate of project implementation has remained low; only 10.5 per cent of licensed projects are under implementation and 7.7 per cent have become operational.

Public sector reform has taken the form of privatization through the sale of assets and through commercialization and increased autonomy of management.

Policy reforms were effected in 1992. The stabilization and structural adjustment measures taken include devaluation of the birr from 2.07 to 5 birr to one dollar. In May 1993 foreign exchange auctions were introduced as a first step towards a flexible exchange rate regime.

Trade policy reform consisted of liberalization measures including the removal of export taxes and subsidies and the restructuring of tariffs.

Infrastructural constraints are further illustrated by the aging fleet of trucks. About half the government trucks and three quarters of private operators' trucks were over nine years old in mid-1993. Since the end of 1992, however, foreign exchange made available through the Ethiopian Recovery and Reconstruction Programme (ERRP) and favourable credit terms extended by the commercial banks have made it easier for private transport operators to import new trucks.

The previous import financing scheme referred to as the Franco-valuta mechanism (scheme of own imports) was operative during 1977-1992 but too few potential investors had access to this facility.

---

[12] See Tadesse, Getahun, "Ethiopian Scenario for Technological Capacity-Building" in the present volume.

The main development objectives of Ethiopia are:[13]

(i) to replace a command economy by a market economy;

(ii) to enhance popular participation in economic activities and the decision-making process with particular attention to decentralization of control over resources for regional authorities;

(iii) to effect the transformation of the existing economic structure;

(iv) to bring about a structural transformation in the productivity of peasant agriculture, and to pursue an agriculture-led industrialization strategy based on the use of local resources including labour (using labour-intensive technology). Among other things, transitional economic policy has stressed the expansion of the rural road network, the expansion of the distribution and use of fertilizers and improved seeds, and the strengthening of extension services for agricultural workers and pastoralists;

(v) to forge links between various sectors of the economy, especially between agriculture and industry;

(vi) to enhance the expansion and diversification of exports.

B. Science and technology

The transitional Government of Ethiopia has identified S&T development and its utilization as one of the priority sub-programme areas under the Human Resource Development and Utilization Programme. It is recognized that specific measures are required to overcome scientific and technological backwardness in order to pave the way for realization of the potential for development.

(a) Science and technology: the institutional framework

The S&T policy document is intended to serve as a basis for formulating detailed policies and programmes for specific sectors. A few sectors have already formulated their policies based on the national science and technology policy (e.g. health, industry, natural resources).

According to the S&T policy document, local technological capabilities have to be built up in several areas: R&D; development of traditional technologies; technology transfer, adaptation and application; engineering design and consultancy; S&T human resources training and development; collection and dissemination of S&T information; and popularization of S&T.

The organizational structure of the S&T system in Ethiopia has four functional levels:

(i) National S&T Council: this is the highest decision-making body for S&T policy and action plans. It is chaired by the Prime Minister and its members include eight sectoral ministers and three prominent professionals.

(ii) The Technical Advisory Committee of the National S&T Council: it is composed of scientists and professionals under the Chairmanship of the Commissioner for S&T. This Committee prepares matters to be discussed and decided upon at the Council.

---

[13] *An Economic Development Strategy for Ethiopia: A Comprehensive Guidance and Development Strategy for the Future*, Ministry of Planning and Economic Development, Addis Ababa, September 1993.

(iii) Science and Technology Commission: this is a government institution accountable to the Prime Minister. It is the central organ for planning, promoting, coordinating, financing and overseeing S&T activities in the country.

(iv) S&T Operational Institutes and Centres: these are responsible for the actual performance of S&T activities in specific sectors.

This organizational structure was proposed in the National S&T Policy of December 1993. It is still too early to assess the operational results.

S&T development is coordinated by a national body, the Ethiopian Science and Technology Commission, which was created in 1975. This body has not had supportive institutions at regional and sub-regional levels. It has also lacked clear policy guidance as the national S&T policy was only issued recently.

The S&T policy sets out policy guidelines, priority sectors and funding proposals (e.g. recommending that 1.5 per cent of GDP be allocated to S&T).[14] The S&T policy emphasized R&D activities in areas of basic research and appropriate technologies for Ethiopia's socio-economic conditions and capacity-building in technology transfer, adaptation and improvement of traditional technologies. The involvement of the private sector in the promotion of S&T activities is also emphasized.

The S&T policy document of December 1993 is a considerable improvement over the past situation when no science and technology policy was documented. However, one major gap is notable in the new policy document in that it falls short of articulating the linkage of economic policy instruments to the guidelines it contains so as to enhance realization of the stated objectives. In addition, it does not engage in a comprehensive review of the experiences (positive and negative) of the past with a view to building on their strengths and tackling their weaknesses. The current science and technology policy is a broad statement, which is intended to guide specific sectors and institutions in formulating their plan of activities. Since December 1993 when the S&T policy was promulgated, the specific sectors and institutions have already formulated their science and technology policies. However, the integration of S&T policy into economic policy has not been realized as yet.

The document on Technology Transfer Regulation No. 12/1993 is intended to encourage, expand and coordinate investment and technology transfer and guide the choice of technology (Tadesse, 1995).

About 12 supportive service organizations were initiated as autonomous organizations or as departments under sectoral ministries. Some 50 R&D institutes exist under various ministries, or under international and regional organizations.

In the agricultural sector, the Institute of Agricultural Research (IAR) is the principal institution engaged in conducting and coordinating agricultural activities at national level. Its research programme covers 12 research areas and is implemented through its 12 centres located in different agro-ecological zones in the country. Other institutions are: universities and colleges engaged in training and research; the National Veterinary Research Institute; the Rural Technology Centre; and the various organs of the Ministry of State Farms, Coffee and Tea Development.

---

[14]The Transitional Government of Ethiopia, Ethiopian Science and Technology Commission, *National Science and Technology Policy*, Addis Ababa, December 1993.

The activities of these R&D institutions are dispersed, and they lack research personnel and facilities and efficient organizational and administrative systems for research activities.

The institutional infrastructure for design and R&D activities in the water sub-sector is weak. The recent establishment of the Arba Minch Water Technology Institute should improve the supply of medium- and high-level trained human resources in water technology, and thereby contribute to strengthening R&D activities in the water sub-sector.

The energy sector is reported to have great potential but its exploitation has been limited. The absence of a clear policy, weak institutional capacity and a lack of coordination have contributed to this situation. The institutions engaged in R&D activities in the energy sector are: the Ethiopian Energy Authority, Ethiopian Light and Power Authority, Addis Ababa University and the Ethiopian Geothermal Survey.

In industry there are a few metal and engineering industries that have some capacity to adapt, develop and produce technologies for the economy. But their capacity is generally limited. Organized industrial research along sub-sectoral lines is just being considered. The Industry S&T Policy which was issued in 1994 aims at facilitating local technological capacity-building through strengthening R&D efforts, improving support services, promoting an appropriate technology transfer system and reinforcing the linkage between modern and traditional sector technologies. Small and medium-sized industries are given special attention (Tadesse, 1995).

The Industrial Project Service offers a multidisciplinary consultancy service to industry in the areas of planning, engineering, project implementation, evaluation and rehabilitation studies, and organizational studies (Tadesse, 1995).

In construction, R&D activities have been conducted in building materials only but these activities are scattered among different institutions and are not coordinated.

In mining, the establishment, in 1982, of the Ethiopian Mineral Research Development Corporation to develop precious and industrial metallic minerals of commercial importance has contributed to the diversification of minerals other than gold and platinum. The R&D efforts require adequate resource allocation and a proper legal framework.

The health sector has R&D institutions which are engaged in research either as their major function or as part of their main activities. The Ethiopian Nutrition Institute, the Institute of Pathobiology, the National Research Institute of Health and the Armans Hausen Research Institute have research as their main function. Others such as the universities, the Ethio-Swedish Paediatric Clinic, the Coordinating Office of Traditional Medicine and the Jimma Health Sciences Institute undertake health research as part of their central activities.

The principal deficiency in the structure and organization of S&T is the lack of vertical and horizontal coordination and integration of S&T efforts. There are over 18 technical and vocational schools and institutes in the country. These are afflicted by quality problems similar to those found in primary and secondary education. In addition there are other specialized institutions. On-the-job technical education is also offered through apprenticeship, in-house training and other types of formal training by enterprises. These training efforts lack coordination and are too confined to their respective enterprise requirements to the extent of compromising on the overall systematic development of technological capabilities.

S&T activities have been rendered less effective by the lack of policy guidance, inadequate human resources training and infrastructure limitations.

The educational system has little S&T content, the quality of education and of teachers is low and the student-teacher ratio is unsatisfactory.

The S&T sub-programme covers three main components: capacity-building for the formulation of the S&T master plan and development of technologies for rural needs; development of S&T support services; and development of selected S&T institutional infrastructure support for industry.

S&T policy planning is most limited at sectoral and regional levels.

(b) The enterprise sector: status and prospects

Interviews with the business community indicated that there is support for the shift towards a market economy and associated policy papers concerned with investment policy, revised labour laws, trade liberalization and exchange rate action. However, there are still problems deriving from land policy, which allows private agents to lease but not to own land.

The private sector expressed further concern over the paucity of information on technology and the weak link to R&D activities in the public sector. The private sector business community perceives that if there is indeed a weak link between public R&D institutions and public enterprises the link is that much weaker between R&D institutions and private enterprises. It was pointed out that officials in most public institutions still prefer to deal with public enterprises and that the private sector is still struggling for recognition. While the intention to carry out reforms has been appreciated in practice it is perceived that the old habits have not changed significantly. Investors continue to face problems of visas and import formalities. In addition, investment procedures are still associated with many bureaucratic hurdles.

Local industrialists in the private sector also referred to the absence of support for transfer of technology and technology innovation efforts.

Local investors noted that it is difficult to gain access to affordable investment finance from development banks and other financial institutions. They expressed concern that the terms of lending are too harsh (high interest rates, too short a grace period) and that venture capital is hard to obtain.

Visits were made to two enterprises. One is an innovative small private sector firm manufacturing rubber parts for other industries. The second is the Engineering Design and Tool Enterprise, a public sector R&D institution which has become a public enterprise since October 1993. The private sector firm began on a very small scale using very simple locally sourced technology. The environment of import restrictions existing at that time had starved industry and transport sectors of the spare parts they needed. This firm started supplying these sectors with a wide variety of the rubber parts they needed. Partly facilitated by import controls and partly because of the limited investment resources available to the entrepreneur, most of the equipment used was also manufactured in-house. This enterprise has been growing steadily and making continuous technological improvements, benefiting from consultations initiated with the local university chemistry laboratories. The technological improvements that this firm has been making have facilitated its survival even in the post-liberalization phase. The entrepreneur behind this successful story, however, admits that the survival of this firm has not been easy and on many occasions he had to struggle against various aspects of a less than favourable policy environment.

The public sector R&D institution has been required to go commercial and to rely less on grants from the Government. The shift from a government department to a public enterprise has led to a shift in its approach in the direction of adaptations and reverse engineering and away from "reinventing the wheel" and duplication, since the immediate objectives of the enterprise are to develop technological capability in design, in the development of prototypes and in the design of tools.

However, trade liberalization has meant that clients have options to import many items. This has contributed to reducing the orders that come from industry. This suggests that under a liberalized trade regime the pattern of demand from clients is likely to alter, posing a challenge to suppliers to come to terms with the changing demand conditions. In such cases the State may also be called upon to manage markets if their unpredictability and volatility are holding back private sector development.

The enterprise in question pursues both R&D activities and purely commercial activities. In the case of the former, some financing is available from the S&T Commission for specific R&D projects.

In its design activities, three possible approaches may be adopted depending on the circumstances: customers may bring samples, they may come with their own designs, or they may come with ideas, which the enterprise can use to make designs and undertake manufacturing.

II. UNITED REPUBLIC OF TANZANIA

A. The economy

The economy of the United Republic of Tanzania enjoyed a reasonably high rate of growth in the 1960s (5-6 per cent), decelerating to 3-4 per cent per year in the 1970s and stagnating at the height of the economic crisis in the first half of the 1980s. During 1980-1985 the growth of the economy averaged 1-2 per cent per year. Agriculture stagnated (growing at 0.6 per cent per year), while the industrial sector declined by 4.1 per cent p.a. with capacity utilization falling to 20-30 per cent. The effect of the stagnation of export volumes was exacerbated by the deterioration of the terms of trade. The economic crisis took a heavy toll on human resource development, especially as the capacity to provide basic health and education services was being eroded.

The structure of the economy is still dominated by agriculture (43.8 per cent of GDP and 80 per cent of employment in 1993). Industry[15] is still quite small, accounting for 16.2 per cent of GDP of which 8.9 per cent was accounted for by manufacturing in 1993 (*Economic Survey* for 1993).

Exports are dominated by traditional primary commodities such as coffee, cotton, tea, cashew nuts and tobacco. These five commodities accounted for about 60 per cent of export earnings in 1993.

For the past 9-10 years the United Republic of Tanzania has been engaged in reorienting the economy away from reliance on administrative control mechanisms (for resource allocation and distribution) towards greater reliance on market forces. The reorientation towards a market economy has consisted of various types of price reform (for foreign exchange, capital and goods and services), fiscal and monetary reform and public sector reform.

Economic performance has shown some improvement, with the growth of GDP averaging about 4 per cent during 1986-1993, up from 1-2 per cent during 1980-1985. This growth performance may not be sustainable, however, unless policies continue to focus on various institutional reforms especially in the financial sector, public sector reform and promotion of private sector investment, trade reform (especially agricultural marketing) and improvement of infrastructure (physical, social and economic) for socio-economic development.

The effectiveness of this growth performance is being called in question, particularly as regards poverty alleviation and economic

---

[15] Industry here is considered to consist of mining, manufacturing, electricity, water and gas and construction.

transformation. This raises the broader question of the role of these economic reforms in realizing longer-term development objectives. The priority long-term objectives for the United Republic of Tanzania consist of revitalizing the productive sectors and raising the level of productivity there, trade restructuring, especially of the export sector, and the pursuance of human resources development. The role of science and technology and the fostering of technological capabilities are central in the realization of these long-term development objectives.

B. Science and technology: the institutional framework

The Tanzania Commission for Science and Technology was established in 1986 as the principal organ charged with the responsibility of advising the Government on all matters relating to scientific research and technology development.

The Commission operates under the Ministry of Science, Technology and Higher Education. The national policy on science and technology, which was first formulated in 1985 and is being revised, is the principal guide for the activities of the Commission. The Commission maintains a system of collaboration, consultation and cooperation with national R&D institutions. Existing R&D institutions are organized sectorally, covering agriculture, livestock, fisheries, forestry, wild life, food and nutrition, building, industry, health and standards.

The Commission has established R&D advisory committees as its principal organs for coordinating the scientific and technological research carried out in the country in the respective fields. The existing R&D advisory committees cover agriculture and livestock; natural resources; environmental research; industrial and energy research; public health and medical research; basic sciences; and social sciences. Every R&D advisory committee is responsible for advising the Commission on research policy and priorities; allocation of research funds; coordination of research and extension services; human resources development; and national and international cooperation.

The Centre for the Development and Transfer of Technology (CDTT) is the principal organ of the Commission responsible for matters relating to the transfer, adaptation, development, absorption and diffusion of technology. The long-term goal of CDTT is to create in the United Republic of Tanzania an enabling environment for self-reliance in technology through technological capacity-building. The functions of CDTT include facilitation of transfer of technology; development, promotion and commercialization of local technologies; technology prospecting and assessment; and technology policy analysis. CDTT has four programme areas: industrial technologies, rural technologies; energy technologies; and new and emerging technologies. The Centre also envisages offering various services, including industrial and technological information services; a technology promotion service; a technology advisory service; and evaluation services on technology transfer agreements.

The Act establishing the Commission provides for the establishment of a National Fund for the Advancement of Science and Technology to be utilized for scientific research, human resource development in science and technology and financing technological development.

C. Science and technology in practice: functions of the institutions and S&T problems

The only R&D institutions that existed in the United Republic of Tanzania before 1970 were the agricultural research institutions. These institutions focused on research on export crops such as cotton, coffee, tea and tobacco. Broader developments of the science and technology infrastructure occurred in the 1970s, starting with the establishment of the faculty of engineering at the University of Dar es Salaam in 1973 and a series of other

R&D institutions in the late 1970s and early 1980s.[16] Most of these R&D institutions are oriented more towards technology development than basic research.

The institutional framework for the development of science and technology has been put in place. In practice, however, the functions of this institutional framework give rise to several issues of concern. The following are some of the key concerns that were raised during the field visit:

(i) The level of technological capability in the United Republic of Tanzania is low, as indicated by the paucity of technological innovation, small output of scientific publications, low levels of productivity in all sectors of the economy and the weak state of human resource development, especially in the scientific and technological fields. In particular, enterprises lack a critical mass of qualified human resources. The situation is aggravated by the inadequate level of managerial capability in some institutions. A major challenge for human resource development is to be found in the educational system. Both primary and secondary educational curricula fail to make sufficient provision for science teaching. Whatever science education is offering may need to be reviewed and restructured to cope with the demands of new and emerging technologies. There is also a need for restructuring in respect of technical education and higher education. Given the narrowness of public sector employment policy, greater encouragement needs to be given to self-employment and other private sector employment opportunities. This shift of attention may call for the reorientation of the educational and training system towards the managerial, business and technical skills that are needed for the generation of self-employment or private sector development.

(ii) The effectiveness of technology transfer through technology flows from outside the country has been limited, and technological learning effects from imported technology have been scanty. What effects there have been can be ascribed mainly to limited technological efforts to adapt, absorb and internalize the technology flows. This is largely explained by the policy environment which, for many years (since 1967), was not conducive to enterprise development and especially to technological innovations. The policy environment was a trade regime characterized by a overvalued exchange rate, high levels of protection and restrictive import licensing, a pricing system based on cost-plus pricing, and widespread replacement of market forces by administrative controls in the allocation of resources (credit, foreign exchange, investment finance, human resources).

(iii) The system of coordination and cooperation among various institutions and other actors in R&D is not as effective as it is supposed to be. In practice, the Commission remains marginalized from the mainstream of government policy-making and decision-making processes. Moreover, scientists and technologists lack contacts with decision-makers.

(iv) Locally developed technologies have been limited but even those that exist have not been fully utilized and developed commercially. The rate of commercialization and utilization of the few R&D results has been low. This is a reflection of the weak link between R&D institutions and the enterprise sector, which inhibits the generation and commercialization of local technologies. In many R&D institutions and even in producing enterprises managerial and marketing capabilities are on the low side.

(v) The flow of industrial and technological information within the country and between the United Republic of Tanzania and the rest of the world leaves

---

[16]These include the Tanzania Industrial Research and Development Organization, Tanzania Engineering Manufacturing and Design Organization, Institute for Production Innovation, Centre for Agricultural and Rural Mechanization and Appropriate Technology and Tanzania Bureau of Standards.

much to be desired. In particular, the technological delivery system serving the enterprise sector is weak.

(vi) The Investment Promotion Centre has little capacity in terms of personnel and information to analyse the technology aspects of investment projects. The IPC is ill-equipped in terms of human resources and physical infrastructure to promote transfer of technology and process application from high technology firms. These deficiencies could be reduced through networking with R&D institutions but such networks have not yet been established. In spite of the efforts at economic reform that have been made over the past 10 years many industrialists and other private investors still believe that the policy environment is not conducive to investment.

(vii) Industry associations have a potentially important role in technological capability development. For instance, MEIDA, with close to 200 members all from the metal and engineering sector, organizes training programmes. However, the training offered is considered too general. Although MEIDA has good contacts with its members, it lacks adequate databases to service them, especially after economic and trade liberalization. Trade liberalization has made it possible for enterprises to have access to imports without having to go through MEIDA and has changed the information requirements of enterprises. Industry associations like MEIDA need to redefine their roles to cope with the needs of their members in the new environment of liberalization, market orientation and private sector development.

(viii) R&D budgets are too small to allow for ventures into new product lines. The main problem is the absence of financing mechanisms for technology innovation. A National Fund for the Advancement of Science and Technology (NFAST) has been proposed by the Commission but it is not yet operative. A Venture Capital Fund was created towards the end of 1993 but it is not yet operational.

III. TECHNOLOGICAL CAPACITY IN ETHIOPIA AND THE UNITED REPUBLIC OF TANZANIA

In both Ethiopia and the United Republic of Tanzania the levels of technological development are low.

In the two countries, the process of building local technological capabilities has been limited by the failure of investment to recover from low levels, inadequate allocation of resources to science and technology for development, failure to expand and restructure the export sector, the lack of diverse and sophisticated skills to cope with challenges from recent technological advancements and weak linkages between efforts of local R&D institutions and the productive sectors.

In both countries it was found that there is a mismatch between the supply of and demand for human resources. While there is a shortfall of some professions and skills there is a surplus of others. It seems that academic and training institutions do not supply trained human resources in response to the demands of users (e.g. industry). This suggests that there is a need to revisit the educational and training system with a view to establishing the new and emerging human resource requirements in the light of new developments in technology and policy reforms.

It was also found that, while training is going on unabated, many graduates are finding it difficult to become absorbed into economic activities while other educated employees are facing retrenchment. The question arises as to what can be done to reduce the gravity of this problem of unemployed educated personnel. The main difficulty is that the Government, formerly the largest employer of graduates and other professionals, is under pressure to retrench while the private sector is still too small to provide sizeable employment. This being so, one option would be to turn these educated job seekers and victims of retrenchment into self-employed people. This option may involve the introduction of crash courses and training programmes for these groups to help them to manage the transition into self-employment.

As regards human resource development, special attention will need to be paid to continuous upgrading of various skills. The public and private sectors have a supportive role to play in training at all levels, including formal education, technical and vocational training and various forms of enterprise level training. In order to cope with the rapid technological changes, training and learning from experience will need to be a continuous activity at the various levels, while closer linkages will need to be forged between training and institution-building and the production sector. It may even be necessary to structure the educational and training systems in line with the changing requirements of the productive sectors.

The problem of low and stagnating investment has important adverse implications for technology flows. The challenge in this respect is to devise ways and means to enhance policies and institutional arrangements that are conducive to the promotion of investment and technology flows. Particular attention may need to be paid to promoting small and medium-sized enterprises to enable them to engage in the transfer and development of technology.

Given that the role of non-government sectors is being promoted in these countries (e.g. through public sector reform), articulation of the needs and requirements of the productive sectors will be enhanced by closer collaboration between the business community, researchers and government in policy formulation.

The transfer and adaptation of foreign technology to local conditions are critical in the process of technological capacity-building. Different forms of technology transfer can be adopted in different combinations as a way of developing technological capabilities. Forms of technology transfer include: foreign direct investment, imports of capital goods and licensing or informal transfer arrangements. While the various forms of investment flows provide an opportunity for fostering local technological capabilities, most of these investment flows can be realized only if the policy environment is conducive to innovation, investment in supportive infrastructure, human resources development and stable macroeconomic policy conditions.

IV. CONCLUSIONS

A. Science and technology policy reviews

Both countries have science and technology policies stated in official documents. In Ethiopia, the science and technology policy has come in the spirit of a fresh start following the change of government in 1991. Largely for this reason it does not engage in a comprehensive review of the experiences (positive and negative) of the past with a view to building on the strengths and tackling the weaknesses. The current science and technology policy is a broad statement which is intended to guide specific sectors and institutions in formulating their plan of activities. However, since December 1993 when the S&T policy statement was issued, the specific sectors and institutions have failed to formulate their programmes of action in connection with science and technology and the integration of S&T policy into economic policy is as yet unrealized. In the case of the United Republic of Tanzania, there was no sudden structural break which necessitated the review that is now in progress. However, although the science and technology policy is under review, this has not been preceded by a comprehensive review of the status of science and technology development in the country. Such an examination would have identified the strengths that need to be built upon and the weaknesses that should be remedied. The formulation or review of science and technology policy in both the United Republic of Tanzania and Ethiopia would benefit from a comprehensive study of the status of science and technology in each one and its relationship with the socio-economic policy environment. This would not only help to instil a broader conceptualization of science and technology policy for the purpose of meeting the basic needs in these countries, but it would also throw light on the role of science and technology in enhancing the international competitiveness of selected export activities.

While LDCs need to harness science and technology to enable them to meet the basic needs of the people, they must also develop their international competitiveness in selected export activities. The balance between these two objectives needs to be addressed, especially in the context of global liberalization and rapid technological advancement. Nevertheless, the science and technology policies do not address this balance either in the United Republic of Tanzania or in Ethiopia. Comprehensive S&T reviews would help not only to set S&T policy in the context of broader development and economic policy, but would hopefully enable such a balance to be achieved.

B. The changing role of the State

In both countries official policy has involved redefining the role of the State with a view to entrusting a greater role to the private sector in economic development. However, the activities of the public sector seem to be receding in both the United Republic of Tanzania and Ethiopia more rapidly than the private sector is developing. There is a danger of gaps emerging in private sector development and in the facilitation role of the State. The new role of the State has not acquired in either country the promotional characteristics that are necessary for private sector development. While considerable progress has been made in macroeconomic policy stabilization, the link between macro-level policy and micro-level activities remains tenuous. This link can be strengthened by State facilitation and building of institutional mechanisms to manage the process of reorientation towards a market economy. At these levels the role of the State and other institutions in facilitating the development of micro-level activities and providing the necessary infrastructural support deserves greater attention. Some of the major elements that need to be put in place are:

(a) appropriate institutional mechanisms for facilitating consultations between the Government and the private sector (and other relevant actors in development);

(b) an increase in the capacity of the State to provide the necessary supportive mechanisms, including education and training and other technological infrastructure;

(c) new mechanisms whereby non-governmental institutions can be engaged more actively in providing the science and technology infrastructure and related supportive mechanisms.

C. Implications of the Uruguay Round

Liberalization in major markets will have the effect of lowering the preferential margins which the LDCs have been enjoying under GSP schemes and the Lomé Convention. This challenges these countries to enhance their international competitiveness with greater urgency than ever before. In response to this increased pressure to attain international competitiveness, the LDCs will need greater technological and financial assistance to raise productivity in the productive sectors and to improve supportive infrastructure.

The Uruguay Round Agreement provides for LDCs to build domestic capacities in critical areas that would enhance their capacity to benefit from the new trading system. Consistent with article 66 of the Agreement on TRIPs, the developed countries are expected to provide incentives to their enterprises and institutions for purposes of promoting and encouraging transfer of technology to LDCs to enable them to enhance their technological capabilities. Support for improving investment conditions and strengthening regional and subregional technology and market links would be instrumental in fostering technological capability-building and in enhancing participation in the new trading environment.

The least developed countries are already facing acute constraints on the resources needed to foster technological capability-building. The implementation requirements of TRIPs place an additional burden on these countries in terms of financial and administrative capacities. Incorporating the new provisions in the national legislation and creating an administrative capacity to manage law enforcement and implementation of enforcement procedures will make undue demands on the already overstreched financial and human resources. The challenge that confronts these countries in endeavouring to foster and reward enterprise development, including stimulation of investment and technology flows, calls for efforts and resource commitments that are not self-sustaining in terms of their resource implications.

D. Private sector development as a vehicle for technological capacity-building

Developed countries can be partners in this process, building on the existing programmes for private sector development. In recent years a number of donors have developed aid programmes in the area of environment. In particular, support (in the form of subsidies, financing, training and information flows) has been given to the transfer of environmentally sound technologies. Some of these programmes have focused on technological innovation and diffusion of environmentally sound or clean technologies. These programmes can be sustainable if they can link partner firms and if the firms concerned find the partnership profitable. The partnership should enhance technological capacity-building in this field. The experience of the OECD countries that have implemented development assistance and technological cooperation programmes in these environmental aspects of technology would be useful. What is needed now is to broaden the scope of technological capacity-building in the existing private sector development programmes beyond the narrower concerns focused on environmentally sound technologies.

(a) Creative partnerships can be envisaged among firms or between firms and the R&D sector involving the blending of various capabilities (capital, technology, marketing, raw materials). Collaborative arrangements can be envisaged in the improvement of the development process, the enhancement of efficiency in the chain of production, learning through information exchange and collaboration to stimulate innovation. Some donor governments already have programmes for subsidizing partnerships between their firms and developing country firms. Experience gained in such programmes should be deployed to design new programmes with a view to enhancing the technological capacity-building components of these partnerships.

(b) Operations of SMEs in developed countries indicate that pooling efforts (resources, information, complementary skills and technologies) have facilitated innovation and enhanced their competitiveness. The experiences built up as a result could be applied to twinning arrangements between LDCs and developed country firms. While the traditional transfer of technology has often involved one-way technological cooperation, the new forms of such cooperation may aim at longer-term mutual benefits involving two-way technology flows based on joint production and sharing of knowledge. Longer-term technological cooperation arrangements of this kind may include training, the introduction of new management systems and various ways of improving technologies. Such partnering should aim at stimulating innovation and accelerating technology diffusion. In the case of new technologies in the area of biotechnology, the LDCs themselves may be well-placed to promote innovations because of factors such as climate and geography, which endow them with genetically diverse raw materials that are not available in developed countries. In this connection, LDCs could make the necessary arrangements to share the commercial benefits from biotechnological pursuits undertaken jointly with developed country firms that may have biotechnological advances to offer. In information technology, the software industry, for instance, offers scope for collaborative arrangements with LDCs offering specific local information needed to adapt and improve techniques to local conditions.

(c) One possible role for the SMEs of developed countries could be to widen the scope of sources of technology possibly in the direction of more labour-intensive and simple technologies. The emerging trends in new technologies also indicate that a number of SMEs are engaging in selected high technologies, e.g. biotechnology, computer technology and other aspects of information technology. However, the more limited managerial and financial resources of SMEs compared with TNCs suggest that the working of technology collaborative arrangements may have to be supported through some kind of promotional arrangements (e.g. financing). The formation of inter-firm linkages or firm-R&D linkages may need to be facilitated by enabling mechanisms such as access to financial and technological resources. Resources may also be required to attract the support of leading international firms.

List of persons interviewed

The United Republic of Tanzania

1.	Prof. M. Sheya	Director of the Centre for Development and Transfer of Technology at the Tanzania Commission for Science and Technology
2.	Mr Chungu	Director of Promotion and Marketing, Institute of Production Innovation, University of Dar es Salaam
3.	Dr Jackson	Senior Economist at UNDP Office, Dar es Salaam
4.	Mr Iddi Simba	Chairman, Tanzania Confederation of Industries
5.	Mr Asmani	Investment Promotion Centre
6.	Mr T. Mteleka	Ministry of Science, Technology and Higher Education

Ethiopia

1.	Ato Asrat Bulbula	Deputy Commissioner of Science and Technology
2.	Ato Shiferan Bekele	Secretary General, Addis Ababa Chamber of Commerce
3.	Ato Berhane Mewa	General Manager, Processing of Polyindustrial Chemicals, Addis Ababa
4.	Dr Taye Berhamu	Coordinator, Ethiopian Private Industries Association
5.	Ato Haile-Masket A.	Head, Trade Promotion Department, Addis Ababa Chamber of Commerce
6.	Ato Amare Wodajo	President, Addis Ababa Private Industries and Handicrafts Association
7.	Dr J. Lonis Hemel	Scientific Affairs Officer, UNECA
8.	Mr T.S. Karumuna	Economic Affairs Officer, Science and Technology Section, UNECA
9.	Prof. Soodursum Jugessur	Chief, Science and Technology Unit, UNECA
10.	Dr Mwanza	Director, Natural Resources Division, UNECA
11.	Ato Bekele Bayissa	Head of Planning Department, Ministry of Industry, Addis Ababa

12.	Ato Yemane Ghidey	Manager, Engineering, at the Engineering Design and Tool Enterprises, Addis Ababa
13.	Ato Gashaw Gebeyeku	General Manager, Engineering Design and Tool Enterprises, Addis Ababa
14.	Ato Tegegnework Gettu	Senior UNDP Economic Advisor to the Ministry of Planning and Economic Development, Addis Ababa.

The Netherlands

1.	Mr R. van den Berg	Ministry of Foreign Affairs
2.	Mr Herman Specker	Technical Adviser, Industrial Development, Ministry of Foreign Affairs
3.	Mr Frans van Rijn	Advisor, Financial Services and Enterprise Development, Ministry of Foreign Affairs
4.	Prof. J.G. Waardenburg	Chief Scientist, Development Cooperation, Ministry of Foreign Affairs

United Kingdom

1.	Ms Stella K. Blacklaws	Deputy Head, Technology Partnership Initiative (TPI), Department of Trade and Industry
2.	Mr Richard Boulter	Small Enterprise Adviser, Overseas Development Administration (ODA)
3.	Mr Collin I. Ellis	Technology Department, ODA

Denmark

1.	Mr Anders S. Rasmussen	Chief Technical Adviser, DANIDA
2.	Mr Leif Christensen	Head of Section, Royal Danish Ministry of Foreign Affairs
3.	Mr Klaus Winkel	Head of Evaluation and Research Department, DANIDA

References

Government of Ethiopia, *Survey of Current Economic Conditions in Ethiopia*. Inaugural Edition, vol. 1, No. 1. A Publication of the Policy Analysis Unit, Ministry of Planning and Economic Development, Addis Ababa, Ethiopia, January 1993.

____ *An Economic Development Strategy for Ethiopia (a Comprehensive Guide and a Development Strategy for the Future)*, Ministry of Planning and Economic Development, Addis Ababa, September 1993.

____ Ethiopian Science and Technology Commission, *National Science and Technology Policy*, Addis Ababa, December 1993.

____ *Economic Reform Programme Impact Analysis*, Addis Ababa, vol. 1, No. 4, May 1994.

____ *Report on Macroeconomic Development in Ethiopia*, Addis Ababa, December 1994.

_____ "Brief Summaries of the National Programmes", Addis Ababa, February 1994.

Mytelka, L.K., "Rethinking development: A role for innovation networking in the "other two thirds", *Futures*, 1993.

OECD, Reviews of National Science and Technology Policy. Portugal, OECD, Paris, 1993.

_____ *Science and Technology and Innovation Policies. Iceland*, OECD, Paris, 1993.

_____ *Technology and the Economy. The Key Relationship.* OECD, Paris, 1993.

Tadesse, Getahun,"Ethiopian scenario for technological capacity-building", paper presented to the Workshop on Selected Cooperation Aspects for Technological Capacity-building in Developing Countries, 10-11 April 1995, Geneva.

UNCTAD, "Report of the Workshop on the Transfer and Development of Environmentally Sound Technologies" (UNCTAD/ITD/TEC/13), Geneva, 1993.

_____ Informal discussions at the second session of the Ad Hoc Working Group on the Interrelationship between Investment and Technology Transfer, Geneva, 1993 (TD/B/40(2)/17-TD/B/WG.5/12), summary report by the UNCTAD secretariat, annex I.

_____ *Trade and Development Report, 1994* (UNCTAD/TDR/14), United Nations publication, Sales No. E.94.II.D.96, New York and Geneva, 1994.

_____ Final Report of the Ad Hoc Working Group on the Interrelationship between Investment and Technology Transfer, (TD/B/40(2)/17-TD/B/WG.5/12), Geneva, 1994.

_____ "Country case study submitted by the United Republic of Tanzania" (TD/B/WG.5/Misc.19).

_____ *Transfer and Development of Technology in the Least Developed Countries: An Assessment of Major Policy Issues* (UNCTAD/ITP/TEC/12), 1990.

UNECA, *The Influence of Economic and Development Policies on Science and Technology in Africa*, Addis Ababa, February 1994.

_____ *Performance Review of Science and Technology Policy Institutions in Ghana, Guinea, Kenya, Nigeria and Tanzania*, Addis Ababa, January 1990.

_____ *Endogenous Capacity Building in Science and Technology in Africa*, Addis Ababa, August 1993.

UNIDO, *Establishment of a National System for Technology Acquisition, Internalization and Monitoring. DP/URT/90/027/11-56. Tanzania. Technical Report: Mission in Tanzania.* Prepared by C. Aguirre Bastos and P. Materu, UNIDO, Vienna, 10 December 1993.

United Republic of Tanzania, The Tanzania Commission for Science and Technology Act, 1986.

World Bank, *African Development Indicators 1994-95*, Washington, D.C., 1995.

ETHIOPIAN SCENARIO FOR TECHNOLOGICAL CAPACITY-BUILDING

by
Getahun Tadesse
Department of Industry
Ethiopian Science and Technology Commission, Addis Ababa

I. GENERAL BACKGROUND

Some important considerations for technological capacity-building in Ethiopia are outlined below.

The massive socio-economic and technological changes needed for the speedy achievement of high priority development goals require extensive and sustained technological capacity-building by enhancing the innovative capacity of the society.

A nation's scientific and technical progress as well as its capacity to utilize the results of S&T are linked to the level of development of its economy. The level of outputs and benefits of overall socio-economic activity in Ethiopia is low, largely because of the inadequacy of technological development in the various sectors concerned.

However, Ethiopia has great potential for development if it can mobilize its human, natural, scientific and technological resources. The universities, colleges and specialized training institutions with their long teaching and research experience are capable of producing qualified professionals. R&D institutions established in different sectors and enterprises could contribute substantially to strengthening technological capacity on the basis of both modern technologies transferred to the nation, and the traditional technologies widely used by the people.

The Transitional Government of Ethiopia has consequently formulated policies, drawn up regulations, and strengthened or established support institutions, with a view to facilitating sustainable technological capacity-building.

II. POLICY AND LEGAL FRAMEWORK TO FACILITATE CAPACITY-BUILDING AND PARTNERSHIP

The following main elements form part of the new policy and legal framework concerning technology in Ethiopia:

The New Economic Policy and Development Strategy were announced by the Transitional Government of Ethiopia (TGE), with the objective of decentralizing and privatizing the economic system. The role of the government is limited to facilitating conditions, building the necessary infrastructure and participating in selected key economic units where the participation of the private sector is marginal and their spill-over effect is high in terms of capacity building.

The **Investment Proclamation issued in May 1992**, liberalized both local and foreign private investment. Foreign investors are especially encouraged to invest or participate in areas and sectors that facilitate the transfer of technology and know-how; in promoting exports; and in resource-based import substituting industries. Investors can set up various forms of business organization including ordinary partnerships, general partnerships, limited partnerships, joint-stock companies, private limited companies or joint venture according to the relevant laws of Ethiopia. The Proclamation offers a generous and comprehensive package of incentives and investment guarantees to investors.

The main objective of **Technology Transfer Regulation No. 12/1993** is to expand and coordinate investment and technology transfer. According to the Regulation, the choice of technology has to be based on the immediate needs and future expectations of national development and on the contribution to be made by technology to the development of national, technical and scientific know-how.

A **Patent Law** has been put into effect concerning inventions and industrial designs. This enables favourable conditions to be created in order to encourage local inventive and related activities, thereby building up national technological capability.

A **National S&T Policy** was enacted in 1993 to serve as a springboard for the formulation of detailed policies and priority actions and programmes for economic and service sectors. The policy guides government bodies, private organizations and R&D institutions in the planning of their respective S&T activities. It also serves as a basis for international cooperation on scientific and technological matters. Based on priority-accorded areas in national S&T policy, S&T policies for agriculture, industry, health and mineral, energy and water have been enacted recently.

An S&T policy for industry was put into effect in 1994 with a view to building local technological capacity through strengthening R&D efforts, improving support services, assisting the establishment of an appropriate technology transfer system, reinforcing the linkages between the modern and traditional sectors as well as between small and medium-sized industry, and coordinating, guiding and assisting all S&T activities in the industrial sector.

III. RESOURCE MOBILIZATION

Financial resources: The Transitional Government of Ethiopia endorsed the annual allocation of up to 1.5 per cent of the country's GDP for S&T development. The Government has also agreed to provide financial and tax incentives to encourage innovative activities and promote local technological capacity.

Human resources: The overall direction of human resources development is established through the Education Policy issued recently. The educational system is to be geared towards the current and anticipated needs of the nation. At present there is a gap in some specialized areas requiring practical knowledge.

Infrastructures: Some are considered to be in fairly good working order although they obviously need continuous improvement. Cases in point are public and private banks and insurance companies, the modern telecommunication system & efficient air transport. At present, considerable attention is being given to improving the electric power system, surface transport and physical infrastructure.

IV. SOME KEY ORGANIZATIONS AND TECHNOLOGY INSTITUTIONS

The following institutions have a critical role to play in technological capacity-building:

The **Ethiopian Science And Technology Commission (ESTC)** is a government institution with responsibility for planning, promoting, coordinating, financing and overseeing S&T activities in the country. It is also required to advise the Government on S&T issues, to implement the Government's S&T policy and to ensure the appropriate and immediate application of R&D results. The highest policy-making body of the Commission is the national S&T Council which is chaired by the Prime Minister. There is a technical advisory committee to the Council and sectoral S&T councils.

The **Industrial Projects Service (IPS)** is a public body, offering a comprehensive multidisciplinary consultancy service to the industrial sector. Such service includes planning, engineering and project implementation of new industrial ventures as well as evaluation and rehabilitation studies of existing industrial establishments, with emphasis on cost reduction, production increases, a streamlined organizational set-up and improved work efficiency.

The **Investment Office of Ethiopia (IOE)** serves as the focal institution for foreign investments in Ethiopia. It is responsible for receiving, reviewing, screening and deciding on applications for the establishment or expansion of enterprises; for approving the purchase or holding of shares in existing enterprises or expansion by a foreign investor; as well as for approving the benefits from incentive schemes. IOE assists foreign investors by providing the necessary information, and project profiles, arranging local partners, and drawing up contractual and related arrangements.

The **Ethiopian Authority for Standardization (ESA)** has the sole responsibility for instituting and promoting standardization activities. Its activities include Ethiopian standards formulation, quality control and classification, materials/product testing and metrology.

The **Ethiopian Management Institute (EMI)** acts as a management consultant, undertakes research and trains management personnel to improve administrative capacity and increase effectiveness. It provides management courses in project formulation, marketing, production, supervision, time management, maintenance, industrial activities, spare parts and general management.

The **Ethiopian Handicrafts and Small Industries Organization (HASSIDO)** provides training and upgrades skills for persons engaged in handicraft activities, and engineering and technical services for cooperatives and small industries.

"The Industrial R&D Centre", to have the sole responsibility for conducting industrial R&D activities based on the immediate and future needs of the country is being set up with the support of the Ethiopian Science and Technology Commission.

There are a number of private consultancy bodies in different areas whose activities are related to technological capacity-building.

Engineering Design & Tool Enterprise (EDTE) is an establishment capable of designing and manufacturing machinery, equipment, tools and other material inputs for the various sectors of the national economy and the international market. It thus has a favourable impact on growth and export earnings. It is equipped with conventional and CNC machines and has well-trained staff.

Akaki Spare Parts and Hand Tools Industry is one of the biggest engineering firms and is engaged in the production of spare parts, components, machinery and different types of hand tools.

Caustic soda, aluminum sulphate and pesticides industries are among the major chemical industries recently established.

There are a number of **small private engineering firms** engaged in the production of durable and non-durable engineering products. The latest technologies are also deployed in the areas of **textiles, cement, leather and beverages**.

The major problem as regards these firms and technologies is their low capacity utilization and limited markets.

V. RECOMMENDATIONS

Recommendations on action to be taken, policies to be enacted, and programmes and projects to be designed should take into account the prevailing situation and future expectations of a given country, such as an LDC, with respect to its regional and international environment at a specific point in time.

The following recommendations therefore concern technological capacity-building and the strengthening of cooperation and partnership within LDCs in general, and with Ethiopia in particular, in the currently prevailing conditions.

A. The role of the State

The State is to formulate appropriate policies and facilitate conditions for implementation; to build and make available the infrastructure urgently required by entrepreneurs; to devise and implement strategies to strengthen support institutions, such as special training, engineering and consultancy firms, R&D institutions, etc., in order to build up local capacity; and to develop appropriate schemes and procedures for mobilizing financial resources effectively and sustainably.

B. The role of economic actors in LDCs

With respect to these actors, the following recommendations are made: foreign investors should be encouraged to develop a local capacity; local enterprises should strive for competitiveness; local entrepreneurs must prepare themselves to participate in and eventually assume economic leadership by building up their local capabilities; entrepreneurs should be ready to absorb short-term risks and work for long-term achievement; and enterprises and entrepreneurs should look for appropriate partners in any part of the world.

C. The role of the international community

Its role should be: to support programmes and projects that are impact-oriented and to appoint the appropriate focal points for their implementation; to design and support national programmes in consultation with entrepreneurs and development experts of developed and developing countries; and to assist in identifying and carrying out need-based training programmes.

D. The role of support institutions

Of particular importance are the functions concerning the documentation and provision of appropriate information; the streamlining of bureaucratic procedures and fast decision-making in their respective domains.

E. Possible practical modalities of partnership

The following aspects relating to partnerships could be considered: joint ventures enabling LDC partners to gain direct access to training and technology, licensing, to encourage local firms to improve their technical capacity; sub-contracting in such a way as to link firms in developed and developing countries; market-outlet schemes, which facilitate the entry of LDC firms into developed country markets; original equipment manufacturing schemes, which would enable LDC firms to manufacture a product to the exact specifications of foreign companies from developed countries; strategic partnership in selected modern technologies which have a greater chance of achieving success in capacity-building and economic returns.

F. Follow-up of recommendations

A follow-up mechanism should be instituted by selecting and appointing appropriate institutions and national coordinators. UNCTAD, together with the national institutions designated, should draw up a plan of action for the implementation of the recommendations, including the development of a system of periodic reviews.

A SUMMARY NOTE ON TECHNOLOGICAL CAPACITY-BUILDING ASPECTS IN THE UNITED REPUBLIC OF TANZANIA

by
Titus Mteleka
Director of Science and Technology
Ministry of Science, Technology and Higher Education, Dar es Salaam

INTRODUCTION

This paper briefly examines technological capacity-building aspects in the changing policy and macroeconomic environment in the United Republic of Tanzania, and explores the implications of these changes for technological capacity-building in the future.

As the technological revolution is now well under way, the principle of science as the shared heritage of humanity is being systematically eroded. Knowledge is being increasingly privatized and the South is being excluded. Thus, many countries in the South find themselves less and less able to predict, let alone regulate, the technology flows (South Commission *Report*, 1990). In general, the new technologies open up dramatic new capabilities to humankind which could be deployed to remove serious obstacles to development but their uneven distribution is likely to increase the global inequalities and dependence of those who do not have control over their potentialities. The challenge for the countries of the South, in particular in Africa, which are least developed among them, is how to take advantage of the new opportunities created by new technologies. The answer appears to be that Africa must build up its own capabilities to apply these new technologies to its development and make informed choices between the technologies on offer.

This observation is reinforced by the experience of countries that have succeeded in upgrading their domestic technological capability, and also seem to have acquired the ability to jump from conventional to frontier technologies (South Commission *Report*, 1990).

I. CHANGES IN POLICY AND THE MACROECONOMIC ENVIRONMENT

A. Structural adjustment and technological capacity-building

In the early 1980s the United Republic of Tanzania started to implement structural adjustment programmes (SAPs). The flow of foreign resources helped to improve the supply of goods through higher capacity utilization and imports of consumer goods. Initially, donor aid showed positive signs of improving industrial capacity utilization. However, this was only a temporary improvement, and with time the problem has become more serious as domestic resources mobilization, including revenue generation through taxation, continue to falter.

It should be borne in mind that, during the application of the structural adjustment programmes, there was an increase in the supply of imports of all types, including intermediate inputs for domestic production. To a certain extent, this jeopardized the opportunities of enhancing technological capacity-building.

B. Import liberalization

During this period it was assumed that the restructuring of industry in the sense of increasing technological capability and competitiveness would take place. But this did not happen, basically owing to the failure to make the necessary private and social investment in technology and its supportive infrastructure.

C. The private sector

The private sector is supposed to play an increasing role in the economy, and the Government is currently withdrawing from certain areas, especially the productive sector. The Investment Code of 1990 endorsed the official support given to the private sector. In these changed conditions, in which the emphasis is being laid on private sector development, it is expected that both managerial and technological capacities will be enhanced.

II. THE CHANGING POLICY CONTEXT AND TECHNOLOGICAL CAPACITY-BUILDING

The policy context has changed. As a result, the State is redefining its role in economic management while encouraging the private sector to play a greater part in the production of goods and services in the economy and recognizing the importance of market forces.

In order to attain competitiveness in the production of goods and services, firms in the United Republic of Tanzania should be helped to do so. The assistance should primarily be given through inter-firm relationships with firms that are technologically more advanced. In many cases these will be firms from the more developed countries. The nature of inter-firm relationships should reflect the relative capabilities of the cooperating firms, but the primary aim of those in the United Republic of Tanzania should be to reach higher levels of technological capability and competitiveness. As far as possible inter-firm cooperation arrangements should be based on commercial principles.

Even when the private sector is playing a greater role in investment and in the economy in general, the Government will need to undertake certain public investments (e.g. in supportive infrastructure). Foreign assistance should be given in this case too, with a view to facilitating capacity-building. The general aim should be to develop the capacity to perform those activities in which local capacity is limited or needs strengthening. The success of foreign assistance should be measured by the results achieved in terms of building the technological capabilities required.

INVESTMENT IN TECHNOLOGICAL CAPACITY-BUILDING IN BANGLADESH AND NEPAL

by
Meine Pieter van Dijk
ING Bank International and Erasmus University, The Netherlands

INTRODUCTION

Local technological capability has been identified as one of the fundamental factors for economic development. In order to assess the exact relationship between investment and technological capacity-building in least developed countries (LDCs) in particular, the author of this report visited Bangladesh and Nepal. In the light of his findings policy approaches have been developed and specific recommendations have been made for a project to foster technology capacity-building in these two LDCs. The report has been prepared with the terms of reference of the Workshop in mind.

In Bangladesh and Nepal investment policies and science and technology (S&T) policies were discussed with government authorities, chambers of commerce and industry, some local entrepreneurs, and institutions supporting research and development (R&D) and technology adaptation in these countries. The report begins by reviewing the present economic situation there and current policies with respect to science and technology. The major actors are then identified and local technological capability evaluated. Lastly, the conclusions reached are set out and recommendations formulated.

I. THE PRESENT ECONOMIC SITUATION IN BANGLADESH AND NEPAL

A. Bangladesh

The present economic situation in Bangladesh can be summarized by the theme of the discussions in the country at this moment: Bangladesh, emerging tiger? The country feeds itself and exported rice during the last two (good) agricultural seasons.[17] Bangladesh has increased its exports of industrial products substantially and has a well-managed economy. Inflation is low and average economic growth was 4 per cent during the last 20 years. The country has created sufficient foreign exchange reserves for almost a year of imports. It was generally confirmed that Bangladesh has a more important entrepreneurial culture than before.

Another very positive indicator of the achievements of Bangladesh is the high level of self-financing in the annual development programme. It used to be totally donor financed, while 35 per cent is now financed from government sources. Concerning the country's future the optimism felt is based on the Government's liberal policies, the healthy macroeconomic situation, the low cost of labour (one dollar per day) and the saturation of the labour market in other Asian countries. These factors make investments in Bangladesh more attractive. Bangladesh already adjusted its economy in the 1980s and is now reaping the benefits. The budget for the fiscal year 1994-1995 continued the trend. It has already announced a broadening of the tax base, streamlining the tax administration, and stated that the Government will serve as a facilitator for arrangements for an outward-oriented economy. The country also pursues an active emigration policy as it considers exporting manpower to be a way to earn foreign exchange (Sobhan, 1994).

---

[17]The potential for further agricultural intensification is limited in Bangladesh. More investment may lead to more capital-intensive production, which nobody would like in Bangladesh.

On the negative side there are the recent political unrest and stagnating foreign investment. More importantly, the very traditional educational system may not be giving people the skills needed in an emerging economy. These factors are undoubtedly inhibiting the growth of the private sector in Bangladesh, although it is debatable how far political instability is important. The private sector complains about the lack of infrastructure and that the nationalized banking sector is a constraint for development.[18] Again, productivity of labour is low in Bangladesh. Labour is often unionized, or used by different political parties for strike purposes. Finally, the top-heavy bureaucracy and the lack of more sophisticated industrial activities in Bangladesh may also be important factors.

Administrative practices are not always straightforward and decision-making is very slow at the lower levels in the Government often because responsibilities are not always well defined. It is difficult to import certain raw materials despite the right to do so. Similarly the one-window service for new investors does not really work because other agencies are still involved. Privatization is expected to continue, but a number of firms will need to be restructured before they can be sold (particularly the jute factories, where the trade unions are strong). In the banking sector, there is not enough competition at the moment. Industrial loans are hard to obtain and loan processing is very cumbersome. Rates of interest are high and working capital is hard to obtain, particularly for small and medium-sized enterprises. Foreign banks are largely concentrating on trade finance.

The picture differs between subsectors, however.[19] Exports of ready-made garments have increased rapidly to more than half the current exports. Underwear accounts for an additional 10 per cent of exports. Next in line come fruit and food products, mainly frozen shrimps. The leather sector is also developing. The strategy is to produce more, and preferably products with a higher value added.[20] This means that instead of exporting wet blue, Bangladesh wants to export tanned leather or, even better, leather products.

The local textile, carpet and leather industries all face European and American markets with higher environmental standards than those of most countries in the region, but no coordinated response has been prepared so far. Tanning, for example, is a very polluting activity. Bangladesh fears its tanned leather exports may be refused in Europe or the United States on the basis of environmental arguments. The tanning industry is aware of environmental protectionism and would like to do something to improve matters at an early stage.[21] Germany and the Netherlands have helped India with environmentally friendly technologies to improve the quality of their leather.

Ceramics are also important for exports, like the traditional export products - jute and tea. Jewellery and handicrafts rank fifth and sixth in export significance. Technology is important in various sectors (see Box 1). In the jute sector, the traditional export product of the country, demand is declining and Bangladesh is searching for alternative uses for this product.

---

[18]For example: "inadequate power to inhibit industrial growth" (FBCCI Newsletter, May 1994).

[19]The World Bank is conducting a large industrial sector study, which will be issued shortly.

[20]The challenge in Bangladesh is to increase the value added of its products. In the garment sector it is estimated that at present the value added is only 20 per cent.

[21]Environmental factors are not yet an important consideration in Bangladesh. It is even more important to supply environmentally friendly technologies to this country, as agreed in general in the framework of the UNCED Rio conference.

Green jute is now used for the production of paper, which seems to be promising.

The informal sector is very important in Bangladesh and entrepreneurs can be highly innovative (Khunder, 1989). In the agricultural sector the question is whether there is scope for further labour-intensive development of agriculture. In many places three crops per year are possible, and high yielding varieties have been introduced. However, the scope for introducing cotton at the wishes of the textile industry is limited, because it would be at the expense of two of the three crops that are planted now. Two years ago some cotton was planted experimentally in the hill area, where the climate is better for this crop.

Box 1. Examples of technology choices in different sectors in Bangladesh

1. The development of the treadle pump supported by the Swiss is important for irrigation purposes
2. The improvement of brick ovens based on Chinese examples (Swiss aid) is relevant for economizing on the consumption of wood
3. Efforts to increase the life span of bamboo would help the building sector
4. Experiences with agro processing would help the conservation of certain products
5. The textile industry is interested in Swiss machinery for making cloth
6. The promotion of dried fish would limit spoilage
7. Improved ovens can reduce energy costs (NGOs are active)
8. The introduction of biogas (NGOs) can also reduce expenditures
9. There is a need to expand fertilizer production capacity (bilateral assistance will be provided)
10. Ferry boats are being constructed (bilateral assistance)
11. Many donors transfer means of transportation of all kinds through their development cooperation
12. Technology support is given to simulate water flows through computers, as part of the Flood Action Plan (FAP)
13. In the private sector a large machine tools factory tries to produce the largest possible number of tools, machines and spare parts locally

Fishing has an enormous potential, particularly fish farming (shrimps). The Government Fisheries Development Corporation is playing an important role in this sector, but the hatchery is run by the private sector and provides the technology.

Important industrial sectors are fertilizer and pharmaceutical products. Bangladesh hopes to attract electronic industries and is considering the possibility of developing a software sector.[22] The question is whether the experience of the garment sector can be repeated in other sectors. A daily wage of one dollar does make the country attractive. However, to become a tiger economy, a growth rate of about 7 to 8 per cent would be necessary.[23] That would entail higher savings and investment quota, which does not seem very likely at the present time.

---

[22]Sectors in which technology does play an important role are: jute, textiles, and the use of water resources (see also Box 1).

[23]The criteria for designating a country a Newly Industrializing Country (NIC) are the size of the industrial sector in GDP (over 25 per cent) and the growth of industrial exports (a two-digit figure).

B. Nepal

The economic situation in Nepal is very different from that of Bangladesh. Liberalization of the economy started more recently (Sharma, 1994). The economy is less outward-oriented, and characterized by production for the local market. Nepal is still a very rural society in the sense that many people live in rural areas and are active in agriculture (mainly irrigated rice and fruit and vegetables in the urban areas). The country also earns some money from international tourism.

Nepal faces a number of problems at present: declining exports,[24] low value added in garment manufacture, foreign domination in the two major export sectors: carpets (Tibetan refugees) and garments (Indian investors). Political confidence may also be decreasing. This is the only Royal Communist Government in the world, or more precisely, a social democratic government, since no industries have been nationalized and the quite liberal policies of the previous Congress Party Government remain in force. The parties in power are styled Marxist-Leninist, however. In practice they form a minority Government with limited possibilities to introduce drastic changes. The Government is in power for a period of five years.

Traditional manufacturing activities process primary products of agriculture, forests and mines. Rice milling, oil pressing, brick and tile making, textile weaving and the preparation of traditional medicines may be mentioned. At present the two major export industries are carpet weaving and ready-made garments.

The building sector is an example of a sector using largely local building materials: local cement, local windows and doors, and baked bricks. Only electrical elements and products related to plumbing are imported. There is a proposal to set up a Centre for Building Technology, which would look more closely into these issues.

The leather sector, for instance, could be expanded further. Too often raw hides and skins are exported instead of the beautiful leather products available in the tourist shops in Nepal. There exists also a potential market for jewellery, in particular silver and gold work. Tourism-related activities could also be developed much more. The garment and carpet sector could try to produce more of the goods demanded by tourists, or facilitate the export of these products by tourists. Unfortunately the raw material for carpets is imported Tibetan or New Zealand wool. Ready-made garments are exported to the United States (90 per cent) and Europe (10 per cent). The competitiveness of the sector needs to be enhanced, particularly after the conclusion of the Uruguay Round when it was decided that the Multi-Fibre Arrangement will be phased out.

In some sectors (hydropower for example) relatively advanced technology has been introduced, while in others the technology is relatively simple. A number of interesting cases of appropriate technology were found in Nepal. In the case of pumps, hydropower and other alternative sources of energy, some local adaptation has taken place. NGOs and donors play a major role in the latter case, by, for instance, promoting appropriate technologies such as water pumps and simple agricultural implements, which can be produced locally. As in the case of Bangladesh, the process of choosing a technology needs to be studied in the major sectors of the economy, such as agriculture, electricity, water, textiles, carpets and leather.[25]

---

[24] "Nepal's exports decline sharply first 9 months of 1993/94" Nepal Rastra Bank quoted in FBCCI Newsletter, May 1994.

[25] New technologies with some potential in Nepal are solar energy and environmentally friendly tanning.

Nepal would also like to develop a software industry, but it has a long way to go.[26] There are not many trained software specialists, nor are there large numbers of small computer-related industries, as, for example, in Bangalore (India). The Nepalese would like to train the necessary human resources, but this is rather a long-term project.

Pollution considerations have led to the Kathmandu beautification project and the efforts to improve the traditional method of brick making in wood burning ovens. There are at least three reasons for the highly polluted air in Kathmandu: the means of transportation embody an old technology and use bad quality petrol which is often mixed with used carter oil. The old technology is not only a question of capital stretching; it also reflects the fact that many of the scooter taxis in Nepal were imported after they were no longer allowed in India.

In general, export promotion should be given more attention in Nepal, particularly since the two main export products (garments and carpets) face severe problems at the present time.[27]

II. CURRENT POLICIES WITH RESPECT TO SCIENCE AND TECHNOLOGY

A. Bangladesh

Waliuzzaman and Haque (1993) have prepared a case study of technological capability in Bangladesh, indicating the number of Universities (nine) and research institutes (58), among others a Chemical Industrial Cooperation Institute and an institute for appropriate technology for the rural areas.[28] The authors also mention a special UNDP-financed programme, entitled the Transfer of Knowledge Through Expatriate Nationals (TOKTEN),[29] under which a number of Bangladeshi scientists living abroad visited the country for a certain period to work on a specific subject (for example, on how to deal with used polyethylene bags in Dhaka).

The first National S&T Policy document is very short (19 pages); it dates from 1980 and was reviewed in 1986 (Ministry of Education, 1986). It is clear from this that scientific R&D is a vast field in which various ministries, government and semi-government agencies, universities and private enterprises participate.[30] The many constraints that exist are listed and objectives are formulated, although in rather general terms. Some examples of these are:

- To attain scientific and technological competence and self-reliance;
- To strengthen cooperation in science and technology between developed and developing countries;
- To provide guidelines for institutional R&D arrangements to attain the above objectives.

---

[26]See J. Mill: "Online to Kathmandu". In: *New Scientist*, February 1995.

[27]See "Don't boast about our fragile export trade". In: *Rising Nepal*, 20 February 1995.

[28]Md. Waliuzzaman and M. Mainul Haque, "Technological capability-building: the case of Bangladesh", study prepared for the UNCTAD secretariat, October 1993.

[29]The project has been stopped for practical reasons.

[30]In Bangladesh much of the R&D is taking place in sector-specific institutions, such as jute and rice research institutes.

In the 1980s the Ministry of Science and Technology was abolished, but the present Government re-established it four years ago. The general feeling still seems to be that Bangladesh is not really equipped to formulate an active S&T policy itself, but rather depends on what is made available by donor countries and organizations. One of the major handicaps for the development of local S&T are the very weak links between the educational sector and industry. The major elements of the S&T policy are summarized in Box 2 (Ministry of Education, 1986).

BOX 2. Bangladesh S&T policies: objectives

1. Organize and coordinate all R&D work concerning S&T in Bangladesh
2. Identify the problems facing the country in each vital sector, where solutions are likely to have a significant impact on the country's economic and socio-cultural development
3. Promote research and strengthen the competence and capability of research institutions, including universities
4. Establish scientific and research institutions/laboratories/ centres of excellence, where research of high quality can be carried out in areas of national importance
5. Improve the standard of scientific knowledge at all levels from school to university
6. Train personnel and specialized S&T staff
7. Ensure a suitable environment for S&T research
8. Foster scientific awareness among the people in general through popularization of S&T and the encouragement of innovative activities especially among the younger generation
9. Establish a national capability for the development of indigenous technology and the attainment of a national capacity for the acquisition, adoption and adaptation of foreign technology
10. Create centralized facilities for collection and dissemination of scientific information and research findings
11. Ensure adequate funding for the S&T sector aimed at the development of infrastructure for R&D activities
12. Promote bilateral, subregional, regional and international S&T collaboration

Recommendation 9 is the most important for our purposes. The objectives are to develop indigenous technology and to promote the efficient assimilation of imported technology. They are formulated in a more detailed way as "attaining national capacity for autonomous decision-making in technological matters" and "ensuring the transfer of research results to the production sectors". The suggestion is made to blend indigenous and imported technological resources but also to generate technologies that are internationally competitive.

The recommendations remain quite general and there are no indications how the objectives are to be achieved. Waliuzzaman and Haque (1993) conclude that the most important instrument of technological development in the case of Bangladesh is foreign direct investment. They suggest that the Ministry of Science and Technology should prepare a more elaborate S&T plan for Bangladesh, once the priorities have been established by the Council for Science and Technology. In 1995, however, the prevailing idea appears to be that the Ministry of Science and Technology will deliver an input to the medium-term plan instead.[31]

---

[31]The Ministry for S&T is currently working on a position paper to be submitted to the NCST concerning the long-term planning of S&T in Bangladesh. Eventually it will be part of the five-year prospective plan.

B. Nepal

Technology policies and planning at the national and sectoral levels in Nepal have been reviewed by the Asian and Pacific Centre for Transfer of Technology (APCTT, 1986). In Nepal's Seventh Development Plan (1987-92) two bodies are designated for the implementation of general S&T activities in the country, namely the Royal Nepal Academy of Science and Technology (RONAST) and the National Council for Science and Technology (NCST). S&T activities are also carried out by the sectoral ministries and specialized agencies. The NCST formulates the national policy for S&T, while RONAST is charged with developing S&T capacity for the all-round development of the country. According to APCTT (1986), Nepal has explicitly recognized the need for, and made a commitment to, technology for development during the last two decades.

In 1992 the Eighth Five-Year Plan for 1992-1997 called for increased private and non-governmental efforts to attain sutainable economic growth. The Government would serve as a catalyst to develop science and technology in support of this goal, especially with regard to rural development sectors (agriculture, cottage industries, small-scale enterprises), and would encourage imports of useful foreign technologies.

National S&T policies are influenced at a lower level by the rules and regulations drawn up by different government institutions such as ministries responsible for building codes, environmental regulations and energy policy (for example UNCTAD, 1987). This makes it difficult to develop a coordinated approach.

The Investment Act (Ministry of Industry, 1992) distinguishes between cottage and small industries on the one hand and large-scale enterprises on the other. Permission is required from the Department of Industry or of Cottage and Small Industries for foreign investment or technology transfer. Transfer of technology is only allowed in cottage and small industries and in medium-scale industries with fixed assets of up to 20 million rupees. Industries with fixed assets of up to 10 million rupees are classified as small industries and those with more than 50 million rupees as large industries.[32]

This distinction is made because the hand-loom carpet weavers are forbidden to use mechanical equipment for fear of destroying the quality reputation of Nepalese exports. In the case of medium-sized enterprises joint ventures have often been set up. The Government does not influence the choice of technology in these instances. The Investment Forum held in 1992 fell well below expectations, achieving only 10 to 20 per cent of its objectives. The impression is that the Government is not really promoting Nepal as a country that is attractive for foreign investors. In general an outsider has the feeling that much more could be done locally and that the tourist sector, to take one example, could be developed to a far greater extent, if only because of its unique character.

III. THE MAJOR ACTORS

A. Bangladesh

The major actors in Bangladesh are the Ministry of Science and Technology, the Board of Investment, the Export Promotion Bureau, individual Bangladeshi, in particular returning migrants, a number of donor countries and organizations and the large number of R&D institutions. They will be discussed in this order.

---

[32]For example the Udaipur cement industry, which produces 850 t per day and exports some of it. It is considered to be of good quality and local demand is high.

In terms of its budget the Ministry is not very important. According to the Implementation Division, the Ministry received Tk. 3,540 Lakh (for 18 projects) for the fiscal year 1993/94, which is about 80 per cent of the allocation in the Annual Development Programme for that year and one fifth of the allocation received, for example, by the Ministry of Industry in the same year for 38 projects.[33]

The Ministry of Science and Technology has no wish to influence the choice of technology in the private sector, but it does want to build a technological base, as the end result of the human development efforts undertaken, and informed the UNCTAD consultant that it would welcome a S&T review. The priorities of the Ministry are to:

1. Increase investments in S&T from 1.17 per cent of GDP to about 2 per cent in the next 15 years.

2. Create a pool of scientists and technology graduates. The Ministry would like to see about 1,000 Bangladeshi studying abroad for a Ph.D degree in this field.

3. Integrate S&T policies with national development policy.

The Board of Investment has been active, organizing, for example, an investment conference in 1994. The vital question, however, is how much foreign investment will flow into the country. For 1994 the figure of US$ 200 million has been mentioned. This is what India received in 1993 (corrected for a population seven times larger). Foreign investments are strongly promoted in Bangladesh. A number of examples are given below of regional projects mentioned in the Newsletter of the Federation of Bangladesh Chambers of Commerce and Industry (May 1994). Some of these may be called technology partnerships:

- Viet Nam is anxious for closer cooperation in the textile, jute and shrimp sectors.

- Indian investors are urged to take part in industrial projects.

- The creation of a Thai-Bangladesh Joint Commission to promote the private sector.

Programmes are to be established with these and other countries (for example, concerning shrimps with Indonesia), and some of them will be genuine partnership programmes.

The Export Promotion Bureau claims that the choice of technology is made entirely by the investors.[34] The Bureau has a matching grant fund to share the total cost with the investor. For example, technical assistance by Italians in the leather sector is paid from the fund. UNDP has assisted with exports (an ITC project) and the World Bank has funded an export development fund located in the Bangladesh Bank, which can be used to obtain credit in foreign exchange for imports of raw materials. It is hoped that the project will finance spare parts and machinery in its second phase.

Other actors are returning migrants. The fact that many Bangladeshi work abroad enables them to get to learn about new technologies, which they sometimes bring home. Non-governmental organizations (NGOs) are also important

---

[33]Very little or no R&D is carried out in the industrial sector in Bangladesh.

[34]The core technology may be the most modern one, but the activities around it (treating raw materials and packaging the final product) may be more labour intensive.

in this connection and very active in Bangladesh, the three biggest being BRAC, Grameen and Proshika. A number of NGOs would like to promote silk production in Bangladesh, but high quality production is still a problem.

Donor countries and organizations are also important. In several interviews with Bangladeshi organizations it was claimed that tied aid leads to the supply of inappropriate technologies. The examples given by Bangladesh related to the number of lorries (and other equipment) in the country and fertilizer factories, all of which embodied the technology of the donors. The major donors in these cases acknowledged the problem and said they were trying to solve it, in one case by buying local equipment for vocational training centres (the Swiss), or by referring to the request made by the Bangladeshi Government (Denmark) in the case of gas-based fertilizer production).

The donor group is also an important actor. It meets annually in Paris, and the background report, prepared by the World Bank, often provides a perspective on the problems of Bangladesh. Like-minded donor countries have enabled a group of local researchers to prepare in 1995 a report reflecting the point of view of Bangladesh, instead of accepting the World Bank view without any critique.

Given the number of R&D organizations in Bangladesh, some coordination is required. Agricultural research policies, for example, are coordinated by the Bangladesh Agricultural Research Council. Similarly, research in the natural sciences is coordinated by the Bangladesh Council of Scientific and Industrial Research (BCISR).

B. Nepal

RONAST is responsible for the formulation of the national science and technology policy. It is convinced that the type of technology chosen is catalytic for the development process in Nepal and it tries to influence this choice. Contrary to Bangladesh, in Nepal the choice of technology is not so much determined by the need to produce for the world market as by the specific needs of a mountainous, relatively densely populated country, with limited natural resources. Logical research priorities are the optimal use of water resources, high altitude research and the exploitation of comparative advantages based on the altitude (for example, the processing of aromatic plants which can only grow at great heights). RONAST has a station in the Himalayas for research purposes. Medicinal herbs are found in Nepal's forests and vegetable and potato seeds can be cultivated at higher altitudes.

Research supported by RONAST concerns, among other projects, a biofertilizer project with the University of Amsterdam, energy projects and a project on urban quality (a metropolis improvement project financed by the World Bank, with inputs from Norway and the Netherlands). RONAST does not deal with the social sciences.

The Research Centre for Applied S&T (RECAST), one of the specialized agencies of RONAST, is working on appropriate technology. RONAST also promotes S&T via radio and television programmes. The ideas are there, but money is lacking. The organization only receives 30 million Rupees from the Government to run the office and it is beset by financial and administrative problems. There is no chairman at present and the institute is trying to execute projects so as to be eligible for further donor money.

The first college was founded in Nepal in 1918. The first university opened its doors in 1959 and RECAST was established in 1976. The NCST also dates from 1976, while RONAST was constituted in 1982.

Hydropower is an important source of energy in Nepal. The question of the choice of technology in this sector is currently on everybody's agenda because of the Arun dam, which is to be financed by the World Bank and the Asian Development Bank. The dam would entail expenditure equal to the national income for one year to produce electricity for the national grid and for export. This choice means a break with the past, when small-scale hydropower was promoted in Nepal. Micro hydropower allows the women to do the rice husking with machines and to use a mechanized press to extract oil from mustard seeds (UNCTAD, 1987). Ten per cent of the population has access to very decentralized schemes, involving for example the use of a small pipe weighing about 35 kg, which yields one kilowatt if put in a river. In some cases the technology is combined with the provision of drinking water and irrigation. The United Mission of Nepal has played an important role in the development of hydropower electricity.

An important programme to finance activities in the field of micro hydropower has been submitted to the Global Environment Facility (GEF) for financing. The idea underlying it is that Nepal possesses the necessary technology, but does not have the machinery and funding to disseminate the results by selling them to other countries. The project intends to set up an Alternative Energy Production Centre (AEPC) as an autonomous body. Some sources are, however, pessimistic that Nepal will be able to export hydropower technology. Its situation is very different from that of other countries. The size of the area which is similar to Nepal may be small and often the grids are better developed elsewhere in the developing world, because this is easier if mountains are less steep.

In Nepal the choice of technology is often characterized as donor driven. Many projects are financed by the donors and this does bring in new technologies. However, some of the donors also try to introduce appropriate technologies for small enterprises (GTZ for example). As a reaction to the practice of bringing in technology which is not adapted, much more emphasis is now placed on the 'ownership' side.

UNDP has gone so far as to finance programmes executed by local government services, often with as little technical assistance as possible from abroad. Such programmes may also transmit a certain amount of technology as is illustrated by the project on decentralization of municipal services. This UNDP-supported project is designed to reinforce the capacity of the municipalities to undertake the necessary infrastructural or other improvements in living conditions (see Box 3). Funds are made available to allow municipalities to subcontract work.[35]

---

[35]Straightforward examples are constructing roads, building bridges or markets, helping the municipalities with water and electricity supplies. In the future, consultants may be found to look at solid waste management and suggest appropriate composting technologies.

Box 3. Reinforcing municipalities to undertake infrastructural work

Municipalities have received some training in formulating terms of reference, supervising the activities undertaken and hiring consultants for specific types of work. The project teaches municipalities how to get the maximum out of these consultancy assignments. Its philosophy can be summarized as: "Involving local consultants is building local technological capacity".

A unique element in this case is that a limited amount of foreign aid (UNDP finance and UNCHS execution) helps to develop this novel approach. Some technical assistance was provided in the beginning, but basically the institutional capacity to deal with the private sector was built up locally. Secondly, funds were made available to finance the use of local consultants. In this way support was given to the creation of a local technological capability. Work was given to small private sector consultants who were thus able to progress in their specialization. Finally, the system will continue in force after the project because the municipalities have their own funds, and have learned to work with the private sector instead of using those funds to create their own bureaucracies. The project is also compatible with the decentralization approach chosen in Nepal, whereby the consultants will have to go to the 36 municipalities (with more than 20,000 inhabitants) instead of remaining in the capital.

Other actors are NGOs, which are very active in Nepal. Discussions were held with one of them, involved in community irrigation, and linked to the activities of the Agricultural Development Bank (ADB). In fact the staff are mostly former ADB employees, who set up this NGO after taking early retirement three years ago. Contrary to the Grameen approach, which is characterized as credit only, they offer saving and credit facilities, skill development and infrastructural development. Their approach can be described as one of area development with credit included as the final activity. This NGO receives financial support from GTZ and their experiences with technology are summarized in Box 4. An international NGO (ATI, 1995) has a programme to help villagers in the rugged Himalaya to conserve biodiversity. The programme is styled a partnership, in which conservation is linked with the economic well-being of the people.

Box 4. Technology activities of a Nepalese NGO

(a) In the case of irrigation activities, the challenge is to find a system suitable to the area. It is even more important to create a capacity in the community to run the scheme. This structure should be sustainable to make it last. In one case the NGO introduced a sprinkler system linked to drinking water. They are also trying out drip irrigation at the farmer's level.

(b) As regards increasing agricultural productivity, the NGO aims to introduce improved seeds and organic fertilizer.

(c) In the case of water and energy projects, the NGO has plans to introduce micro hydropower, a technology available in Nepal, on the grounds that the cost of electricity generated in this way is one fifth the private sector price. One kilowatt capacity would be US$ 1,200 versus US$ 4,000 to 9,000 in the private sector.

(d) With respect to biogas, some farmers are even using biogas sludge as a fertilizer as they find that it produces good yields.

(e) This NGO is also involved in tree planting (community forestry, which requires training and the introduction of appropriate species). In one area there are 15 community forests. This activity is carried out primarily by women.

The Nepalese Government subsidies for hydropower schemes account for 25 per cent of the total cost. Most of the components (such as generators and turbines) are produced locally. Only the governors and local controllers need to be imported. The Government subsidizes the generators, the belts, the control boxes and the cables. The ADB is the mechanism through which this technology is transferred to the users via a subsidized loan. In more marginal areas a larger subsidy is required. The Agricultural Development Bank of Nepal complains that the loans are not always repaid, but it does not use the equipment as collateral for the loans. There may be various reasons for the payments difficulties, but in every case there is a lack of financial management training in Nepal.

IV. AN EVALUATION OF LOCAL TECHNOLOGICAL CAPABILITY

The situation in this small, landlocked least developed country is undoubtedly very different from that of Bangladesh. The choice of an appropriate technology is even more important in this case. It is less determined by the need to produce for the world market but depends much more on the needs in this specific local situation.

It is important to look at the mechanisms of technology transfer, the local capacity to adapt and develop technologies and the degree to which government, private sector associations and donor organizations can influence the process. As Enos (1991) has noted, the appropriate degree of local technological capability varies at different stages of economic development.

Some consider foreign direct investment as the front runner and main vehicle of technology transfer in Bangladesh. Most of the technology in Bangladesh is imported. In the case of international tendering, BCIC may advise. The criteria used are whether the technology is the latest and the most efficient. In Bangladesh there are clearly differences in the process of technology transfer and adaptation between the formal export-oriented industrial sector, local small and medium-sized enterprises and the NGO sector. Briefly it can be said that the export-oriented industries want the most modern technology at least for the core of their activity, so as to remain competitive on the world market.[36] Meanwhile the handling of raw materials or the final product may well continue in a very labour-intensive way.

A number of donors are active in the local small and medium-sized enterprises and in this sector a local technological capacity has been built up. Small enterprises can copy a number of imported tools and machines and most of the spare parts (for example, Huq *et al.*, 1993). In fact the capacity to copy machines and spare parts is highly developed in these private mechanical workshops.

In the NGO sector there are many projects for income generating activities for poor people. Appropriate technologies are often introduced and sometimes local technological capacity is developed to produce the newer technologies and maintain them. Examples are biogas equipment, improved hand looms, energy saving technologies and the introduction of crop rotation.

Examples can also be found of local innovations, although they are not always fully commercial yet. For instance, instant tea is locally developed, natural tanning products are grown and green jute is used as paper pulp.[37] Researchers complained that it is difficult for new technologies to get accepted outside the agricultural sector where there is a complete extension service for that purpose.

In both Bangladesh and Nepal, of course, the fact that the budgets available for S&T policies are limited has played a role. More importantly, however, the development of a real national S&T policy does not seem to be a priority in either of these two countries. It may be linked to the general loss of faith in planning, or it may be because so many vested interests are involved that any attempt to change science and technology policy in a drastic way evokes determined opposition.

Rana (1989: 78) notes that in Nepal there were hardly any cases in the industrial sector in which technologies were tested and assessed before importation. In general no consideration was given to alternative technology options, or to the necessity of adopting or assimilating imported technologies.

V. CONCLUSIONS FOR BANGLADESH AND NEPAL

In a liberalized economy the choice of technology is left very largely to the private sector and the Government has limited possibilities of influencing the process of choice. However, to take East Asia as an example, the Governments can create the necessary conditions for the development of the economy.

The fact that in Bangladesh the S&T policy of 1985 has not been updated indicates that the country has other priorities, such as food production, industrialization and developing the social sectors. It can also be said that there is no real technology policy in Bangladesh. As one of the people interviewed remarked: "People do not look at S&T as a tangible instrument that has real value". Originally S&T was mainly a government activity. In the

---

[36] In export processing zones the technology is certainly chosen by foreign investors. Local knowledge of specific parts of production, such as the design process or marketing, is very limited, however.

[37] "Dhaka to save TK. 1.2 billion producing 25,00 MT pulp from green jute by fiscal 94/95 in three pulp and paper mills of BCIC" (FBCCI Newsletter, May 1994).

liberalization process the private sector and in particular all kinds of specialized institutions play a more important role.[38]

Discussions about ownership of technology have a positive impact on the issue of technology transfer. Ownership increases when technologies are developed locally, are owned by local companies and adopted through local entrepreneurs. This requires respect for local technology needs and the stimulation of local technological capacity.

Both countries feel excluded on the information high road. For example, electronic mail is not available and even access to recent publications is often difficult. Nepal faces a few extra constraints, such as its location and the size of its internal market. Consequently a large number of Nepalese have opted for emigration (Rana, 1994).

C. Fortín, Officer-in-Charge of UNCTAD (1995) rightly points to the risk of marginalization of certain LDCs in a liberalized global economy. It is important therefore to emphasize policies that stimulate technology flows and promote technological innovation. Flexible specialization and the creation of industrial districts can contribute to that type of industrial development (Van Dijk, 1993 and 1994).

Certain projects could be selected that are appropriate to the needs of the LDCs and pre-feasibility studies could be carried out. Nepal and Bangladesh could also benefit from the Global Environmental Facility, a UNDP-World Bank administered fund to which LDCs have preferential access.

Information on opportunities to invest in LDCs should point more specifically to the options for more labour-intensive technologies, which may be more attractive in this specific situation. Many LDCs are so eager to attract foreign investment that they forget about their comparative advantage.

Science and technology policy reviews have gained prestige through the efforts of the OECD (OECD, 1993). A review of the existing policy measures and regulatory framework of LDCs with respect to technology may be useful, although, as was evident in the two countries visited, not all LDCs have an elaborate regulatory framework and well-defined policies. Consequently, it does not seem to be a priority to review the S&T policy of the two countries concerned, given the fact that the policy is outdated (Bangladesh) or not really defined (Nepal).

Planning is less popular than before and private sector involvement allows for very little planning. Hence the question that must be asked is to what extent the process of technology transfer and adaptation can be influenced. Donor organizations certainly play a role, although not always a positive one if tied aid leads to a supply of inappropriate technologies. Donors have played an important role in Bangladesh and Nepal as far as the introduction and diffusion of new technologies is concerned. Tied aid leads to a large number of different brands of certain technologies (lorries, buses and pumps for example). In this situation it is clearly important for donor countries and organizations at least to cooperate more than before in relation to S&T and technology transfer.[39]

---

[38]The tea and jute institutes were mentioned; a similar institute for the leather sector is missing.

[39]Stimulated by the Maastricht Treaty, EU member countries exchange more information on their activities in Bangladesh than in the past (the EU office in Nepal is very small). Other efforts to achieve donor coordination are also undertaken in Bangladesh. There are groups for different sectors, such as health activities (led by the World Bank), and interventions in the water sector.

Both countries fear the effects of the conclusion of the Uruguay Round of GATT, as, in both, a booming sector (garments) is now facing problems. The development of the garment sector in the two countries is closely linked to the lack of a quota for exports from these countries. In the future they will have to compete with the most effective producers in the world. As they have to import most of the cloth it will be difficult for them to be efficient producers. The problem may be more general and these countries may need additional assistance. In Bangladesh a technology information system would certainly be useful. The importance of promoting trade in the region is also emphasized.[40]

Building up local technological capacity in two LDCs is undoubtedly more difficult than trying to do the same in one of the East Asian tigers. At the end the question to be asked is what should be the role of UNCTAD in this field. It can, for instance, function as a catalyst, making others aware of the importance of technology and making available experiences in building up local technology capacity. For poverty alleviation, employment creation remains crucial and hence also the introduction and development of appropriate technologies.

VI. CONCLUSIONS ON THE ROLE OF S&T FOR LDCs

From the studies on Ethiopia, the United Republic of Tanzania, Bangladesh and Nepal six conclusions can be drawn.

A. The need to review the present science and technology policies

Some countries do not have a S&T policy, or, where they do, it is not implemented. In some cases nothing has been foreseen for the so-called meso level (see (e) and D. below). An evaluation should be undertaken, preferably by independent experts, to try to assess to what extent the S&T policy reflects the priorities of the country, is being implemented and has been successful in achieving its objectives. Points of attention could be:

(a) How broadly or narrowly has the policy been defined?

(b) What were the needs and priorities defined and are they still valid?

(c) Has attention been paid to implementation and has the policy been implemented successfully?

(d) What has been the role of foreign assistance in implementing the policy?

(e) Have polices been elaborated at the meso (sectoral, regional and institutional) level?

(f) Have the basic needs of the population been adequately addressed? (see E. below)

B. The need for assistance to be given in formulating comprehensive science and technology policies

A review as suggested under A. may reveal the need to formulate different types of S&T policies in LDCs. The differences between these S&T policies and those of a more traditional nature could be of four types:

---

[40]For example in the FBCCI Newsletter, May 1994, see "Myanmar for enhanced trade" (suggestion to create a Free Trade Zone on the Bangladesh/Myanmar border).

(a) S&T would be defined more broadly than usual. Instead of limiting its scope to the natural and physical sciences, attention would also be given to the social sciences.

(b) Instead of concentrating on R&D, attention would also be paid to the issue of dissemination of R&D results and the use made of them.

(c) The needs of the users would be taken more into consideration (see E. below).

(d) Instead of concentrating on academic research, the importance of including the roles of primary and secondary education and of vocational training would be stressed. It may be necessary to change the content of these forms of education and training. In vocational training the innovative mentality of the students may have to be stimulated, so that they become more dynamic entrepreneurs at a later stage.

Least developed countries should receive technical assistance to evaluate their present policies and to formulate more comprehensive S&T policies. Countries making the transition to a more market-oriented economy will face a number of specific problems that would need to be taken into account.

C. Identification of a different role for Governments

In the case of S&T policies, East Asia can be taken as an example. Governments can create the conditions for the development of the economy, but this requires a new role for the State in the economy. Instead of controlling and directing, the State would be creating the appropriate conditions for the development of certain sectors and activities. The major elements would be:

(a) Consultations with the private sector.

(b) Concentration by Governments on providing infrastructure, education and training and an appropriate macroeconomic framework.

(c) Account to be taken in S&T policy of the resources of the country and the results of the consultation process with the private sector (see (a) above) with respect to the future development of the economy.

D. The need to pay attention to the meso level when implementing S&T policies

S&T policies need to be elaborated at the sectoral, regional and institutional levels. In the larger countries in particular the number of different (sub) sectors, the number of provinces (or states) and the number of institutions involved may be very large.

Projects tend to be at the macro level, while, in fact, however, implementing policies is more difficult than formulating them. It requires considering the institutional capacity of the different actors concerned, making funds available, and ensuring that there is coordination among the different institutions involved.

E. The importance of identifying the S&T needs of farmers, small entrepreneurs, women and the poor

The identification of these S&T needs poses problems in every country. Taking into account the problems of poor people is particularly complex. Too often a small group, belonging to the upper layers of society, determines the priorities. Consequently many countries have either no S&T policy or only very specific ones. In this connection the question that must be asked is to what extent science and technology policies have contributed to the satisfaction of the basic needs of the population.

F. Projects could be started in the following fields

(a) Evaluation of S&T policies of LDCs;

(b) Support for the formulation of S&T policies aimed at addressing the basic needs of the population;

(c) Projects furthering the implementation of S&T policies;

(d) Assistance to governments in periods of transition in defining a new role for the Government in the development process;

(e) Identification of the S&T needs of the population.

References

APCTT (1986): Technology policies and planning, Nepal. Bangalore: Asian and Pacific Centre for Transfer of Technology.

________(1993): Technology exchange at APCTT. New Delhi: Asian and Pacific Centre for Transfer of Technology.

ATI (1995): Creating incentives to conserve biodiversity. Washington: Bulletin Appropriate Technology International.

Enos (1991).

ERA (1989): Impact study of some activities of the United Nations system in S&T in Nepal. Kathmandu: UNDP.

Fortin, C. (1995): Statement at the second part of the forty-first session of the Trade and Development Board. Geneva: UNCTAD secretariat.

Huq, M.M., K.M.N. Islam and N. Islam (1993): Machinery manufacturing in Bangladesh, An industry study with particular reference to technological capability. Dhaka: University Press Limited.

Khunder, N. (1989): Technology adaptation and innovations in the informal sector of Dhaka. Geneva:ILO Working Paper.

Ministry of Education (1986): National Science and Technology Policy. Dhaka: Science and Technology Division, February.

Ministry of Industry (1992a): Industrial policy, 1992. Kathmandu: Singha Durbar.

________(1992b): Nepal foreign investment opportunities. Kathmandu: Singha Durbar.

OECD (1993): Reviews of national science and technology policy, Portugal. Paris: OECD.

Pedersen, P.O., A. Sverrisson and M.P. van Dijk (eds., 1994): Flexible specialization. The dynamics of small-scale industries in the South. London: Intermediate Technology Publications.

Rana, R.S. (1989): Science and technology development in Nepal. Kathmandu: RONAST.

________(1994): Employment and migration in Nepal, some long-term implications. Helsinki: United Nations University, World Institute for Development Economics Research (UNU/WIDER).

Sharma, S. (1994): Economic liberalization and agricultural development in Nepal. Kathmandu: Ministry of Agriculture/Winrock International.

Sobhan, (1994): Labor exports from Bangladesh. Helsinki: UNU WIDER conference paper, June.

UNCTAD (1987): Technology issues in the energy sector of developing countries: Small-scale hydropower projects in Nepal (UNCTAD/TT/62), New York. United Nations .

________(1993): Technological dynamism in industrial districts: an alternative approach to industrialization in developing countries. (UNCTAD/ITD/TEC/11), United Nations publication, Sales No. E.94.II.D.3, Geneva.

UNDP (1994): Development co-operation, Nepal 1993 Report. Kathmandu: UNDP.

Van Dijk, M.P. (1993): The interrelations between industrial districts and technological capabilities. In: UNCTAD (1993).

________(1994): New competition and flexible specialisation in Indonesia and Burkina Faso. In: Pedersen *et al.* (eds., 1994).

Waliuzzaman, M. and M.M. Haque (1993): Technological capability building: the case of Bangladesh. Geneva: Study prepared for the UNCTAD Ad Hoc Working Group on the Interrelationship between Investment and Technology Transfer.

List of persons interviewed

Bangladesh

1.	Mohammed Iqbal Karim	Economist, UNDP Office
2.	M. Waliuzzaman	Chairman, Bangladesh Council of Scientific and Industrial Research (BCSIR)
3.	MD. Akmal Hossain	Director General, Export Promotion Bureau
4.	Ton Schutte	Netherlands Embassy
5.	Bram van Zwieten	Netherlands Embassy
6.	Depariya Bhattacharya	Research Fellow, Bangladesh Institute of Development Studies (BIDS)
7.	Peter Arnold	Head, Development Cooperation, Swiss Development Cooperation
8.	S.M. Al-Husainy	Secretary General, Federation of Bangladesh Chambers of Commerce and Industry
9.	Abdus Salam Bhuyan	Project Director, RDL Cell, Federation of Bangladesh Chambers of Commerce and Industry
10.	Richard Dictus	Assistant Resident Representative, UNDP
11.	Maksud Khan	President, Dhaka Chamber of Commerce and Industry
12.	Hossain Akhtar	Senior Vice President, Dhaka Chamber of Commerce and Industry

13.	Syed Toufique Ali	Vice President, Dhaka Chamber of Commerce and Industry
14.	Salman F. Rahman	President, Federation of Bangladesh Chambers of Commerce and Industry
15.	Muhiuddin Khan Alamgir	Secretary, Ministry of Science and Technology
16.	M.A. Quaiyum	Chairman, Bangladesh Atomic Energy Commission (BAEC)
17.	Mrs Watanabe	Resident Representative, UNDP
18.	Peter Grant	First Secretary (Economic), Aid Management Office, British High Commission
19.	Knut Nielsen	DANIDA, Dhaka
20.	G.L. Narasimhan	UNIDO
21.	Nick Roberts	Economic Adviser, European Union (EU)
22.	T.I.M. Nurunnabi Khan	Programme Officer, ILO, Dhaka
23.	A.B.M. Siddique	Division Chief, Socio-Economic Infrastructure Division, Planning Commission
24.	Gunilla Goransson	Technical Assistant to Planning Commission

<u>Nepal</u>

1.	Manoj Bahadur Basnyat	Chief, Programme Unit 1, UNDP
2.	B.K.L. Joshi	Senior Programme Officer, UNDP
3.	Caroll Long	Resident Representative, UNDP
4.	B.N. Sapkota	Secretary, Ministry of Commerce
5.	Madhav Ghimire	Joint Secretary, Ministry of Finance
6.	P.P. Dahal	Secretary, Ministry of Industry
7.	H.P. Sharma	General Manager, Trade Promotion Centre
8.	Andrew John Little	Project Adviser, MSUD Project, Ministry of Local Development
9.	Rishi Shaha	Secretary/Member of Royal Nepal Academy of Science and Technology (RONAST)
10.	Frederik Prins	Programme Coordinator, Netherlands Development Organisation (SNV)
11.	Sri Krishna Upaddhyay	SAPROSC (NGO)
12.	K.R. Pandey	National Training and Extension Adviser, Decentralization Project
13.	Badri Prasad Ojha	Officiating Secretary General, FNCCI
14.	R.S. Rana	Centre for Economic Development and Administration (CEDA)
15.	Bikash Pandey	Programme Manager, ITDG

16.	Umesh Malla	Joint Secretary, Ministry of Housing and Physical Planning
17.	L.R. Upadhyay	DG, Building Department
18.	Jigber Joshi	DG, Department of Housing and Urban Development
19.	Y.B. Thapa	Member, National Planning Commission
20.	Bongol	Assistance to National Planning Commission
21.	Michael Alcock	First Secretary, British Embassy
22.	Ernst Wicki	Assistant Coordinator, Swiss Development Cooperation
23.	Bruce Campbell	Senior Technical Adviser, UNFPA
24.	C.F. de Stoppelaar	Royal Nepalese Honorary Consul
25.	Herman Grimminck	Representative, Intercountry Child Welfare Organization (Netherlands NGO)
26.	Egbert Pelinck	Director General, International Centre for Integrated Mountain Development
27.	Eric Kamphuis	Director, SNV
28.	Bert Hamming	Holland Medical Services, NGO
29.	Ram Kumar Sharma	General Manager, Agricultural Development Bank of Nepal
30.	Hari Raj Pant	Section Officer, Department of Cottage and Small Industries
31.	Hirak Ghosh	Subregional Adviser, ILO International Programme on the Elimination of Child Labour
32.	Punya Prasad Lamsal	Division Chief, Agricultural Development Bank of Nepal
33.	Binod Hari Joshi	Federation of Nepalese Chambers of Commerce and Industry
34.	Badri P. Ojha	Officiating Secretary General, Federation of Nepalese Chambers of Commerce and Industry
35.	Arjun K. Upadhya	National Director, UNDP
36.	Basant Subba	SASCON Pvt. Ltd., Sand and Stone Consultants
37.	JPO UNCDF	UNDP Office
38.	J.H.J. Jeurissen	Netherlands Ambassador to India and Nepal

<u>Switzerland</u>

1.	Jamaluddin Syed	Minister (Economic Affairs), Permanent Mission of Bangladesh, Geneva
2.	Marcel van der Kolk	First Secretary (Economic Affairs), Permanent Mission of the Netherlands, Geneva

3.	Mussie Delelegn Arega	First Secretary, Permanent Mission of Ethiopia, Geneva
4.	Frank Joshua	UNCTAD, Geneva
5.	David Dichter	Technology for the People, Geneva
6.	Laurent Guye	Head Section, Development Policy Division, Office Fédéral des Affairs Economiques Extérieures, Bern
7.	Banmali Prasad Lacoul	Chargé d'affaires, Permanent Mission of Nepal, Geneva
8.	Lewin Mombemuriwo	CPC, Harare, Zimbabwe
9.	Msuya Waldi Mangachi	Minister Counsellor, Permanent Mission of the United Republic of Tanzania in Geneva
10.	K.P. Nyati	Confederation of Indian Industry, New Delhi
11.	G.S. Prosser	WS Atkins Environment, Surrey, United Kingdom
12.	A.S. Prasada Reddy	Research Fellow, RPI, Lund
13.	M.M. Sakbani	UNCTAD, Geneva
14.	Roger Short	Short and Associates, Songy, France
15.	John H. Skinner	Senior Adviser, UNEP, Paris
16.	Simon J.H. Smits	First Secretary, Permanent Mission of the Netherlands, Geneva
17.	P. Spycher	Head Department, Section Desk Asia II, Office Fédéral des Affaires Economiques Etrangères, Bern
18.	A. von Wartensleben	UNCTAD, Geneva
19.	Niklaus Zingg	Head, Bangladesh Desk, Office Fédéral des Affaires Etrangères, Berne

London

1.	Stella K. Blacklaws	Deputy Head, Technology Partnership Initiative, Department of Trade and Industry
2.	Richard Boulter	Small Enterprise Adviser, Overseas Development Administration (ODA)
3.	C.I. Ellis	Divisional Engineering Adviser, ODA

The Hague

1.	Piet de Lange	Sector Programmes Coordination and Technical Advice Department (DST)
2.	Frans van Rijn	DST
3.	H. Specker	DST
4.	J.G. Waardenburg	Chief Scientist, Development Cooperation, Ministry of Foreign Affairs

Copenhagen

1.	Leif Christensen	Head of Section, Royal Danish Ministry of Foreign Affairs
2.	Anders Serup Rasmussen	DANIDA
3.	Klaus Winkel	DANIDA

EXPERIENCES AND SUGGESTIONS FOR TECHNOLOGICAL CAPACITY-BUILDING IN BANGLADESH

by
M. Waliuzzaman
former Chairman, Bangladesh Council for Scientific and Industrial Research, Dhaka

I. EFFECTS OF GLOBALIZATION OF TRADE AND INDUSTRY

In the context of global liberalization of commerce and industries the Government of Bangladesh has adopted the policies of a free market economy. Emphasis is being placed on accelerated industrialization for economic development, which calls for increased national investment and technological capacity-building if the country is to be competitive in the international market. A long-term policy instrument to facilitate foreign investment for technology transfer is being considered as part of the Government's current industrial policy. It is likely that the open market policy embraced by Bangladesh will initially have an adverse effect on existing industries as well as on the growth of indigenous technologies, but in the long run it is expected that local industries will succeed in adjusting to the new and emerging technologies necessary for their survival. This is the ultimate goal of investment policy liberalization.

II. NATIONAL TECHNOLOGICAL DEVELOPMENT TRENDS

Bangladesh has a population of over 120 million, and offers good opportunities for foreign investment in the various sectors of the economy. The Board of Investment recently organized an International Investment Forum in Dhaka to attract foreign direct investment (FDI) and pave the way for joint ventures between local and foreign entrepreneurs. Although the interest displayed was more muted than anticipated, with the growth of the democratic system in the country and the investment incentives that are being offered, it is expected that sizeable foreign investments be made in Bangladesh in the near future. It is hoped that FDI and joint ventures in the industrial sector will create opportunities for technological capacity-building, but the results achieved will depend on the volume of investment and extent of the R&D activities carried out locally by the foreign investors. Multinationals carry out innovations and technology development either centrally or in their subsidiaries which are licensed in developing countries. Although this system is helpful in technology transfer, R&D in the country of investment would be an advantage for technological capability-building. As regards environmental considerations, these have now been provided for in the approval process for the setting up of new industrial units as well as for the improvement of existing units. Prior clearance by the Department of Environment is required for approval of a project.

At present, development planning in Bangladesh is not based on a centrally formulated technology plan. Different Ministries have their own planning units which are responsible for sectoral development planning. The central coordinating planning body is the Planning Commission. This scrutinizes the sectoral development projects and facilitates the process of obtaining the approval of the highest authority for national development — the Executive Committee for the National Economic Council. However, there is no explicit coordinating activity for technological capacity-building through a planning commission. There is a UNDP-funded programme known as TOKTEN, which is handled by the planning commission for technology transfer through expatriate Bangladeshi nationals, but its benefits are hardly perceptible as yet.

Current industrial policy has no specific provision for technological capacity-building or technology transfer except through FDI or joint ventures.

Nor is there any organizational activity for technology assessment or the study of reverse engineering.

Some sectoral technological capacity-building has taken place in agriculture, health and population control, pharmaceuticals and cosmetics. Although there has been a certain amount of investment in the primary energy and power sector, technological capacity-building leading to transfer of technology has not been achieved.

Export Processing Zones (EPZ) have been set up by the Government over the last decade to facilitate technology transfer and creation of employment opportunities. There has been some foreign investment in the EPZ for reasons of low labour costs, but there has been no transfer of technology nor have any contributions been made to GDP.

III. ROLE OF THE MINISTRY OF SCIENCE AND TECHNOLOGY

The Ministry of Science and Technology, which was elevated from Divisional status two years ago, is now coordinating S&T activities for technological capacity-building. It has emphasized the importance of developing more need-based research projects and more industry-institution interaction by R&D organizations. The Ministry of Science and Technology has recently sponsored a project to set up a technology transfer centre but it has yet to be approved by the National Council for Science and Technology.

In addition, the Ministry is actively considering a scheme to send 1000 scientists and engineers abroad for higher studies leading to doctoral degrees with a view to building up R&D capacity in various sectors over a period of five years.

IV. ROLE OF THE PRIVATE AND PUBLIC SECTORS

The private sector's role in technological capacity-building is insignificant. R&D is virtually non-existent, and there is little need-based research cooperation between private sector industry and public sector R&D organizations. As the private sector is virtually unaware of R&D benefits, their products hardly undergo any change for purposes of quality improvement, but this situation is expected to change in the near future in view of the current open market policy of the Government.

In most cases, the private sector employs under-qualified people with less productive capability. The reason is obvious: the cheap cost of labour. The capacity to operate machines is considered to be sufficient for running plant machinery set up under turnkey arrangements. These inefficient industries have continued to make money while the technologies have remained static and the efficiency of the plans has declined abysmally. As there has been no obligation to modernize, the enterprises have continued to operate the plant machinery even though it was fully depreciated long before. However, some technological capability has developed in private-sector workshops (roadside or organized), which can replicate certain foreign technologies and make spare parts for machinery.

Scientific technological capacity-building activities are virtually limited to public sector R&D organizations. There are several of these in the country, but the mechanism of R&D funding is unsuitable and inadequate. At present, all R&D expenditures are funded by the Government, and, in the absence of any industry-institute cooperation, there is hardly any income forthcoming from industry or non-governmental sources for the R&D institutions. Public sector industries as such do not have any R&D establishments.

A. Obstacles to technological capacity-building and suggested remedies

The industrial credit financing institutions have limited technological capability to assess the technological competitiveness of FDI or joint ventures or of local entrepreneurs' investment projects. Therefore the investments made have not been helpful for technology transfer. The human resource development programme is not being geared to the needs of the economy. Although Bangladesh has eleven universities, in both the public and private sectors, for education in engineering, science and technology and management, their curricula are not adequately need based and designed for technological development. Therefore the prime need now is for suitably trained personnel to meet the requirements of industry and other sectors of the economy. Technology development is expensive, so only the best human resources should be selected for the process of technological capacity-building.

However, at present, the public sector R&D institutions are the main technology providers. They also provide jobs for university graduates and publish a number of scientific papers.

Limited career prospects for research workers often lead to frustrations and ultimately jeopardize R&D activities and results. If public sector R&D personnel were given career building opportunities in line with those of other professionals and of civil servants, this would make an important technological capacity-building contribution to R&D institutions. An efficient research management and evaluation system would also be an essential element in technological capacity-building.

The Bangladesh Council of Scientific and Industrial Research (BCSIR), a public sector body, developed a large number of processes/technologies, over the years, primarily to develop import substitution industries and introduce innovative processes based on locally available raw materials. However, most of the processes and technologies faced problems in finding buyers. In many cases, the technologies could not be exploited as they were not competitive in terms of quality and production cost vis-à-vis the imported product. The reasons given for the difficulties of marketing the indigenous technologies may explain why the efforts of many other R&D organizations were not fruitful. As a result, local entrepreneurs in both the public and private sectors have come to doubt the effectiveness of such organizations. In most of these organizations the absence of any institutional mechanism for feasibility studies of research projects caused frustration among scientists when they found that the end products of the research and technology were not commercially viable. Besides, delay in the development of processes and technologies due to the limitations of modern R&D infrastructure facilities and lack of trained personnel rendered many of the indigenous technologies uncompetitive for commercial exploitation. In such situations, governmental commitment and venture capital for the exploitation of indigenous technology would act as a catalyst.

B. Lessons drawn from previous technological projects

For the last three decades the lack of technological capacity-building in Bangladesh has led to technological stagnation in industry. This is exemplified by two major industrial units set up about 20 years ago, with substantial capital investment, which are now operating at a loss or are inoperative, for the simple reason that the technology imported is outdated, and gives rise to problems of technological management and product marketability. In the absence of any in-house R&D and a need-based human resource development programme, the two projects, in each of which several hundred million dollars have been invested, have become liabilities for the Government. Had there been any awareness of the need for technology capacity-building at the time of project conception and implementation those two projects would still be operational today. Similar concern exists regarding the technological status of the urea plants.

C. Role of domestic and foreign capital in technological capacity-building

Domestic capital in the private sector has not been forthcoming for development of technological capacity-building. The flow of foreign direct capital has not been significant in the private sector either.

In recent years, the Government has been able to mobilize more domestic resources than before. This has enabled it to provide more financing for the annual development programme in the public sector. Several projects have been undertaken in the health, agriculture and fertilizer sectors with funding from foreign donor agencies in the public sector, and this will no doubt help to promote technology capacity-building.

Since it has been demonstrated in many countries that science and technology are a prime mover for economic development, capital investment, whether domestic or foreign, private or public, is clearly a prerequisite for technological capacity-building.

V. R&D MANAGEMENT FOR TECHNOLOGICAL CAPACITY-BUILDING

No achievement in R&D is possible without providing for: (a) the proper development of human resources; (b) the requisite physical facilities for S&T research; (c) an effective mechanism for selecting economically viable R&D projects; (d) an effective system for research management and evaluation; (e) collaboration between R&D institutions, universities and users of R&D output, particularly industries; (f) an effective system for the dissemination of research output; and, above all, (g) government commitment for fiscal, legal and institutional support.

Human resource development could be made possible through cooperation between the developed and the developing countries as the former have better institutional infrastructures for training scientific personnel.

A judicious selection of R&D projects in developing countries can promote technology development. The importation of new technologies and their adoption, with or without modifications through reverse engineering, could be helpful in developing technological capability. However, a "make some and buy some" technology policy for developing countries is likely to be the most suitable strategy for development and transfer of technology. Nevertheless, it must be kept in mind that the technological gap between the developed and developing countries is substantial and that the developed countries are always competing among themselves for technological superiority. In view of this, it sometimes seems as if the technological gap between the developed and the developing countries will never be narrowed. In fact, there is a saying that "Technology is a game for the rich and a dream for the poor".

VI. SOME SUGGESTIONS AND RECOMMENDATIONS FOR TECHNOLOGICAL CAPACITY-BUILDING

The major economic actors in the process of technological capacity-building are the State, industrial entrepreneurs, R&D organizations, universities and the international community. Their roles may be summed up as follows: (i) the Government must promote and support technology development programmes and integrate technology plans into the national planning process to accelerate economic development; (ii) the Government must provide sufficient funds for R&D and formulate favourable fiscal, industrial and commercial policies to facilitate the development of technology-oriented industries; (iii) the political environment must be congenial enough to attract both local and foreign investment; (iv) there should be increasing public awareness about the benefits of science and technology; (v) there should be effective collaborative research between R&D institutions and industry; (vi) foreign capital, either directly or in the form of joint ventures, must flow from the developed to the developing countries; (vii) developing countries must have access to the technological information of the developed countries; (viii) the efforts of the United Nations, and particularly UNCTAD, to provide financial and expertise support for technological capacity-building in the developing and least developed countries are praiseworthy.

In view of the liberalization of economic policy by the Government, it is anticipated that private sector investment, both foreign and local, will soon be forthcoming in the various sectors of the economy involved in technological capacity-building in Bangladesh. However, in order to assess the development trends and technology transfer, a review of the relationship between investment and capacity-building will be necessary, for which international organizations such as UNCTAD can provide the requisite support.

ASPECTS CONCERNING TECHNOLOGICAL CAPACITY-BUILDING IN NEPAL

by
Ramananda Mishra
Joint Secretary, Ministry of Industry, Kathmandu

I. A GLANCE AT THE SOCIO-ECONOMIC SCENARIO

With a population of 18.5 million, a growth rate of 2.08 per cent per annum, and a literacy rate of 32 per cent, Nepal, a land-locked country, falls into the category of least developed countries and is facing tough challenges in terms of development.

Nepal is predominantly agricultural. This sector absorbs more than 80 per cent of the total labour force of the country. Although Nepal is rich in mineral resources and well-known for possessing abundant water and forest resources, about 90 per cent of its people live in the rural areas, and 41 per cent of the households are living below the poverty line. In the industry sector, Nepal is well behind the others in this South Asian region. This sector in Nepal accounts for 5 per cent of GDP and employs only 1.1 per cent of the total labour force. The difficult Himalayan ranges create geographical constraints but these are offset by the beauty of the scenery which attracts tourists from all over the world. The Himalayas are also famous for the medicinal herbs that grow there and that require a systematic approach to exploitation for commercial purposes. The handicrafts sector has not yet found its right place in the world market.

II. GLOBALIZATION AND LIBERALIZATION TRENDS

The change-over in the political system in 1990 from the Panchayat to the present multi-party system, called for a new outlook to the economic growth of the country. The Eighth Five-Year Plan (1992-1997) for attaining the goal of economic development has set a policy of sustainable economic growth through a market-oriented, liberal economy, as the basis of the Plan. Hence, in those areas where there are viable prospects for private and non-governmental efforts, the Government's role will be confined to that of a catalyst.[41]

In inviting foreign investment to Nepal, the present Deputy Prime Minister of Nepal, addressing a recent reception hosted by the Japan-Nepal Association at Kansai, Japan, stated: "Our economy is open, liberalized and market-oriented, where privatization has its due role to play. In furtherance of our economic goals by following the policy of economic liberalization, we accord due priority to foreign capital, technology and management."[42] The Government, through several high-level missions, including those led by the Head of the Government, has invited industrialists and entrepreneurs at international forums to consider investing in Nepal where they can enjoy the incentives and facilities provided for the establishment of industries and other ventures.

III. INDUSTRY AND TRADE POLICIES

Realizing that the industrial sector plays a vital role in economic development, Nepal has adopted policies for the growth and promotion of this sector. In line with globalization and liberalization trends, Nepal has

---

[41]The Eighth Five-Year Plan (1992-1997), His Majesty's Government, National Planning Commission, Nepal.

[42]*The Rising Nepal* (national daily newspaper), Kathmandu, 28 March 1995.

pursued dynamic policies to stimulate local capability-building and encourage local entrepreneurs. It has also encouraged foreign capital and technology to come to Nepal. It is gradually reducing its custom barriers and giving the local industries some breathing time to improve their competitiveness, import better technology and increase their overall productivity.

The Industrial Enterprise Act 1992 has graded the industries of the country into four categories, according to the investment pattern: (a) cottage industry; (b) small-scale industry; (c) medium-sized industry, and (d) large-scale industry. In cottage industry, small and medium-sized industries with fixed assets of up to Rs. 2 million NC are open to technology transfer, and foreign investors have been given ample possibilities of investing in large-scale industry (with fixed capital NC, Rs. 5 million or US$ 1 million or above). For the promotion of the industrial sector, a high-level Board has been set up, headed by the Minister of Industry. The One Window Committee set up under the Act, has been formed to provide quick and efficient service on infrastructural and other matters of primary concern to industrialists. This Committee attends to the needs of investors as regards water supplies, electricity and telecommunication facilities, imports of machinery, raw materials and spare parts, the issue of import licences, the release of foreign currency and all other facilities required by investors. The Committee has the authority to make binding decisions on these matters. (The industries to be given priority are listed in annex 1).

The Government has adopted the role of a facilitator rather than an entrepreneur. It has been encouraging the private sector in nearly all fields of economic activity except defence. At the same time, it has kept a close watch on environmental aspects. This has demanded relatively advanced technology to meet the norms set by the Government's guidelines for environmental protection.

The private sector is free to select and enter into technical collaboration agreement with any foreign party. The agreement, however, must be recorded with the Government and should specify a few essential conditions such as duration, terms and conditions, royalties and technology transfer arrangements. The duration may be extended by mutual acceptance and upon ratification by the Government. The foreign Investment and Technology Transfer Act 1992 provides for legal support and facilities to be available to parties entering into joint ventures whether in equity or merely technical collaborations. More than 150 establishments are now operating as joint ventures/technical collaborations in Nepal.

The trade sector is undoubtedly a linch-pin for the economic development of any country. Nepal, as a land-locked country, has a Trade and Transit Treaty with India to gain access to the sea for export and import purposes. The lack of exploitation of its natural resources and the small industrial base have curtailed the possibilities of foreign trade to act as an engine of growth. As a result, the balance of payments has not been favourable. The Government has adopted policies for the promotion of foreign trade, and framed its trade policy in keeping with the open, liberal and market-oriented nature of the economy. Incentives and facilities have been provided to promote exports.

IV. THE OBJECTIVES OF THE PLAN, TECHNOLOGICAL CAPABILITIES AND THE CONDITIONS FOR PARTNERSHIPS

The objectives for the development of science and technology during the Eighth Plan (1992-1997), are (a) "To develop science and technology in such a way as to support the all-round development of the nation"; (b) "To support rural development sectors such as agriculture, cottage and small-scale industries by enhancing the scientific and technological capabilities available in the country"; and (c) "To encourage the import of foreign technologies that have a direct bearing on the country's economic development".

Although a least developed country like Nepal cannot afford to spend very much on S&T research, the efforts made in this respect demonstrate the importance it assigns to such work and to the need to create the necessary conditions for the utilization of modern technology. Nepal established the National Science and Technology Council in 1975, and the Royal Nepal Academy for Science and Technology was founded in 1992. The Tribhuvan University has been involved in the development and expansion of science and technology. Research is also being carried out in various government research laboratories, mostly in the fields of agriculture, botany, mining and pharmacy.

There are discrepancies and flaws in the process of research and implementation, and, as a result, the achievements have not been sufficiently fruitful." There is an obvious lack of coordination in the activities of various units that were existing or were created for the development of science and technology. In addition, another major concern has been the inability of scientific and technological development to be geared towards increasing production and productivity. The necessary contact between the researcher and the user seems to be lacking. Similarly, the results of research have not been able to be brought into practice on a sizeable scale. There is neither sufficient imports of appropriate foreign technology nor is there any attention being paid to the development of traditional indigenous technologies".[43]

Forms of technology partnership have been attained very successfully in a number of cases of industrial establishments concerned with textiles, sugar, cement, bricks, steel rods and sheet re-rolling, cigarettes, paper, etc., which are now wholly managed by Nepalese. In other cases in the private sector arrangements have been made for regular visits for purposes of technical consultation, but the local staff takes charge of the respective enterprises in normal periods.

As regards the different technology transfer modalities, the private sector in Nepal has preferred equity schemes in most cases. This may be due to the idea that, being financially involved, the foreign investors will naturally be serious about the adoption of the appropriate technology for such joint venture projects to compete successfully. However, enlightened entrepreneurs have sometimes preferred technical collaboration only. The Government has imposed no restrictions on technology transfer modalities which are to be decided by the parties concerned in mutual agreement.

The present industrial policy has envisaged setting up an Agency for Technical Transfer to streamline technological flows and their adaptation to Nepalese conditions. The Ministry of Industry now has a technology transfer section which needs to be strengthened and developed. The development-oriented international agencies such as UNCTAD, UNIDO, UNDP, etc. should make information on technology collaboration and related aspects available to the Ministry on a regular basis.

V. THE ROLE OF HUMAN RESOURCE DEVELOPMENT

The human resource situation in Nepal is dichotomous: while on the one hand Nepal has unskilled surplus labour, on the other hand it has a scarcity of skilled labour, and suffers from shortages of technical and managerial human resources.

In the transfer of technology the skill element is central. LDCs, such as Nepal, require experts to train local staff how to use and adapt technology to increase productivity. Most of the ministries and departments have their own training centres to produce the skilled personnel necessary to cater to the needs of their plans and programmes. Agencies could support such

[43] The Eighth Five-Year Plan (1992-1997), *op. cit.*.

development activities, making critically needed experts available under assistance packages, with arrangements for the local costs to be met by the recipients of the technological know-how if necessary.

NATIONAL PRIORITY INDUSTRIES

1. Modern sugar and Khandsari mills
2. Modern oil mills processing local oil-seeds
3. Integrated dairy (including animal husbandry) industry
4. Fruit and vegetable seed production industry
5. Tea and coffee farming and processing industry
6. Fruit processing industry
7. Herb farming and processing industry
8. Baby food and hygienic food producing industry
9. Cotton, woollen and silk yarn industry and textile industry based thereon
10. Leather processing and leather goods producing industry
11. Commercial and professional tools and equipment industry
12. Slate, stone and concrete blocks industry
13. Paper industries (writing, printing and newsprint)
14. Educational materials and stationery industry
15. Pharmaceutical industry
16. Medical equipment and instruments industry
17. Engineering industry (including agricultural and industrial tools and equipment)
18. Pesticides industry
19. Chemical fertilizers (excluding blending and mixing) industry
20. Industry manufacturing fuel saving devices
21. Industry manufacturing pollution control devices
22. Solid waste or waste product processing industry
23. Hydropower generation and distribution
24. Hotels, resorts
25. Roads, bridges, tunnels, ropeways, flying bridges, railways, trolley buses and office and residential complexes, etc.
26. Mineral-based industry
27. Caustic soda, chlorine, aluminium smelter, etc. Industries using electricity as its main input
28. Hospital, nursing home
29. Computer software industry
30. Export-oriented agro-based industry
31. Precision goods

TECHNOLOGICAL CAPACITY-BUILDING AND TECHNOLOGY PARTNERSHIP ASPECTS IN ZIMBABWE

by
Lewin Mombemuriwo
Director, National Cleaner Production Centre, Harare

INTRODUCTION

Despite the critical importance of technology and its development in developing countries this issue has long been neglected. However, the situation has changed with the advent of independence. The new States are trying to bridge the technological gap created over the years by methods now largely outdated, while they are at the same time beset by poverty, debt and unemployment. The developed countries attempt to narrow the gap by exporting technology through various forms of agreements but it nevertheless continues to widen in the absence of strong economies and R&D institutions to encourage local technological capacity-building in the recipient countries. The technically trained people in the developing countries should be taking advantage of the available technology to form companies at various levels to stimulate R&D. Many, however, are preoccupied with immediate survival in harsh economic environments and would rather concentrate on establishing themselves in multinational conglomerates where opportunities are still available. Efforts must be made to ensure that up-to-date technologies are available to the developing countries to help their industries, both large and small. In turn, the developing countries must make an effort to create favourable environments for the transfer of technology.

In the case of Zimbabwe, the realization by the Government that development without a technological foundation would be unsuccessful has prompted the establishment of institutions and programmes, in conjunction with international organizations, to spearhead technological development and technology transfer. During the long period of isolation experienced by the country from 1965 to 1980, technology was pirated or procured with very few standards and specifications attached to it. Owing to the economic sanctions applied by the international community when the Unilateral Declaration of Independence (UDI) was in force, the only area in which technological development took place was agriculture. This sector thrived even in the absence of partnerships with foreign investors because, unlike industry, it was given institutional support.

I. CURRENT CHALLENGES TO TECHNOLOGICAL CAPACITY-BUILDING IN ZIMBABWE

The attainment of full independence in 1980 ushered the country into a new era in which the emphasis was on consolidation of political power in the face of a strong apartheid-based opposition, a sector whose technological development had not been held back by isolation. The Government had responsibilities to fulfil, such as the promotion of education and health while technological development was fully supported through the establishment of agencies to foster it.

Nevertheless, the achievements of some R&D institutions, particularly in agriculture, where Zimbabwe still excels, were not completely lost from sight. R&D institutions have contributed, for instance, to high tobacco and cereal production. The success of these research centres is evident throughout the country and the technologies developed by them are used by commercial and rural farmers. Industry, on the other hand, mainly consists of multinationals that developed their technologies in industrialized countries, as UDI and the political issues of the 1980s prevented industry from benefiting in any way from the changes taking place elsewhere. The core of small and medium-sized enterprises (SMEs) in Zimbabwe were purely recessive types of pre-UDI technologies that had originally sprung from multinationals and therefore tended to perpetuate obsolete technologies.

The current economic development measures, against a setting of globalization and liberalization, which industry has been pressing the Government to implement, have exposed the weaknesses of the pre-1991 policies of a closed economy, with local industry over-protected. Market forces were never given the chance to develop because there was no competition in either pricing or quality of products (standard products), set prices being imposed on the consumer whether the products on offer were sub-standard or not. Market forces have now taken root. Consumers can compare prices, qualities and technology, and thus have the power to determine the survival of industry through the economic structural adjustment programme (ESAP).

Higher quality products are infiltrating the markets at reasonable prices, leaving local industries in disarray. The immediate victims were the individually run SMEs and SMEs which had been incorporated but not fully assimilated into multinational conglomerates. And yet this is the sector that the ESAP programme was supposed to nurture and promote. Employment creation opportunities which the ESAP programme was expected to generate vanished. The market envisioned as the result of that programme has dwindled as employment and hence income are no longer forthcoming. The prices of basic commodities (food, clothing, schooling, interest rates, services) started to soar, making commodities even harder to find on the local market.

Where new technology had been acquired by some big companies, in the areas of textiles and clothing, for example, over-production flooded the market. Moreover, SMEs with little technology and know-how were winding up business and thereby reducing the market, so the companies were forced to close down regardless of their advanced technology. This illustrates the need to make technology available throughout the economy rather than limiting it to a small sector. Rates of exchange were adjusted in an attempt to export the surplus goods, and thus reduce imports, but the targets necessary to sustain economic growth were not reached. The downward trend of the exchange rate made imported technology unaccessible to the SMEs because of its prohibitive cost.

Technological advancement is imperative, however, and the Government has initiated the construction of an R&D centre to service industry to enable it to develop products to international standards. This will stimulate SME development as this is the sector that desperately needs such assistance, while large companies already have R&D facilities and financial capacity.

As the majority of people in Zimbabwe, as in many other developing countries, cannot acquire resources such as skills, finance and technology, Zimbabwe has consequently embarked on a technological capacity-building programme to stimulate economic growth, including the establishment of a Scientific and Industrial R&D Centre and of a National University of Science and Technology. The concept of managerial skills development had been misconstrued at all levels as consisting solely in the management of finances and labour, and had never been extended to include the understanding and management of technology. Promoting the development of SMEs in developing countries should start by technical management skills. Once the concept of technology has been grasped, management skills can be learnt on that basis.

The maximum assimilation of technology takes place in the firms where technology is applied in the course of production. This should be the arena in which capacity-building efforts should be concentrated. The old plants and outdated technologies should be replaced by new and efficient models, and the managers and workers should have sufficient skills to understand and appreciate the changes taking place. The success of such a capacity-building programme depends on the supportive role played by the State. For example, as regards the training of apprentices, the Government gives incentives in the form of tax rebates to the companies that offer attachment facilities. It also encourages the establishment of institution-funded NGOs to operate under very favourable conditions.

The area still suffering from teething problems concerns the role played by the private sector in conjunction with the public sector. Here the division is apparent, with the private sector resenting government initiatives because of the divergencies in their political views founded on ethnic problems.

The Government is pressing for black entrepreneurship, but most of the possible candidates lack technological knowledge after being marginalized for so long, and are only just beginning to enter the economic mainstream. And, because of the pressures exerted on the Government, those who do finally take off with its assistance fail to maintain a viable business. Meanwhile, the small enterprises are being drawn by multinationals into high credit schemes coupled with abnormal interest rates, which push them further into debt.

The role of the private sector should be to enter into joint ventures with the SMEs, particularly the up-and-coming black entrepreneurs, and to encourage technology transfer and the acquisition of managerial skills. Economic growth will then be a meaningful concept because employment and market opportunities will be created that will eventually benefit big and small enterprises alike.

II. TECHNOLOGY PARTNERSHIP ASPECTS

At the same time, partnership between the SMEs (where risk is minimal but business opportunities are higher) and technologically advanced foreign organizations should be encouraged in order to help the developing countries to catch up with the others as regards their economies and technological level, and thereby lessen their debt burdens. These joint ventures will reduce the financial burdens on SMEs, especially the capital inputs and crippling interest rates which are as high as 45 per cent in the case of Zimbabwe. These factors naturally act as a deterrent to aspiring entrepreneurs. Other proposals in capacity-building would be for the international community to support least developed and developing countries by introducing options of interest to them, e.g. programmes that relate to technology transfer and information accessibility, and arousing the interest of the developed countries in assisting developing countries.

Without examining the cause of the diversity between the developed and least developed countries, it is difficult to think of technology partnerships as an instrument to foster entrepreneurship through effective technology transfer and the development of managerial skills and as the only means to deal with the problems and changes in international economic trends. The transfer of technology and the development of managerial skills may simply add to basic features that already exist: even if the economic setting is sound, with the poverty that prevails throughout the country these skills will serve no purpose.

It is almost impossible for the majority of people in developing countries to save up in the hope of investing in some form of business, because their governments tax them heavily, and suppliers of utilities such as electricity, telecommunications, water, etc., are inefficient. Moreover, as they are government controlled and thus have no competition, their service charges are set very high to offset their losses.

The culture developed over the years of colonization has had far-reaching effects on developing countries, which still suffer from the class structure that continues to exist there. It is the top levels of this structure that form the core of the leadership in industry and in politics. This very group is the main source of the technically trained people who constitute the backbone of the multinationals, but do not take the risk of starting businesses and adopting the technologies that might be available as they would in developed countries. They possess the skills required for existing types of business but have not acquired those needed to negotiate contracts, particularly for technology. It is thus necessary for this group to develop a spirit of confidence in business, because they are the only people equipped to do so, but they continue to be too fearful of the hazards involved in becoming independent entrepreneurs outside the sphere of the multinationals.

A large number of project proposals based on different modalities, particularly at the inception of ESAP, have been approved, (e.g. the Zimbabwe Investment Centre (ZIC) approved 366 project proposals in 1994). The projects included 267 joint ventures between local and foreign partners, 86 were wholly foreign owned while 12 were wholly owned locally. The success ratings were 100 per cent for wholly foreign owned, 96 per cent for joint ventures and 10 per cent for locally owned ventures, mostly SMEs. The reasons for success included non-equity terms involved in the wholly foreign owned, technological agreements, effective transfer of technology, and the acquisition of new organizational skills in the joint ventures, while failures were due to lack of new, competitive technologies. The joint ventures established between government-owned companies based on political grounds may result in technologies being misunderstood because appointments to the companies are normally political.

III. CONCLUSIONS AND RECOMMENDATIONS

Policy-oriented proposals for the identification of the best conditions and incentives for promoting effective technology partnerships should emphasize the importance of taking an integrated approach in the formulation of the country's policies by the major actors in the economy. This requires the Governments to facilitate an open attitude to issues of technology, such as the provision of support to technological institutions, by allocating funds for technological development. The private sector should look at these institutions as developmental resources and make use of them. Research and development at enterprise level should be tested and the repeatability of the results should be endorsed by research institutions and made available.

Technically trained persons should be encouraged to form the basis of the SMEs because of their ability to translate and appreciate technology. This can be achieved by making the business environment favourable in terms of financing, taxes, interest on loans, the final cost of acquiring technology and transparent terms of partnership.

The international community, and particularly the developed countries, should redouble their efforts to source technology and disseminate information on it in order to make it accessible to countries. They should also encourage the Governments of developing countries to support technological capacity-building projects.

BUILDING TECHNOLOGICAL CAPACITY IN THE DEVELOPING AND THE LEAST DEVELOPED COUNTRIES - THE CASE OF SMALL AND MEDIUM-SIZED ENTERPRISES IN CHILE

by
Hugo Cubillos
Ambassador of Chile to the Government of Sweden, Stockholm

BACKGROUND

The UNCTAD Ad Hoc Working Group on the Interrelationship between Investment and Technology Transfer highlighted, at its various sessions, some important elements linked to technological development in developing countries.

Perhaps the most important conclusion was that the objective of investment and technological development was competitiveness which developing countries must achieve within the productive capacities of their enterprises. A year after the deliberations of the UNCTAD Ad Hoc Working Group, the factors of competitiveness and productivity seem to be more and more closely intertwined. In order to achieve increased productivity, an enterprise must also endeavour to improve its competitiveness and this applies equally to enterprises that have domestic markets and those with international target markets.

In order to raise its competitiveness, the enterprise must introduce new technologies that improve the product thereby making it more attractive to the consumer and user. This is not easy to implement in small and medium-sized enterprises (SMEs) in developing countries, and particularly difficult in the least developed countries.

I. STRENGTHENING TECHNOLOGICAL CAPACITY IN SMALL AND MEDIUM-SIZED ENTERPRISES

Developing countries which applied structural reforms from the 1980s onwards have observed that State financing of R&D activities has significantly declined. As a result, these activities are nowadays the responsibility of business and academia. Governments have fewer resources to contribute to R&D activities than in the past. Moreover, Governments must be wary of making contributions to support the R&D of enterprises because the Governments of the importing countries could consider them unacceptable incentives or subsidies.

In low or medium-income countries, the establishment of small and medium-sized enterprises (SMEs) has grown substantially. They provide a very specific impression of the technological problems in these countries.

In Chile, SMEs try to fill a gap in national production, but they have restricted access to elements that are critical for the improvement of their competitiveness, such as, access to technology, capacity-building and loans from the banking system and domestic financial circles. Chilean SMEs may be grouped in three main categories:[44] (a) innovative and quality-based SMEs (group 1); (b) quality-targeted SMEs tending towards quality (group 2); (c) mature and conservative SMEs (group 3).

Enterprises in Group 1 are those whose main objective is the transfer of "know-how" and their main motivation is quality. These SMEs use technology as a vital tool for competition. They regard investment in R&D as good

[44] PYME, Un desafío a la modernización productiva (A challenge for productive modernization), Corporación de Fomento de la Producción (CORFO), 1994.

business and the best tool for ensuring the survival of the enterprise. In Chile, these enterprises usually seek funding from the Fondo de Desarrollo Technológico (FONTEC) and this enables these enterprises to have a high technology base, to be innovative and to enjoy vigorous growth. However, this group of enterprises accounts for only 1 per cent of SMEs in Chile.

Enterprises in Group 2 are very interested in quality. Their basic concern is information. These SMEs are equipped with standard, medium-level technology and they need technology transfer, both hard (hardware, such as processing equipment) and soft (training of the work force and mid-level management and software). A recent study revealed that 8 per cent of the enterprises interviewed were stressing quality management. Approximately 9 per cent of SMEs in Chile belong to this group.

Ninety per cent of Chilean SMEs belong to Group 3, the conservative enterprises. Their main concern is financing. Their entrepreneurs do not see the importance of technology, quality is not valued and these enterprises have a low technology base.

There are numerous factors within SMEs that affect their innovative capability. In Chile, the following have been identified:

(a) A lack of business management and appropriate organization of the existing factors of production. In the case of SMEs, there are many cases in which the owner and the manager are one and the same, and this can have negative repercussions on technological investment. The non-separation of capital between the individual and the enterprise presents many problems for the success of the business since technical decisions run the risk of becoming personal and subjective; this can often curb opportunities for technological change. Personal experience - frequently undocumented - is the main source of information for the owner. On the other hand, the employment of a technical manager can greatly influence the efficiency of technological innovation, the management of information and the design of business strategy.

(b) Another negative aspect of SMEs is the scarcity of technical capabilities within the enterprise. There are no professionals or technical specialists because of the limited size of the operations. Furthermore, their scarce resources do not allow these enterprises to resort to consultants or to external technicians.

(c) In Chilean SMEs there is also the problem of the ability to choose the appropriate form of new investment in infrastructure and equipment. This situation occurs because of the lack of strategic analysis of the enterprises' productive integration and potential. In addition, there is a dearth of information on demand in the target markets that would enable the SMEs to avoid the acquisition of obsolete, inefficient or high-cost technologies.

(d) SMEs have few resources at their disposal for R&D within the enterprise. This is a weak point that derives not only from the precariousness of resources but also from the difficulties they encounter in gaining access to bank loans.

(e) Besides, in Chile and many developing countries, there is no formal or informal link between academia and business. We are aware that UNCTAD has a project in this fundamental area, but there has not yet been any international organization "with a calling in development assistance" that has demonstrated the urgent interest that such a project represents to developing countries.

The above description of SMEs in Chile gives an accurate picture of the situation of SMEs in other developing countries, in particular, the situation of technological capacity in the least developed countries and many low-income countries.

II. THE CRITICAL ROLE OF HUMAN-RESOURCE DEVELOPMENT

Numerous factors are required in order to overcome the above-mentioned difficulties in creating, promoting and modernizing technological capability in developing countries, and the State, now more than ever, must be an efficient promoter in the relationship between the private sector and academia. In the author's opinion, several elements that provide the technological function with some degree of dynamism are required.

First of all, the State must mobilize services in support of enterprises to improve their access to financing, technology, training, information and the market place.

Technological dynamism for the modernization of productivity means placing greater emphasis on changing the thinking of the actors involved. These include not only entrepreneurs but also the workers in an enterprise. In order to achieve this, the following are essential: training and capacity-building of entrepreneurs, technicians and workers throughout the country, and the process of association between local, regional and international enterprises.

The main goal for enterprises in the coming years is to increase their levels of productivity. This means investment in the capacity-building of entrepreneurs, technicians and workers and in innovation, adaptation or the acquisition of technology.

The second goal is the proper integration of the enterprise in domestic and international markets. To achieve this, certain State incentives are needed, but the essential factor is the training of human resources, in both quality management and in the harnessing of technologies than can be most effective for business.

The goal mentioned in the previous paragraph could be the key to the modernization of technological capability in developing countries. This objective should start with education at the primary level, and continue through the secondary and tertiary levels.

In order to reach that goal, it is necessary to reformulate the educational systems in developing countries, as in the developed countries. The educational systems in the developing countries must respond to the challenge of technology and modern science without resorting in the future to the heavy cost of purchasing licenses, delaying the training of engineers, entrepreneurs, technicians and workers. The technological capability of a country will ultimately be measured by the quality of the people that participate in R&D and those who promote technological development in enterprises. Consequently, the productivity and competitiveness of a country should, of necessity, be a product of its educational system.

III. ASSOCIATIONS BETWEEN ENTERPRISES

While the reforms of the educational systems can be fruitful, many enterprises in developing countries will find it necessary to receive technology from other sources. The most important of these sources nowadays seems to be the association between enterprises which can take several forms, as outlined below:

(a) Investment in joint development;

(b) Strategies or strategic alliances between enterprises related through R&D, markets, design or exchange of technicians, workers or management personnel;

(c) The most popular form of association nowadays is the association of enterprises working on similar products or in similar markets.

(d) There can also be an association between enterprises in which the most technologically strong industry agrees to transfer certain technological advances to an industry operating in different markets;

(e) There are other types of associations whose objectives often cannot be made known because of convenience or confidentiality clauses.

In any event, investment and the target market or markets have a fundamental role to play in the enterprises' decision to form an association.

IV. PROBLEMS AND POSSIBILITIES FOR THE LEAST DEVELOPED COUNTRIES

The most serious problem within the framework of association of enterprises arises in the least developed and other low-income countries. It so happens that enterprises in the more advanced or industrialized countries are relatively less inclined to associate with small enterprise in these low-income countries. This is understandable since some World Bank and UNDP studies have shown that institutions created in low-income countries have broken down quickly or closed down for lack of support from the State or because the foreign institution that set them up in the first place withdrew earlier than planned.

It is therefore the duty of the international community to demonstrate active concern for this problem, particularly since there is an awareness that the least developed countries do not have the minimum economic resources needed to create or maintain institutions that can ensure the development of their technological capacity. Their GNP growth is also poor, if not negative, and many developed countries have lost interest in providing major economic and technical assistance because the least developed countries do not have the capacity to maintain their institutions.

This vicious circle must be broken. The international community cannot remain indifferent to the widening of the technological gap between industrialized and poor countries. International cooperation should promote activities to stimulate the least developed countries to embark on the road to technological progress in the areas of production and services.

There is one formula that could be established with those least developed countries that are prepared to enter into agreements with the Governments of developed countries on the establishment and maintenance of their technological capacity. A commitment could be established between one State from among the least developed countries and one or more developed countries for the latter to promote and finance the building of R&D institutions and enterprises engaged in the production of goods and services. This could be done on condition that they are responsible for the process for a sufficiently long period and that the least developed country will entrust the management of the technological institutions and the enterprises to the Governments and enterprises involved in the project. In this way, the least developed country will be assured of financing and efficient management while the industrialized countries' resources will contribute effectively to the technological progress of the least developed States.

This implies that one State will have to agree to concede certain essential decisions to another State. But, in studying the current situation in international cooperation and the security considerations that enterprises require for their investments abroad, there does not seem to be another formula to assure in the present international economic circumstances the least developed countries that their technological capacity and, consequently, their equitable development with the rest of the world will be promoted.

BARRIERS TO THE TRANSFER OF ENVIRONMENTAL TECHNOLOGIES IN ARGENTINE INDUSTRY

by
María del Carmen Longa Virasoro
President, Asociación para el Desarrollo de la Gestión Ambiental
Buenos Aires

I. LIBERALIZATION AND PRIVATIZATION TRENDS IN ARGENTINA AND TECHNOLOGICAL DEVELOPMENT

A. Deregulation

In the period 1991-1993, a market economy was created by eliminating controls on prices, wages, interest rates, foreign exchange rates and capital flows, by removing subsidies and by reducing the weight of the public sector in the economy. A massive privatization programme placed public services under the discipline of competitive markets, or, in the case of monopolistic markets, under the oversight of regulatory frameworks. This privatization process has led to an upgrading in four areas: (1) training and managerial skills, (2) equipment and infrastructure, (3) technological progress, (4) productivity. One example of these effects is the development by the Argentine telephone company of a training programme for suppliers to upgrade their technical skills; this will imply ISO 9000 certification for next year. Another example is that of a textile company, which, through its association with a foreign company, will be introducing new information systems to make their fiber quality more homogeneous.

At the same time, the globalization of the economy has left much less room for the development of in-house capabilities. In many cases, firms have increased the import content of their production activities and have moved "backwards" towards the final assembly of imported components.

B. Investment and trade liberalization

Foreign investors and local investors are governed by the same legal conditions and there are no restrictions on the repatriation of capital and dividends. Investment guarantee treaties have been signed with a number of countries. During the period 1988-1992 foreign investment rose from US$ 1.1 to 4.1 billion. The main sectors concerned are automotive production, food products, agriculture and agroindustry, oil and natural gas, mining and telecommunications. In foreign trade, nearly all non-tariff barriers and export taxes were eliminated, while the tariff structure was simplified and tariffs were sharply reduced. There are no duties on imports of capital goods.

Concerning investments in environmental technologies, of the 300 firms studied in a recent survey, 67 per cent plan to invest in environmental measures, of which 30.3 per cent intend to invest directly in technology transfer related to the environment.

II. BARRIERS TO TECHNOLOGY ADOPTION

The recent survey of 300 companies conducted in 1993-1994 identified the following barriers for the adoption of environmental business management systems and cleaner technologies: (a) lack of information; (b) lack of qualified personnel; (c) lack of know-how for the use of cleaner technologies; (d) a confusing regulatory framework; and (e) financial needs.

The barriers perceived by developing countries are as follows:

(a) Patent holders prevent environmentally sound technologies (ESTs) from being used in developing countries by refusing to license, and setting prices at levels that are too high for the local market.

(b) Developing countries are discouraged from using ESTs for the following reasons: the costs of new ESTs are greater than those of existing "polluting" technologies; there are insufficient financial resources to cover the incremental costs; there is a lack of new resources, or information about existing resources, that are specifically for ESTs; spare parts and equipment servicing are not available at a reasonable cost or on a timely basis.

(c) Insufficient information disclosure by producers of ESTs weakens the developing country's product choices and negotiating advantages, and reduces the likelihood of appropriate environmentally sound technology transfer decisions.

III. RECOMMENDATIONS

The actions taken should address the following priorities: (a) dissemination of information; (b) training and human resources development; and (c) institutional strengthening.

A. Public policies for the transfer of technology from abroad

Some caveats are set out below with regard to the aims and effects of government policies introduced in developing countries to import more advanced technologies from developed countries.

Successful transplanting of advanced technologies may have important externalities in building up a stock of knowledge in the developing country, which will make it easier to transfer technically related innovations. The development of technological competencies in a field such as information technology can have pervasive applications across a range of industries and sectors.

There is a need for careful prior empirical analysis of the entire decision-making system that may be affected by government policies to promote technological progress in particular industries or sectors (interaction between diffusion and innovation phenomena).

Efforts to speed up the rate of innovation in industries supplying capital goods can lead to fears of larger capital losses through obsolescence for firms that are considering adopting the new technology, thus retarding the current pace of diffusion of available technologies and slowing the rate of productivity growth.

Tax and other subsidies for R&D can reduce the costs of imitation and lead to the wider diffusion of a new technology through an industry. But if it is anticipated that most other industries will also adopt the technology quickly, there will be less inducement to bear the cost of adopting it early on. The initial speed of diffusion would be slowed down, even if the eventual extent of the technology's adoption were increased.

Public funding for the dissemination of information to users of innovative technologies may induce supplying firms to set their prices initially at a higher level than they might otherwise have chosen to do.

The demonstration value of exposing more potential adopters to information about new products is critical.

The design of market-based policies can stimulate the private sector to develop new pollution-control technologies and expertise. Because investments in pollution control can increase profit-making by firms through incentive-based systems, firms will be encouraged to adopt superior pollution-control technologies. This in turn will create incentives for research and development of cheaper and better pollution-abatement technologies.

B. Private sector

Owing to the widespread acceptance of the "polluter pays principle" in developed countries, subsidized programmes of environmental industrial reconversion are no longer the rule, and the private sector in Argentina has been requested to adopt a more proactive role in this process of change. In this respect, technical assistance takes priority over financial assistance, even if the latter is also deemed necessary.

Tacit or codified knowledge involved in technology transfer (details of processes and material specifications, technical expertise of managers and workforce) is a vital factor in a successful process. In this respect, the workforce in Argentina has the competitive advantage of having an acceptable scientific and technical level. "Training for trainers" programmes have proved useful in achieving a capacity-building goal.

C. International community

The following activities might be undertaken by the international community.

(a) Start-up of technology transfer centres. In this connection, the aims would be to increase the access of developing countries to ESTs, mainly in the small and medium-sized enterprise sector, and help to bring about the much needed technological shift. These centres should have a small and effective structure and a very active marketing profile in order to promote business and technology at the same time. Large databases do not fulfil the purpose of facilitation and diffusion, and they have a poor record in Latin America. The support of international agencies is crucial to obtain the requisite level of excellence in the training of the professional teams involved. In this case, too, training for trainers is necessary to duplicate successful experiences in the region.

(b) Assistance in sectoral projects. Technical and financial assistance should be given in the implementation, measurement and evaluation of environmental technology projects, in order to draw lessons from them and to duplicate them throughout the region.

(c) Training programmes for young professionals. Young professionally trained people should be the agents of tacit knowledge transfer. They should also maintain cultural links with developed countries and keep in contact with the sources of supply of goods and services.

D. Options to facilitate the transfer of ESTs

The various types of options to be considered are set out below:

(a) Options using new sources of global revenues: environmental premiums based on tradeable pollution permits; revenues from a global carbon or greenhouse gas tax; international environmental offset investment programmes; and debt-for-nature swap programmes.

(b) Options using market mechanisms: raising global demand for ESTs by agreeing to international standards in a range of existing technologies; the same applies to bulk-purchase agreements by developing countries, and to purchase guarantees by developed countries; transferring patent rights to an international organization to allow the technologies to be used in developing countries; redefining patent rights with the aim of excluding crucially needed environmental technologies; and a price discount incentive for developing countries to increase EST markets.

(c) Options using investment and trade agreements: placing a limit to supplementary charges for environmental technologies and services destined for developing countries; arrangements relaxing limitations on the repatriation of income derived from ESTs used in developing countries; standardizing methods for environmental costing and projected environmental savings; and adopting export constraints on environmental costing and projected environmental savings.

(d) Options using regulatory systems: requiring commercial banks to prepare environmental cost and benefit statements for large commercial loans; and creation of an international centre to settle investment disputes regarding EST transfers.

(e) Options using national tax and tariff systems: creating tax incentives for the transfer or use of ESTs in developing countries; creating tax disincentives to restrain the use of environmentally hazardous technologies; creating tariff incentives to increase the flow of ESTs; and creating tariff barriers to reduce trade in environmentally hazardous technologies.

(f) Options using development assistance: bilateral official development assistance programmes; multilateral official development assistance programmes; establishing environmental purchasing standards for multilateral banks and international organizations; and expanding multilateral bank assistance for projects using ESTs.

PHILIPPINE EXPERIENCE IN TECHNOLOGICAL CAPABILITY-BUILDING FOR SMES IN THE AREA OF ENVIRONMENTAL MANAGEMENT AND SUSTAINABLE DEVELOPMENT

by
Grace Favila
Executive Director, Philippine Business for the Environment, Manila

INTRODUCTION

The first signs of public concern for the environment became evident in the Philippines in the late 1970s. However, business and industry remained aloof from such concerns, and it is only in the last five years that business in the Philippines has become actively involved in environmental matters.

I. THE GRADUAL INTEGRATION OF ENVIRONMENTAL CONCERNS

Among other reasons, the following are three major factors that led the Philippine business community to face environmental issues squarely:

(a) **Demands of the foreign and domestic markets.** It began to be necessary for export manufacturers with markets in Europe to certify that their products were made under sustainable processes and from sustainable materials. Today, with the successful conclusion of the Uruguay Round, environmental responsibility in processing is an essential element in global competitiveness. A growing number of local consumers, influenced by schoolchildren who had learned the principles of environmental protection and sustainable development, started to demand more environmentally-responsible products.

(b) **The United Nations Conference on Environment and Development at Rio in 1992.** The Rio Conference, through its media coverage and the special participation of international business, caught the attention of local businessmen.

(c) **Increasing evidence that "Environment makes good business sense".** Aside from the reports of such foreign companies as 3M and AT&T, of increased profits or savings due to corporate environmental responsibility, a number of local experiences have also borne out the same proposition.

Convinced that environment is a valid business interest, many business entities have started to integrate environmental concerns in their decision-making processes, in their strategic planning and in other corporate practices. They have also begun to seek out information on possible courses of action to make their processes clean or environment-friendly.

II. RELEVANT POLICIES AND LEGISLATION

A brief description of the policy and regulatory environment in the Philippines is necessary at this point. It is generally accepted, by foreign as well as local experts that Philippine policies and laws pertaining to the environment are quite adequate. What is sadly inadequate is the effective enforcement of these policies and laws. The Government suffers from a shortage of resources for acquiring appropriate monitoring equipment and providing proper training for enforcement personnel. As a result, businessmen are easily tempted to violate the law, and just pay the fine or bribe the inspectors if and when they are caught. Big companies, which cannot afford the bad publicity of non-compliance, complain of the absence of a "level playing field".

Since 1992, the Government has embarked on a multifaceted capability-building programme to improve its enforcement of environmental policies and regulations. These efforts focus on the Department of Environment and Natural Resources (DENR), particularly its Environmental Management Bureau (EMB). Financing for these capability-building efforts is augmented by funding from international donors and bilateral/multilateral agencies like the United States Agency for International Development (USAID), the United Nations Development Programme (UNDP), the Asian Development Bank (ADB), the World Bank, the Danish International Development Assistance agency (DANIDA) and others.

Because of the poor enforcement of environmental laws by the Government, companies are hesitant to spend much money to improve their environmental equipment. They prefer instead to choose options that improve their environmental performance with as little capital investment as possible. This has led to the high popularity of the concept of **Pollution Prevention** or **Waste Minimization.**

A. Programmes to promote pollution prevention: IEMP and AEIP

There are now a number of programmes that promote this concept. Two of the most successful are funded by USAID under the Industrial Environmental Management Project (IEMP) and the ASEAN Environmental Improvement Project (AEIP). The former focuses on small and medium-sized companies like pig farms, sugar millers and fish canners, while the latter aims to help big industries such as the steel industry and textile industry.

B. Pollution management appraisals by companies

The IEMP is really a capability-building project with EMB, but one of its components is promotion of the practice of Pollution Management Appraisals (PMAs) by companies. Under a PMA, an outside expert visits a processing plant, together with its in-house operations manager and/or supervisors, to identify the areas and opportunities where waste minimization could be introduced. The expert then prepares a report for the company management, including a set of recommendations for adoption. The expert will make another visit later to follow up on any action taken.

In the beginning, companies were very hesitant to volunteer for a PMA, which was originally given free of charge by IEMP. However, because many of the early volunteers reported tremendous savings shortly after such an appraisal and the adoption by the companies of the expert's recommendations, there has been a surge of volunteers who are even willing to pay for a PMA. However, IEMP can no longer absorb all the volunteer companies under the terms of its project. What has happened instead is that a market for PMA consultants has evolved and local scientists and engineers are starting to respond to this demand. To sustain the practice of PMAs in the long term, IEMP also conducts training courses for local consultants. What is emerging is a new field of commercially valuable expertise. It is relevant to the theme of this Workshop to point out that many of the recommendations resulting from PMAs, such as the separation of waste streams, efficient use of raw materials, installation of pressure-control valves, and addition of weirs to separate solid wastes, cost little or nothing. In each case, the adoption of these low-cost or no-cost recommendations has yielded significant savings in operating costs, in the case of the former after a few months only. It is important to note that the PMAs also made high-cost recommendations, many of which have not been adopted. More time is needed to convince small businessmen and their creditors that such expenditure would eventually be recouped through the savings that would materialize if the recommendations were put into effect. Some businessmen are also waiting until law enforcement becomes truly efficient to justify the high cost of such recommendations.

The AEIP too has had a number of successful experiences with PMA.

C. Self-monitoring

Self-monitoring is another low-cost practice that has proved to be environmentally successful. Under a programme funded by the Swedish Government, a cement company and a pulp and paper company volunteered to install self-monitoring systems in their plants. Monitoring equipment and Swedish consultants were loaned to these companies and their personnel were trained. The training concerned process control with the focus on pollution prevention rather than on end-of-pipe solutions. After a year, there were dramatic improvements in both companies' pollution levels.

D. Environmental Impact Assessment

Environmental Impact Assessment (EIA) is another technology that has been transferred to the Philippines. Its assimilation has been long and painful taking 15 years, but today most sectors of society accept that strengthening the country's capacity to carry out EIA can make a major contribution towards improving environmental natural resources management. A law now requires EMB to implement the EIA system. Once again, however, a major barrier to full implementation is inadequate government enforcement. To a lesser extent, there is also the need to upgrade the technical analytical skill required to carry out EIA.

It is encouraging to note that over the last 15 years, as a result of the exposure of local scientists and engineers to the EIA system, there is now a growing pool of local experts who can carry out EIAs satisfactorily. In the beginning, EIA projects were given exclusively to big foreign consultant companies as required by the bilateral/multilateral agencies funding the projects. However, these companies hired local scientists and engineers to carry out the tests and surveys required by the EIA system, many of whom thereby acquired enough experience and confidence to found their own local consulting companies. Because their rates are much lower than those of their foreign rivals, they are often hired for locally funded EIA projects. Their commercial success has also made science and engineering courses attractive to young students, which augurs well for the further development of local capability.

III. SUCCESS FACTORS

The above experiences suggests that the factors leading to successful technological capability-building in a developing country are as follows:

(a) **Evidence of profitability.** This factor is essential to the success of any new technology to be introduced to a developing country. Given the scarcity of capital and other business-related resources, local entrepreneurs cannot afford to invest in undertakings whose returns are more social than economic. The PMAs have been highly successful in the Philippines because they have effectively improved the companies' financial situation by, among other things, reducing their operating costs. The surge of interest in scientific and engineering careers is, in fact, largely due to the economic attractiveness of the emerging environmental consultancy business rather than its socially-oriented rationale.

(b) **Initial demonstration by foreign consultants** *in situ*. In each of the above examples, the technological capability-building effort succeeded because foreign consultants effectively demonstrated the process in the local environment. No doubt, the foreign experts gathered insights from the local trainees that enabled them to adjust the technology to the peculiarities of the local situation, making the whole effort one of positive cooperation.

(c) **A reasonable level of local capability for science and engineering.** This is another important success factor in the above examples of technological capability-building. The Philippines' pool of scientists and engineers has actually shrunk in the last decade or so. The number of students going into the sciences drastically dipped in the late 1980s due to the fact that careers in business management and law were more economically attractive. The science graduates of a generation ago have found employment in other countries. Nevertheless, a number remained and it is they who were tapped and trained by the visiting consultants, and are now passing on what they learned to other local experts.

(d) **Sufficient financial assistance.** Because one of the main reasons for the local Government's inadequacy is lack of financial resources, the fact that the above examples of technical assistance were coupled with generous financial assistance was an extremely important element in their success. The IEMP alone has a total budget of US$ 20 million, an amount which allows them to obtain the best local and foreign human resources, adequate equipment and a good operating environment.

BUILDING TECHNOLOGICAL CAPACITY IN DEVELOPING COUNTRIES: THE CASE OF INDIA

by
K. P. Nyati
Head, Environment Management Division, Confederation of Indian Industry, New Delhi

INTRODUCTION

The technological capacity of each country is different, be it for addressing environmental issues or for meeting the basic needs and requirements of the population. An appreciation of this fact is crucial, especially in the context of building such a capacity in developing countries. There are many reasons that explain why an understanding of country-specific peculiarities should be the bedrock for action plans and initiatives in this regard. Some of the most important are as follows:

- The overall status of the existing technological base in a particular country determines the starting point for action.

- The technological capacity-building process implies progressive adaptation, integration, assimilation and final absorption. The sustainability of progressively higher levels of technological capacity is thus assured.

- For any process to take roots an enabling policy framework is an essential prerequisite. An understanding of the existing policy environment in the given country concerned is thus the key to the success of technological partnership processes.

- Technological capacity-building process cannot be imposed from above. It has to be driven by the needs and aspirations of the people. In other words, it is the market and the macro-economic scenario that condition the climate for technological modernization, its direction and pace.

- Given that natural endowments, infrastructure and other associated support mechanisms are at different levels of development in different countries, action plans and technology cooperation processes must take these differences and the underlying strengths and weaknesses into account.

- The level of institutional infrastructure and the quality of the human resources, including the academic institutional base, in the country concerned will obviously determine where the thrust of the technological capacity-building process ought to be.

- Lastly, there has to be a clear-cut objective for technological capacity-building that will mesh with the ongoing developmental strategies of the developing countries. However, a certain amount of moderation may be necessary if the ultimate aim of technology cooperation is to help developing countries to restructure their national economies with resource-use intensities.

I. SMALL AND MEDIUM-SIZED ENTERPRISES (SMEs)

In most developing countries SMEs constitute the bulk of the industrial base and contribute very significantly to their exports as well as to their GDP or GNP. For instance, India has nearly three million SMEs, which account for almost 50 per cent of industrial output and 37 per cent of India's total exports. It is these features of SMEs that make them an ideal target for technological cooperation with foreign and local enterprises, with multinationals, and with R&D institutions and centres of technology development, as well as for purposes of commercialization.

Most of the large companies, even in developing countries, have a financial as well as a technical capacity to identify technological sources and evaluate alternate technologies that would suit their requirements. Unfortunately, this capacity is conspicuously missing in most SMEs. It is for this reason that SMEs need special assistance and the technology capacity-building process must address this huge but desirable requirement.

It is not easy to devise a mechanism that would be useful for all this vast number of geographically scattered and culturally dissimilar enterprises. In order to develop an effective mechanism, it is helpful to determine the barriers and other factors that hinder the process of widespread technology cooperation on a commercial basis. The list is long, but some of the most important are: (a) lack of access to technology information; (b) non-availability of in-house or institutionalized expertise to evaluate technologies; (c) the high cost of hiring consultant services; (d) lack of finance; (e) the desire to avoid risk (the "not-me-first" syndrome); (f) weak supportive infrastructure; (g) lack of willingness to part with technology information; (h) an uneven playing field; (i) non-availability of technically trained human resources; (j) a shorter life-span for products and technologies; (k) a policy framework not conducing to technology cooperation; (l) the risk of violating intellectual property rights; (m) the high cost of better technology; (n) small plant size; (o) emphasis on production and not on production costs.

II. TECHNOLOGY INFORMATION - A POWERFUL TOOL

It is very clear that most of the SMEs do not have access to well-researched technology databases that provide information pro-actively on a regular pre-determined basis. Some of the development assistance projects in a few countries have helped to set up such data banks. However, the information usually remains in the banks untapped, while the purveyors of the information wait for the targeted beneficiaries to request it. The element of pro-activity is often disregarded completely. It is obvious, in fact, that despite enormous inputs and the wealth of information available, the efforts made rarely deliver the desired results.

Familiarity with the ground conditions in which the targeted beneficiaries operate, and the faith and trust inspired in small industries by such technology information clearing-houses are very important in ensuring that technology cooperation is successful. It must be added that it would be very useful if technology information providers could also contribute to the adaptation efforts.

A. Seeing is believing

Many studies undertaken by the Confederation of Indian Industry, the National Productivity Council, UNIDO and other international agencies in the past make it clear that the mere act of passing on technology information does not give rise to specific technology partnerships among enterprises. Even the glossy brochures fail to convince would-be technology acquirers. The entrepreneurs who run small businesses nearly always want to see a technology in operation and delivering the goods before they decide to acquire it.

B. Practical demonstrations

A demonstration of the technologies available therefore has to be an integral part of any technology cooperation process. It may be worthwhile to think in terms of establishing technology parks where entrepreneurs can obtain first-hand information. The technology parks need not become white elephants. On the contrary, once a given technology is accepted and becomes widely used, it should be replaced by a newer technology that has the potential for acceptance in the same country. Since these technologies would actually be working plants, the produce of such a park should be sold in the open market and the profits generated could be ploughed back to expand the parks or to establish similar centres elsewhere in the country.

In order to attract entrepreneurs, these technology parks should organize training programmes, workshops and seminars, as well as sector-specific trade shows so that technologies rapidly become well known and proliferate. It might be useful for technology databases to be housed in these technology parks.

III. FINANCING

Business is business and should be conducted in a business-like manner on commercial terms. However, some financial support from government and technology possessors may be necessary for initially equipping technology parks with manufacturing systems and hardware in industrial sizes.
The availability of financial resources on affordable terms and in a non-bureaucratic manner is yet another problem the SMEs must confront. It is imperative therefore to influence existing financial networks and, if need be, to set up a separate mechanism for funding smaller enterprises, especially those categorized as micro-enterprises.

IV. INSTITUTIONAL SUPPORT SYSTEMS

In order to create a business environment in which the adoption, adaptation, and ultimate assimilation of diverse technologies that are resource efficient and have little waste output become a normal business proposition, the supportive infrastructure will inevitably have to be strengthened in many developing countries. The institutional networks in question are required to address a vast array of concerns from ensuring the availability of trained human resources to continuous technology innovation and upgrading over time. In most developing countries, in fact, there is a need for such institutions to deal exclusively with the myriad problems that SMEs face in their day-to-day work.

V. CONCLUSIONS

In a nutshell, any effective technological capacity-building exercise will have to address issues that can be broadly classified under the generic heads of information dissemination, technology demonstration, a conducive policy framework, and financing and institutional support systems. In each of these categories, the barriers must be clearly identified and enabling strategies developed so that the technological capacity-building process becomes meaningful, in terms not only of international trade and business or of the environment, but also of making it responsive to the needs and aspirations of the people in developing countries.

PART TWO

PROGRAMMES AND INITIATIVES

This part presents contributions on programmes and initiatives for the promotion of technological capacity-building and technology partnerships

BUILDING CRITICAL TECHNOLOGICAL CAPACITIES IN AFRICA

by
T. S. Karumuna
Economic Affairs Officer, Science and Technology Section,
Economic Commission for Africa, Addis Ababa

INTRODUCTION

The African region has the largest number of least developed, land-locked, and most seriously affected developing countries. The vast majority of its population lives in rural areas, and large parts of the region are stricken by or susceptible to drought and natural disasters. On the whole Africa has the lowest share of scientific and technological capabilities of any region in the world. In other words, it is a continent beset by a multitude of extremely serious problems. On the other hand, Africa possesses important though largely underdeveloped potentialities. Its vast natural resources offer enormous opportunities for the application of science and technology in their exploitation and use for the benefit of its people. However, in the absence of such developments, poverty and deprivation prevail and economic and social condition are steadily worsening for many. This situation was strongly deplored by Africa's Heads of State and Government, in 1980, in a policy declaration which highlighted the major impediments to, as well as policy and other requirements for, the creation of a scientific and technological base in the member States.

A more recent and comprehensive initiative took place in connection with S&T in May 1994, when participants the twenty-eighth meeting of the ECA Conference of Ministers deliberated on the theme: "Building critical capacities in Africa for accelerated growth and sustained development." This was partly in recognition of the fact that the lack of critical capacities had been instrumental in limiting the achievements of the economic reforms undertaken so far by the member States, and also of the evident need for improved capacities in view of the increased competition resulting from current changes in the structure of the world economy.

I. CURRENT SITUATION IN THE AREA OF S&T

The least developed countries in Africa suffer from a shortage of scientific and technological personnel owing to the limited educational facilities for training them in the required numbers and mix. The economic and social crisis that began in the early 1980s led to declining government budgetary provisions for education and training. The devastating results, such as the deterioration of infrastructure, ill-equipped laboratories and libraries, and uncompetitive wages received by teaching and research staff, have all contributed to the decline in the technological capacities of educational institutions. The observed preference of donor agencies and foreign investment programmes for hiring expatriate technical personnel frustrates the effort to increase the utilization of local capabilities in African countries, and to stem the problem of brain drain.

The ongoing structural adjustment reforms and the liberalization of the economies will have important repercussions on the technology capacity-building process. While there are explicit measures regarding capital ownership, safeguards for employees of former State enterprises, technological dimensions are not treated as major issues in the complex process of privatizing public enterprises. Thus, negotiations on such aspects as future choice and sources of technology, use of local technical personnel in the core operations of the enterprises, acquisition of skills by and training of local experts, local production of parts and components for the gradual replacement of import and promotion of local inplant research and development, are not likely to be given due prominence. Measures are required to ensure that the liberalization of economies is accompanied by safeguards for the development and use of local technology capacities.

The investment of resources is essential for technological capacity-building. In spite of the many sectors competing for the limited financial resources available, such an investment cannot be avoided if governments wish to achieve realistic gains for their people. The success of countries like Japan and the Republic of Korea in their industrialization is often spoken of without, however, full cognizance of the commitments which brought it about. Heavy investment was necessary in order to create local capabilities and a supportive infrastructure of technical institutions, organizations and services. Of no less importance was the critical role played by the leadership and government in providing direction, initiatives and support.

II. PROBLEMS AND CHALLENGES IN CAPACITY-BUILDING

For the least developing countries in Africa, technological capacity-building poses many and varied challenges. At the top of the list is the lack of political commitment, beyond the declarations of intent in conference resolutions, declarations, and plans of action. Such commitment should be spelled out in action-oriented national, subregional or regional policies and strategies, which should be supported by the allocation of the necessary resources to achieve the stated goals in technology capacity-building. The necessary institutional framework for policy making in science and technology matters is virtually non-existent, else ineffectual and unable to provide leadership in terms of policy formulation and implementation or to galvanize the scientific and technological community in public institutions, universities and scientific establishments to contribute to creating a strong technological base in the member States.

A critical component of technological capacity-building is skilled personnel. Currently literacy rates for Africa, which were around 61 and 41 per cent for males and females respectively in 1991, are among the lowest in the developing countries. School enrolment has been declining since the 1980s. Technical training activities have yet to build strong linkages with industry. There is a severe shortage of conventional education and training. While science education is constrained by lack of teachers and of proper laboratories and equipment, so the output and level of graduates in scientific and technical fields are inadequate. The development of managerial skills as part of the conventional training for scientists and technologists has been advocated and courses in these fields should become a regular feature of engineering and technical training. Other aspects which need to be upgraded relate to R&D; consulting and engineering design; policy analysis and management; standardization and quality control; production, repair and maintenance of scientific and technical equipment; management of technological information; technology acquisition - searching and sourcing for technology negotiation; adaptation.

Notwithstanding the present state of industry in Africa, it has the potential to contribute to the creation of technological capacity. Through attachment programmes in industry, students at universities and research institutions can add to their practical experience and professional skills by working with professionals in real life environments. Purposeful linkages between industry and institutions of higher learning can promote the exchange of expertise and enhance the quality and relevance of both training and research. New linkages of this kind should be established and the scope of those in existence expanded as regards subject coverage and number of institutions involved. The programme of University-Industry-Science Partnership (UNISPAR) in Africa needs to be vigorously promoted throughout the region. Furthermore, governments should initiate policy reforms to offer incentive packages for industry to increase their participation in such schemes.

III. CONCLUSIONS AND RECOMMENDATIONS

The importance and hence the necessity of creating appropriate technological capacities in the member States cannot be overstated. To achieve sustained growth, African Governments must embark on enhanced capacity-building through greater utilization of the human resources available and the strengthening of national institutions and infrastructure. This is an immense challenge to developing Africa and more so to the LDCs. Yet this task must now begin in earnest. In so doing, it is important for technological capacity-building to be viewed as an integral part of the overall long-term national plan and strategy for socio-economic development. National governments have the primary responsibility for initiating appropriate policy reforms to ensure the strengthening of existing technological institutions and the creation of new ones. The quality of education and training at all levels must be improved, including the expansion of employment opportunities with income generation activities for young graduates. This effort should empower as many people as possible through the upgrading of education and skills.

Government policies should encourage industry and the private sector to participate in training and upgrading the skills of their employees through inplant or external training programmes. Enterprises should also undertake joint research and training programmes with universities and technical institutions by providing facilities for the practical training of graduates, and by carrying out joint R&D activities in priority areas. Financial incentives should be made available to enable participating firms to recoup part or all of their training costs from the training levy collected by some governments. Tax exemptions should be given to firms as a reward for attaining specified levels of R&D effort in designated areas. The establishment of indigenous private sector institutions such as consulting and engineering design organizations, which could provide a wide range of technical services to investors, could be usefully promoted. They should have access to special funds for installation purposes, and be offered incentives, e.g. concessions on the duties and taxes levied on machinery and equipment necessary for their operations. Foreign firms seeking to provide technical services should engage in joint ventures with local equivalents; in this connection, clear directives should be given for the upgrading and use of local capabilities.

The development of appropriate policies, plans and strategies for technological capacity-building must emerge from an informed view based on analysis and understanding of member States' requirements. Technology policy research and analysis should be strengthened in the member States through the national nodes of the African Technology Policy Studies Network, based in Nairobi, Kenya, which is already coordinating the work being undertaken throughout the African region. Its national nodes should be strengthened to become training centres for technology policy analysis and management in the member States.

Many of the expectations for the development and application of science and technology beyond the year 2000 cannot be realized in the absence of medium- to long-term investment programmes, which are prerequisites for the establishment of a sound technological capacity. Such strategies must be based on a comprehensive policy reform that will place science and technology at the core of the socio-economic development process, and promote the development of an endogenous science and technology capacity. The ECA strongly advocates a broad view of science and technology, to include such aspects as: assessment of technology, searching for alternative technologies and for alternative suppliers of technology, negotiating with suppliers of technology, unpackaging of technologies, design and application of incentives for technology development and application, conduct of R&D, and management of S&T programmes and institutions. Thus, the promotion of technological capacity-building in Africa should focus on a comprehensive list of technological functions and their requirements in terms of human resources and institutional needs. Important current initiatives are being undertaken through the Presidential Forum on Science and Technology to generate greater awareness of the need for action in pursuit of a science-led development process in Africa, efforts to establish new funding mechanisms for science and technology at national and regional levels, and the conclusion of the Treaty establishing the African Economic Community. All these help to create a new climate for renewed efforts to develop a viable science and technology base by African member States.

United Nations bodies and organizations have a special opportunity and role to play in assisting member States in creating the necessary technological capacities. Their role could consist in: (a) Support to national dialogues for building a consensus on technology policy and strategies. This should involve a view of long-term overall national technology development directed towards increasing the ensuring effectiveness of science and technology in Africa by linking it firmly to the mainstream of economic activity rather than pursuing it on ineffective, narrow and rather disjointed fronts; (b) Development of national, subregional and regional policies and institutions to exploit new technologies, most of which are devised outside Africa; (c) Promoting a deeper understanding of the technological capacity-building advocated among member States. This is necessary in order to spell out the forms and functions of the different elements of the technological capacities to be created; (d) Provision of long-term experts and advisers, or facilitation of their identification and recruitment in response to the needs of member States; and (e) Organization, jointly with the ECA, of regional seminars and conferences in specialized issues, to educate policy-makers and develop a science and technology culture.

SELECTED COOPERATION ASPECTS FOR TECHNOLOGICAL CAPACITY-BUILDING IN DEVELOPING COUNTRIES IN ASIA AND THE PACIFIC

by
the Economic and Social Commission for Asia and the Pacific (ESCAP), Bangkok

INTRODUCTION

The New Delhi Declaration on Strengthening Regional Economic Cooperation adopted by the Economic and Social Commission for Asia and the Pacific at its fiftieth session held in April 1994 identified technology transfer as an effective means to achieve the specific purpose of raising the standards of living of the people in Asia-Pacific developing countries and sustaining the dynamism of the region.

Developing countries of the region face a multitude of socio-economic problems, many of which can be overcome by the effective exploitation of technology which could play a strategic role in providing solutions to the two seemingly conflicting goals of raising the living standards of the population and at the same time ensuring sustainable development. The central issue for developing countries, which are mainly importers of technology, is how to utilize technology transfer channels and related technology flows to exploit opportunities available now and in the future to achieve these goals. However, strategies and modalities for addressing the emerging challenges and opportunities are likely to differ in different regional countries as the Asian and Pacific region currently has the following economies and geographic groupings; the newly industrializing economies (NIEs), the Association of South East Asian Countries (ASEAN), the South Asian Association for Regional Cooperation (SAARC), the Pacific Island Countries (PICs), the Central Asian Republics, the Indochinese countries and the economies in transition, least developed, land-locked countries of the former groupings.

The main issues and concerns which must be addressed, keeping in view the recognized differences cited earlier, include promotion of transfer of technology and related capital to the region and among regional countries, building-up of S&T capabilities and infrastructure, participation of the private sector in S&T development, upholding of the competitiveness of small and medium-scale industries in an open and liberal economic environment, application of technologies for sustainable development and use of regional and international cooperation for technology transfer and building up of technological capabilities.

I. ROLE OF THE PRIVATE SECTOR IN TECHNOLOGY TRANSFER AND TECHNOLOGICAL CAPACITY-BUILDING

As firms, both local and external have emerged as the central actors in technology transfer transactions, their technological capabilities have a considerable influence on the whole spectrum of technologies used and their efficiencies over time. Equally, technology transfer transactions can contribute to the enhancement of the technological development of local firms and industry.

Technology transfer arrangements may include two broad flows of technology. The first is an aggregation of the flows of capital goods, operation know-how, maintenance and repair, etc. which are usually incorporated into a new unit of production capacity. The second constitutes the broad type of flows, which contribute to the expansion of the technological capability of the importing firm. This type consists of the system-related knowledge incorporated within the production system purchased and the various kinds of skills, experience and technical and managerial knowledge that are required for controlling, modifying and improving the system over time.

Technology sellers usually transfer to the recipient firms the basic knowledge and skills needed to establish and operate the new production facilities, but hardly ever relinquish control of the so-called core technology. However, there are technological resources which fall between these two categories. Such resources are rarely willingly transferred by technology suppliers, but their availability for transfer is open to negotiation. Other means can also be employed to capture them. Maximizing this flow is not only a supply-side issue. It can be argued that the size of the flow of the more dynamic and in-depth knowledge to firms depends, among other things, on some prerequisite conditions within and around the recipient firms themselves and on the efforts they themselves make during the period of technology transfer for investment. A key factor determining the existence and effectiveness of such technical efforts is the availability and utilization of technological and managerial capabilities within the firms. Furthermore, the technical principles, know-how, engineering specifications and designs, etc. which underlie the particular production facilities may be transferred alongside those facilities. But whether they constitute an effective component of the firms' capability will depend, first, on the firms' success in obtaining them and secondly on their ability to absorb them. The structure of technology transfer in investment projects also depends on the balance between imported and domestic supplies of various flows and can be greatly influenced by a range of techno-managerial decisions.

The new international competitive conditions in many industries, arising from the combined effects of changes in the international economic environment and trends in technological change of an immensely complex and rapid nature, are leading to major changes in corporate strategy. In the domain of technological innovation, many developed country and sometimes developed and developing country firms are forming *strategic alliances* to gain access to complementary technologies. Consequently, for many developing country firms, although the chances for entering into strategic alliances with TNCs are limited and considerations of strategic control over core corporate technology still set limits to the content of the technology transferred by TNCs, there may be new opportunities for making much greater use of those firms as vehicles for transferring the forms of technology that would add to developing countries' capabilities for managing and generating technical change.

II. ENDOGENOUS TECHNOLOGICAL CAPABILITIES AND TECHNOLOGY TRANSFER

The experiences of most advanced developing countries in the region demonstrate that the ability of a country to attract, adopt and benefit from foreign technology depends mostly on the national situation and that it relates to the general economic and policy framework, the level of endogenous technological capabilities and the availability of qualified human resources. The interaction of these and other factors creates a favourable technology climate supportive of technology-based development. It is therefore important for a country seeking to acquire technological capabilities for export manufacture to take well-coordinated and measured steps to develop such abilities.

The existing technology climate of a country can be further improved through technology transfer and, in particular, foreign direct investment (FDI) consisting of a package combining capital, technology and access to international markets and their contributions to economic growth and, more especially, the enhancement of endogenous technological capabilities.

III. TECHNOLOGICAL INFRASTRUCTURE AND PRIVATE SECTOR DEVELOPMENT SUPPORT

Ultimately, an effective way to achieve sustainable industrial development in developing countries is to allow them to improve the technologies they imported and in the long run to create their own technologies relevant to their problems. Therefore, there is a need for *technological infrastructure development* including R&D institutions with links to the production sector, standardization and quality control and industrial engineering design and consultancy service organizations, technology information patent offices, intellectual property rights regime mechanisms, technological education and training institutions, and an appropriate policy-mix, etc.

However, the experience of many developing countries shows that their scientific and tecnological activities, especially R&D, in public institutes and universities were largely carried out in isolation from the real world of production. Direct assistance in stimulating and supporting private sector capability development is negligible. Beyond the limited support for private sector R&D, no suitable instrument has been designed to stimulate firms to acquire significant knowledge and expertise through international technology transfer or other means. Although consultancy and technical services, etc., are not totally excluded, they are often dealt with much less seriously than allocation of resources for public sector R&D. There is now growing evidence that unless industrial firms have built up significant in-house capabilities they cannot effectively draw on the R&D results of the public sector institutes or make technical demands on them, thus limiting the usefulness of public sector R&D.

IV. TECHNOLOGICAL UPGRADING OF SMALL AND MEDIUM-SIZED INDUSTRIES (SMIs)

While small and medium-sized industries (SMIs) play a very important role in almost all the economies of the region, the traditional economic advantages provided by natural resources and cheap labour are becoming increasingly insufficient to ensure markets for such industries. Their survival and growth therefore depend on their ability to assimilate latest developments in technology to improve their productivity, product quality, versatility, flexibility and competitiveness. Technology blending, aimed at the partial modification of technological systems in developing countries through the selective introduction and use of new and emerging technologies without fully replacing existing traditional technologies, is often seen as the appropriate response to such challenges. The promising feature of this approach is that it enables the conditions that would permit developing countries to derive some of the benefits obtainable from new and emerging technologies to be identified, but does not entail drastic social and economic change beforehand. Biotechnologies, microelectronics, new materials or renewable sources of energy are suitable areas for technology blending through, for instance, the use of new fermentation technologies in agro-based industries to produce alcohols and organic acids, and, in the textile industry, the establishment of microcomputer systems for quality control and the reduction of stockpiling, and the retrofitting of old looms with microprocessors.

SMIs encounter several difficulties in attempting to improve their operations through the application of new technologies owing to their inability to assess market needs and appropriate technologies, their limited access to technological information and funds for financing the acquisition of new technologies as well as their lack of the necessary capacity to adapt and use imported technologies that could be transferred to them.

V. TECHNOLOGY TRANSFER AND SUSTAINABLE DEVELOPMENT

Environmental degradation is not an inevitable consequence of industrialization and economic growth although environmental and developmental goals are sometimes in conflict. Environmentally sound industrial development is not equivalent to constraining the rate of industrial growth. In pursuing any strategy leading towards more sustainable development, developing countries of the region certainly need to make good use of technology for, among other things, solving the serious environmental problems they are facing. In principle, it might even be possible to follow industrialization strategies that differ widely from those followed by most countries of the world. For example, instead of focusing so heavily on demands generated by the higher income and urban segments of society, industrial growth could be made more responsive to the needs of the rural poor.

Given that new technologies such as microelectronics, information technology, biotechnology, new materials, etc., can generate significant productivity and quality gains, they can be expected to spread rapidly to most manufacturing industries. These technological developments may make it possible for developing countries with the capacity to use such technologies to benefit from substantially lower resource inputs and waste outputs in their future industrial growth. Exploiting the full potential of clean and new technologies will require not only the right investment in appropriate and efficient capital facilities, but also the acquisition of technological and managerial capabilities. Therefore, there is a need for change in the ongoing efforts to promote the transfer of environmental technologies to developing countries. These efforts appear to concentrate for the most part on using imported equipment and expertise to achieve a one-shot environmental improvement rather than laying the basis for *self-sustaining* paths of increasing efficiency in the future. Greater attention should be given to the development of the technological and managerial capabilities needed to ensure the continuing improvements in efficiency over the long run.

In order to provide the countries of the region, and particularly their SMIs, with quality information on environmentally sound technology opportunities, the ESCAP secretariat through the Asian and Pacific Centre for Transfer of Technology (APCTT) has been implementing a project entitled Mechanism for Exchange of Technology Information (METI). Activities carried out under this project are: (1) Development of a special format to carry out a market survey on METI-style information services among potential users of the system, followed by the preparation and dissemination of a METI training manual for master trainers in technology information; (2) Development of a low cost system for the exchange of technology information among participants through computer communication; (3) Development of computerized databases such as: (a) METI thesaurus; (b) METI users manual; and (c) METI progress report.

VI. NEED FOR REGIONAL COOPERATION IN TECHNOLOGY TRANSFER AND ENDOGENOUS CAPABILITY BUILDING

Increasing levels of intraregional trade and investment are gradually shaping a truly interdependent regional economy in the Asia-Pacific region, based on the linkage of the production structure of several economies in the region through the development of a dynamically changing regional division of labour. To a significant extent because they succeeded in utilizing the technological revolution to enhance their national comparative and competitive advantages, first Japan and then most of the advanced developing countries of the region have become critical growth centres supplying other economies of the region with FDI and technology. Regional industrial and tecnological development on these lines creates a fertile ground for cooperation in technology transfer among countries of the region, which should be directed by carefully designed incentives and policy measures towards strengthening technological capabilities, particularly, those of the recipient countries. The fact that the ESCAP region as a whole has emerged as the most dynamic part of the world economy, with a dramatic change in industrial structure, export orientation of manufacturing and growing purchasing power, constitutes an important macroeconomic condition for increased transfer of technologies, including new and emerging technologies, to the more advanced developing countries, and from them in carefully identified sectors in the less developed economies. The acquisition of such technological capabilities will go a long way to ensure the export competitiveness of developing countries' manufactures.

The need for cooperation is heightened by the fact that the human and material resources of many of the members and associate members are rather limited for them to act independently in this endeavour. To create sufficient absorptive capacity for imported technologies in priority productive sectors countries facing similar problems should pool their resources in a collaborative effort among donors, governments, R&D agencies and productive sectors. Furthermore, the differences among ESCAP members and associate members with respect to population size, resource endowment, geography, technological development, and level of national technological capabilities, which result in a high degree of complementarity, can be exploited through regional cooperation in science and technology for the benefit of all the countries of the region.

The opportunities for regional cooperation in the endogenous technological capability-building of ESCAP member countries are most important, because of the vital importance of advances in this respect to technological development. While advanced developing countries such as the NIEs have had adequate domestic resources to attract technology and related capital and to expand their local technological capacity, a number of developing countries in the region (LDCs, island developing countries, disadvantaged traditional economies and others) remain outside the mainstream of economic development primarily because local conditions in terms of skills, technological and physical infrastructure, market size, etc. continue to be poor, inappropriate or unfavourable. These same countries also suffer from a lack of information and knowledge, as well as of financial resources. Such countries have therefore been unable to attract adequate volumes of technology and capital. It is argued that concerted efforts in the region aimed at assisting them to develop local technological capabilities through regional cooperation should improve their situation considerably. Furthermore, if serious attempts are made to enhance the flow of investment to the have-nots in the region, more focused attention should be paid at the national level in the disadvantaged countries to increasing the pace of indigenous technological capability-building efforts.

VII. ACTION PROGRAMME FOR REGIONAL ECONOMIC COOPERATION IN INVESTMENT-RELATED TECHNOLOGY TRANSFER

The Commission at its fiftieth session adopted, by resolution 50/9 of April 1994, an Action Programme for Regional Economic Cooperation in Investment-related Technology Transfer. The programme was inspired by the realization that the growing interdependence of production structures, high growth and liberalization of regional economies, coupled with the expansion of regional trade and investment, provided an impetus to greater regional cooperation in science and technology. Furthermore, it was realized that as technology transfer remained the main avenue for most developing countries in their quest for technology-led industrialization and increased product competitiveness in the world market, the ability of such countries to adopt foreign technologies and maximize the benefits from their transfer greatly depended on their endogenous technological capabilities. The higher the level of such capabilities, the greater will be these countries' ability to adopt foreign technologies.

The purpose of the Programme is therefore to facilitate, through regional cooperation, the expansion of flows of technology to the region and among the individual countries concerned as well as the enhancement of local technological capabilities required for technology transfer, adaptation, use and development. The secretariat has initiated and carried out a number of activities and studies to implement the Action Programme in the following areas: strengthening technological capacities in the export of manufactures; enhancing investment-related technology flows to least developed, land-locked, and Pacific island economies, as well as to economies in transition; standardization and quality control; and consultancy services. It has also undertaken studies in relation to technology transfer patterns, environmentally sound technology, and patent laws. The two main studies provided for in the Programme are in course of preparation. They deal respectively, with technology flows and the associated capacity-building and with national policies for the promotion of technology transfer.

Various technical assistance activities have also been undertaken by the secretariat. The Workshops and other meetings held included the following:

A Workshop on the Role of Technological Capabilities in the Expansion of Manufactured Exports was jointly organized by UNCTAD and ESCAP in September 1994, to consider the role of technological capabilities, associated policies and their applications for the export performance of textile/garment and electronics firms. Two Workshops on Matching Investment Opportunities and Industrial Relocation in the Asia-Pacific Region were organized by the secretariat, in close cooperation with the Boards of Investment of the Philippines and Pakistan, and with financial assistance from the Government of the Republic of Korea. They were held in October 1994 and in January 1995 respectively. The Workshops focussed on the factors inducing industrial enterprises to shift production to overseas locations and thereby promote greater integration through increased trade, investment and technology transfer. The first meeting of the Organizing Committee of the Technical Consultancy Development Programme for Asia and the Pacific and the international training programme on consultancy for exports of manufactured goods organized by that Programme and other agencies, was held in December 1994.

Among future meetings and studies, the following are planned:

An expert group meeting on enhancement of technology flows from advanced developing countries to least developed countries, to be held in June 1995; an expert group meeting on promoting regional economic cooperation for industrial and technological skills development including requirements for adopting new and emerging technologies; a workshop on standardization, metrology and quality control for Asia/Pacific countries, in close cooperation with UNIDO; a project on regional cooperation on the adoption of the ISO 9000 series, with financial assistance from the Government of Japan.

TECHNOLOGICAL CAPACITY-BUILDING IN LEAST DEVELOPED AND OTHER LOW-INCOME COUNTRIES: UNDP'S PILOT PROGRAMME IN SCIENCE AND TECHNOLOGY

by
Johann Bäumler
Deputy Director, UNFSTD/STAPSD
United Nations Development Programme (UNDP), New York

INTRODUCTION

UNDP has always focused on capacity-building. While, in the 1970s, the emphasis was on institution-building, it shifted in the 1980s to human resource development and, in the 1990s, the activities have formed part of the broader concept of capacity-building including both institutional and human aspects. In science and technology, this focus was exemplified, for instance, in support for the Consultative Group in International Agricultural Research (CGIAR), in projects to strengthen science education in Africa and in the building of national and regional capacities with respect to the repair and maintenance of scientific instruments, to mention only three examples out of many others.

I. PILOT PROGRAMME ON ENDOGENOUS CAPACITY-BUILDING IN SCIENCE AND TECHNOLOGY

This note concentrates on one aspect of capacity-building in science and technology, i.e. the capacity to make and execute autonomous and informed decisions in the development, acquisition, deployment and diffusion of technologies and to integrate science and technology into the national development process. Six pilot projects in Cape Verde, Jamaica, Pakistan, Togo, Uganda and Viet Nam, which have recently been concluded, demonstrate this approach. Among the countries concerned are four LDCs. The basic concept goes back to a central recommendation by the Vienna Conference on Science and Technology held in 1979. The full title of the programme was "Endogenous Capacity Building in Science and Technology through Policy Dialogues Amongst Stakeholders", to emphasize the broad participation and the required process of dialogue and consensus-building. It was executed under the substantive responsibility of the United Nations Department for Development Support and Management Services (UNDDSMS) and its predecessors, and managed by the United Nations Office for Project Services (UNOPS), while the United Nations Fund for Science and Technology for Development (UNFSTD), which received a trust fund of about US$2 million from Germany, acted as the funding agency.

The main purpose of the programme was to introduce a novel approach to decision-making in science and technology based on a broad consensus of a representative spectrum of society.

Its specific aims were to initiate and produce the following four major outputs:

- an institutionalized decision-making mechanism that is country and demand driven, cross sectoral and coordinated and that makes the best possible use of locally available scientific and technological expertise;

- a portfolio of initiatives to address the local, institutional policy framework under which science and technology is to be applied, including specific programmes/projects, policy adjustments and instruments;

- better coordination at the country level with and within external agencies and the United Nations system;

- mobilization of domestic and external resources for science and technology programmes and projects leading to a coalition of resources for a unified approach.

It is still too early to assess the substantive results of the programme but all six countries succeeded in creating a special infrastructure for the exercise and in contributing to capacity-building with respect to decision-making.

II. IMPLEMENTATION OF THE PROGRAMME

National steering committees were established, headed in Viet Nam by the Chairman of the State Committee for Science and Technology, who has meanwhile been appointed Minister of Science and Technology for Environment. In Jamaica, the Science and Technology Adviser for the Prime Minister chaired the National Steering Committee. In Togo, the Chairman of the Steering Committee was the Minister of Information, while in Uganda, a high government official chaired the Steering Committee. In Pakistan, the Permanent Secretary to the Ministry of Science and Technology assumed this role.

National coordinators of proved technical competence were nominated to supervise the whole process of problem identification and decision-making. Three policy dialogues were organized in each country to identify areas of concentration and other related actions requiring policy formulation, legislation and institutional restructuring. In Pakistan, the emphasis was placed on the development of carbon fibre industrial applications; in Jamaica, on food processing industries; in Viet Nam, on the contribution of science and technology to small and medium-scale enterprises; in Cape Verde, on fishery research; in Togo, on the valorization of local raw materials; and in Uganda, on technology information for rural development.

National consultants carried out about two dozen diagnostic studies to prepare for those dialogues. A broad range of stakeholders participated in the dialogues: scientists, civil servants, bankers, business leaders from large companies and representatives of small and medium-sized enterprises, journalists and concerned citizens. It should be noted that all the actors in the dialogues were nationals of the countries concerned, which reinforced the effect on capacity-building. Although it is still too early to determine the sustainability of the pilot programme in the different countries, there are indications that this decision-making mechanism might be particularly effective in LDCs and/or small countries where it is easier to bring together a representative group of people. It appears that, when indigenous capacity in science and technology is limited, as is the case in most LDCs, there is a stronger need to develop endogenous capacity to decide on national science and technology activities and the proper mix of foreign and local technologies.

III. CONCLUSION

Whatever the long-term results of the programme, the extensive national discussions about science and technology have already introduced a new and unique feature into national policy dialogue on development matters. At the same time, they have provided a rare opportunity for many participants who are normally outside the decision-making process to help in shaping national priorities in science and technology. By so doing, they have been exposed to a very real process of capacity-building.

OECD COUNTRY REVIEWS OF SCIENCE AND TECHNOLOGY POLICIES

by
Jean-Eric Aubert
Principal Administrator, Outlook and Country Studies Division,
Directorate for Science, Technology and Industry, OECD, Paris

This note describes the country review process developed by the Organisation for Economic Cooperation and Development (OECD) in the field of science and technology policy. It addresses three basic questions: (1) Why do Member and other countries request country reviews? (2) How are country reviews implemented? (3) What outputs result from such reviews? A few remarks on the application of this review process to developing countries conclude the paper.

I. WHY MEMBER AND OTHER COUNTRIES REQUEST COUNTRY REVIEWS

The tradition of OECD country reviews – whatever the field concerned – dates back to the early days of the Organisation, as part of a process of mutual information and surveillance. The best-known of these reviews are the "Economic Surveys", which are published every year for each Member country. Unlike the Economic Surveys and the reviews undertaken in other areas (such as environment, energy, aid to development), S&T policy reviews are done on a voluntary basis at the explicit request of interested countries.

Begun in the mid-1960s, they first concerned the largest OECD economies, and requests by other Member countries rapidly followed. A first wave of reviews took place up to the mid-1970s (about 20 being completed by 1975). In the second part of the decade, there was a slowdown in demand. In the 1980s, a new wave started, with most requests coming from small and medium-sized economies, and again about 20 countries were surveyed. In the early 1990s, the Eastern European countries that became OECD partners in transition (Hungary, Poland, the Czech and Slovak Republics), as well as Russia, requested such reviews. Most recently, Mexico, which joined the OECD last year, was reviewed. The Republic of Korea has also just become involved in the process.[45]

OECD countries were primarily interested in these reviews because they saw them as an efficient, and not very costly, tool to help them to build and adapt their institutions and strategies to manage science and technology. The interest manifested by the international community as well as the information given on the individual country's S&T capabilities were seen as facilitating international cooperation. In addition, and this was in fact the most important reason, the advice from outsiders was used to stimulate reforms and change in the country itself. The decline of interest in the larger economies is mainly due to the fact that they have developed their capability for self-evaluation over the years and do not need the support of an international organization, even a prestigious one, to stimulate internal reforms.

As these reviews are voluntary, a specific demand must be made by the country's highest authority (i.e. the minister) in charge of S&T. In most countries, this occurs only after a long and painful endeavour to reach a consensus. Thus, the presence of a motivated group or institution able to

---

[45]For OECD reviews on S&T see: Reviews of National Science Policy (up to the early 1980s); Reviews of National Science and Technology Policy; Innovation Policy (five publications during the 1980s); Science, Technology and Innovation Policies; Science, Technology and Innovation Policies – Special Series of the Centre for Cooperation with Economies in Transition (since the early 1990s).

carry the operation from its early stages up to completion has always been a key factor and a condition of success.

Aware of the limits of analyses concentrated only on the S&T system, OECD proposed in the mid-1980s to replace S&T policy reviews by "Innovation Policy Reviews" that would include investigations into surrounding sectors such as industrial policy, education policy, financial systems, etc. These reviews, however, have found few clients: not only because of resistance from those sectors, but also because in fact no institution deals with those different sectors in a horizontal manner, and the presence of a well-defined institution or ministry seriously interested in the review and able to carry it forward appears to be in fact essential. As a consequence, innovation taken in a narrow sense now unfortunately tends to be considered as an appendix to S&T policy reviews.

II. HOW COUNTRY REVIEWS ARE IMPLEMENTED

In the field of S&T policy, the country review process has traditionally been based on a series of steps which include the following:

(a) Preliminary visit of one week by one or two persons from OECD secretariat, comprising: meetings with main government institutions involved in S&T policy-making, visits of a sample of S&T actors, such as universities, public laboratories, enterprises, etc., to gain insight into the climate in which research and innovation develop; and definition of the parameters of the reviews, including preparation and content of the background report (see (b) below), composition of the review team (see (c) below), and schedule of further steps.

(b) Preparation of a background report by a group of experts and civil servants of the country under review. This report provides a description of the S&T system: it surveys R&D efforts and outputs with appropriate indicators, R&D actors, policy objectives, institutions and programmes, and main policy issues. It is important for the report to provide an informed and neutral description of the system, without avoiding key policy problems identified through a consensus-building process.

The draft report provided by the country — kept to a reasonable size (80-100 pages in usual OECD publication format) — is then further edited by the Secretariat.

(c) Visit of approximately one week by a review team, including three or four senior level experts, called "examiners", who are selected for their complementary competencies (academics, industrialists, policy makers). Through a series of meetings with key organizations and actors, they focus their analysis on the issues they deem most important, with a view to providing policy suggestions to the Government; the OECD Secretariat acts as rapporteur/coordinator of the team.

(d) Preparation of an "examiners' report" by the review team, which is about one-third the length of the background report. The report makes the opinions of the examiners clear and formulates policy suggestions. Preparation of the report generally takes a few months; occasionally the preparation includes an additional visit by a few members of the team or the Secretariat. Once the team members have agreed on a draft, the report is shown on a confidential basis to the authorities who requested the review in order to eliminate factual errors and prevent problems which might be created by judgements lacking political sensitivity.

(e) Discussion of the "examiners' report" in the capital of the country being reviewed, with representatives of OECD governments involved in S&T policy (in principle, delegates of the OECD Committee sponsoring the OECD work on science and technology, including science attachés in the capital concerned). The discussion generally takes one full day; mainly, it brings face to face the team of examiners and the authorities in charge of S&T policy to discuss key problems and possible policy approaches for tackling them. In addition, a half-day meeting is organized to present the reports and the outcomes of the discussion to the S&T community at large and the press. A summary account of this discussion is then prepared by the Secretariat.

(f) Publication of the examiners' report, the background report and the summary account of the review meeting by the OECD (some six months are often needed to prepare and complete the publication after the review meeting). Sometimes another meeting is arranged in the country to encourage politicians once again to focus attention on science and technology policy.

The procedure usually takes 9 to 12 months from the first visit by the Secretariat to the review meeting. The Secretariat is currently considering a revision of the procedure to streamline and shorten the process, give more influence to the Secretariat than to the examiners in the preparation of the evaluation report, and possibly integrate the two types of report (background and examiner evaluation) in order to avoid overlaps and improve the analytical approach.

It should be emphasized that a financial contribution is required from the country requesting the review. It generally covers the costs associated with the travel of the review team and its stay in the country for the review mission and the review meeting at the end. Non-Member countries are requested to pay the full direct costs (including fees for the examiners and travel and stay costs for the Secretariat). In addition, there are "indirect" costs associated with the preparation of the background report.

III. THE OUTPUTS OBTAINED FROM SUCH REPORTS

The most immediate and tangible outputs of the review process are the two reports prepared in the course of the review and later published by the OECD, along with the summary account of the review meeting. The background report offers a relatively up-to-date description of the S&T system with its main components. The examiners' report provides policy orientations.

Generally these orientations concern: (a) strategic aspects of S&T policy and related weaknesses; (b) organizational issues, such as the place given to S&T in the ministerial hierarchy, and the financial and other means at its disposal; (c) balance in funding between different types of R&D (basic, applied, technical, industrial); (d) management of programmes and various support schemes; (e) development of scientific and technical services, such as information, certification and standards, quality control; (f) conditions for innovation and use of research structures and results: this includes a variety of topics such as entrepreneurship capacity and financial channels; (g) mechanisms for international cooperation in S&T; (h) relationships between the central and federal/regional authorities for S&T policy making, funding, etc.

It should be stressed that the report does not include, nor is the review designed for it, any precise assessment of the research capacity in specific institutes or disciplines or any precise evaluation of the technologies on which the country is or should be focusing its efforts. Such evaluations would require specialized competencies and longer stays in the country and would considerably expand the scope and cost of the operation.

The review stays, in fact, at the level of the conditions needed for improving policy making (strategies, institutions, programmes, etc.). In so doing , by formulating critical remarks and making proposals for reforms in selected areas, the report, and more generally the OECD review, stimulate a useful debate in the communities concerned, and thus help to prepare a change in mind sets. This self-analysis process is the most important output of the review, although this is not necessarily well understood by those who benefit the most from the exercise.

Experience shows that the impact of OECD S&T policy reviews is greatest in the smaller "advanced" economies, because they are the ones most able to implement the suggestions arising from the reviews. Nevertheless, the influence of reviews has been far from negligible in less advanced countries in which appropriate follow-up mechanisms have been established. In certain countries, the OECD has in fact been a key actor in shaping and reorienting policy, notably when reviews have been implemented at relatively short intervals (5 to 7 years for instance).

In any event, a general lesson to be drawn from the experience of the OECD Secretariat is that the influence of our analysis and recommendations depends greatly on our understanding of the country's socio-cultural context, i.e. not only the detailed institutional settings but also power structures, management practices, and fundamental values as they appear in the day-to-day behaviour of the actors.

IV. APPLICATION TO DEVELOPING COUNTRIES

The review process, as developed at the OECD, can certainly find useful applications in developing countries. Its limits should, however, be clearly perceived. It is in no way an extensive evaluation of the S&T potential and capability of the country concerned. It is an efficient instrument for catalyzing debate and reflexion. If well founded and politically sensible, the review can also help in establishing the policy institutions and formulating policy orientations.

In applying the process to developing countries, a few options should clearly be adopted: (a) to focus on the country's capacity for technological innovation and diffusion, including technology transfer, imports and use of foreign technology; (b) to pay, even more than for developed economies, the greatest attention to the socio-cultural context in order to maximize opportunities for successful change; (c) to plan a strict follow-up mechanism for reviewing progress made on the basis of policy suggestions and change in the basic parameters influencing the development of the technological capability; and (d) as a crucial point, to involve donors in the review process, as they play a key role for stimulating appropriate reforms.

In conclusion, it is worth mentioning that the OECD was recently associated with a World Bank operation in Brazil to help in assessment prior to allocating a significant amount of structural funds. Such an approach, in which the analytical and policy expertise of OECD would be closely linked to powerful means for stimulating reforms, would certainly deserve to be considered.

SOUTH-SOUTH TRANSFERS OF TECHNOLOGY TO SMALL AND MEDIUM-SIZED ENTERPRISES IN THE LEAST DEVELOPED COUNTRIES

by
David Dichter, Director, and Klaus Netter, Chief Economist, Technology for the People,[46] Geneva

I. THE CASE FOR SOUTH-SOUTH TRANSFERS

In the context of the drive for economic and technical cooperation among developing countries (ECDC and TCDC), many learned papers have been written and resolutions passed extolling the virtues of transferring production know-how and management expertise from firms in the more advanced developing countries (ADCs) to those – largely small and medium-sized enterprises (SMEs) – in the least developed countries (LDCs). With the shift of the world's economic growth pole to the ADCs of East and Southeast Asia, these arguments gain cogency. Regrettably, virtually no systematic efforts have been made so far to test the validity of the thesis.

The underlying argument in favour of South-to-South transfers of technology (SSTT) is based on the proposition that a wide range of technologies that have been tried and tested by ADC firms can be transferred to LDC firms far more cheaply and effectively than transfers of more sophisticated technologies from the North.

The relative cheapness of these ADC technologies in the LDCs can be explained by the combined effect of (a) a labour intensity reflecting more closely the relative capital-labour cost ratios in LDCs than the corresponding capital intensity built into Northern technologies; and (b) the incomparably lower salary levels and more modest standards of comfort regarding housing and transport that are expected by the average ADC – especially Asian – technician as compared to his or her Northern counterpart. The latter factor assumes particular importance with regard to on-the-job training, managerial assistance and maintenance follow-up that can spell the difference between a successful transfer of technology and a failed one. This cost difference allows the purchaser of Southern technology in, say, a Sub-Saharan African country to acquire considerably more technology and technical assistance for the same foreign-exchange outlay as would be obtainable from the North.

The higher effectiveness is the result of (a) the greater adaptability of technologies that have stood the test of time, tropical climate and other harsh external conditions, as compared to technologies requiring highly skilled workers, moderate or even controlled temperatures, ready and continuous availability of power, water and smooth means of transport; and (b) the greater simplicity of the technology, enabling the LDC technology recipients to achieve earlier autonomy with regard to maintenance and repairs. The picture frequently observed in LDCs of factories and workshops standing idle for months on end awaiting the arrival of a busy and expensive Northern technician to repair a minor mishap bears out this point.

Among other factors favouring SSTT, the following may be worth noting:

(a) Plant lay-out and organization of production in LDC SMEs are likely to resemble those prevailing in ADCs more than those common in the North;

(b) By the same token, ADC technicians installing the necessary technology and training their counterparts in an LDC environment will be better able to

---

[46]A non-profit non-governmental organization based in Geneva.

cope with the shortcomings of the external environment than similar technicians from the North, who seldom have to face the problems of spare parts that are unavailable, power cuts or flooded roads. Moreover, the ADC technicians are more likely to focus their training on the critical technical bottlenecks that they have learnt to overcome in their own workshops;

(c) ADC firms are more likely to operate at production scales corresponding to the reduced market requirements and consumer purchasing power of LDCs than the huge, automated plants of the highly industrialized countries.

II. THE OBSTACLES FACING IMPLEMENTATION OF SSTT

The most important single obstacle facing implementation of SSTT – for the time being – is the virtual tying of aid supporting technology transfers to firms based in the donor countries. In this area, the tying is even more rigid than that applied for the procurement of goods. Such tying extends even to supranational donors such as the Economic Union, whose commitment to ECDC in the industrial area is limited to cooperation among its associated countries – the ACP group – which includes virtually no ADC capable of providing SSTT.

The second obstacle, which may become less important with time, is the virtual absence of government-financed investment-promotion programmes in ADCs able to provide SSTT.

Most international aid agencies such as the World Bank and the United Nations Development Programme (UNDP) are strongly regionally oriented and place only a tiny fraction of the technical assistance funds available into global interregional programmes. The consequent bureaucratic obstacles that need to be overcome to convince two distinct regional bureaux to support a particular bi- or multi-regional project are daunting.

As is true of ECDC in general, SSTT projects are unlikely to be mobilized by the interested parties unless neutral institutions exist to promote them. Whereas integration groupings do exist at the inter-governmental level to promote infrastructural and similar ECDC projects vis-à-vis international or regional financial institutions, no such promoting institutions exist for projects designed to bring together SMEs of developing countries located in different regions.

The need for a promoter is not limited to the financial needs – modest though they may be – of SSTT. The promoter is needed even more to overcome the lack of expertise on the part of SMEs in the LDCs regarding access to international markets and sources of technology in other developing countries. Aside from identifying potential technology suppliers and sources of equity loan finance, such a promoter must: (a) arrange technical research and marketing studies; (b) coordinate the activities of the potential partners; (c) organize product testing and field trials, where required; (d) help to draw up the appropriate legal instruments; and (e) join the negotiations as a neutral third party wishing to overcome obstacles threatening to obstruct the final deal.

Whereas specialized technology brokers (banks, law and consulting firms) are readily available to perform such functions at high fees for major firms in the developed countries, such brokers are unavailable for the much more modest projects typically involved in SSTT. Public agencies are generally unable and unwilling to perform such day-to-day hands-on activities for particular pairs of partners on the grounds that they cannot pick and choose.

Nevertheless, enterprise-to-enterprise cooperation, especially in the South-South context, is increasingly being seen as a more realistic and effective way to accelerate industrial development in the LDCs than inter-governmental assistance programmes. This point was reflected in the recent policy statement by the Vice-President of the United States, Al Gore, to the effect that one-half of US development assistance will henceforth be channelled through non-governmental channels, in particular to the private sector.

When account is taken of the fact that a large number of SSTT projects, if not most of them can be implemented for less than US$100,000, and that such projects can help two developing countries simultaneously, SSTT is an opportunity too good to miss.

INCREASING COMPETITIVENESS AND TECHNOLOGICAL CAPACITY-BUILDING AMONG SMALL AND MEDIUM-SIZED ENTERPRISES THROUGH TECHNOLOGY PARTNERSHIP

by the
Division for Science and Technology, UNCTAD

SUMMARY AND CONCLUSIONS

The Workshop aimed at identifying appropriate and innovative ways of technological capacity-building in developing countries, and participants will discussed current approaches to the promotion of capacity-building as well as approaches which are being considered. The major emphasis was on the concept of technology partnership as a new strategy of technological cooperation, a concept which can be of particular interest to small and medium-sized enterprises (SMEs).

An initial review of the literature and of experiences in this domain shows that a comprehensive analysis of cases specifically dealing with technology partnerships among SMEs from developed and developing countries is lacking. The conceptual definition of such partnerships as a way of fostering entrepreneurship and technological capacity-building in developing countries is a first step in that direction. The promotion and "operationalization" of this approach, in specific countries and economic sectors, including choosing "would-be-partners", developing agreements and identifying appropriate incentives to form partnerships may be a next step.

A number of issues require further examination. These include the forms such partnerships could take among SMEs and their role in technological innovation, including R&D and competitiveness. Mutual interests between small and medium-sized enterprises from developed and developing countries should be identified as well as measures to counterbalance and upgrade asymmetric relationships between partners from different levels of industrial and technological development. Furthermore, obstacles to such new strategies (market limitations, policies and regulations, disincentives, lack of technical infrastructure and services, lack of necessary qualified human resources) should be taken into account, in order to design the environment conducive to technology partnership.

Clearly, to foster the development of technology partnership arrangements between firms, particularly SMEs, from developing and developed countries, it would be essential to sensitize and mobilize all economic actors involved in this process, and to activate effective interaction among them. In this context, the examples cited in this note of technological partnership arrangements practised among developed countries' enterprises could be considered as models of such cooperation with SMEs in developing countries, where enterprises are major actors of economic activity. Technology partnership arrangements could be promoted by supportive activities on behalf of the developed and developing countries' organizations concerned, including investment promotion centres, chambers of commerce and industry, industrial producers associations, and technology and R&D institutions. Particular policies and programmes of support to SMEs in the developed countries, currently largely oriented to export promotion, could include a broader, future-oriented technology perspective and develop into technology-based cooperative ventures with developing countries. Specific host-country conditions, such as local technological infrastructure, including technology and R&D institutes, technological level and specific capacity of enterprise partners, and market size could be influential in promoting the process of technology partnerships.

Eventually, the operationalization of the concept of technology partnership will require the attention of diverse national and regional economic actors and institutions with the objective of supporting the necessary analysis and the possible development of policy-oriented pilot projects. In addition, it will be crucial to draw the attention of the international community to the strategic dimensions of technology partnership for increased competitiveness and technological capacity-building.

INTRODUCTION

The term "technology partnership" arose in discussions at UNCTAD's Ad Hoc Working Group on the Interrelationship between Investment and Technology Transfer where greater cooperative arrangements among enterprises were considered as key factors in the current international economic environment. While among developed countries' enterprises such types of arrangements through the sharing of technological capabilities and particularly of R&D-related investments for innovation have been termed "strategic alliances", the question was posed of how developing countries' enterprises may take advantage of similar cooperative arrangements in the area of technology.[47]

The present note aimed at introducing the subject of technology partnership into the discussions of the Workshop. The Workshop's intention was to explore aspects concerning the scope of technology partnership, promote an exchange of experiences among diverse interested actors in this domain, and consider the possible follow-up for promoting technology partnership so as to allow developing countries' enterprises to take advantage of such arrangements, particularly in cooperation with SMEs from the developed world.

The note reviews the literature and selected experience in the area of technology partnership and draws some conclusions for consideration at the Workshop.

I. THE SETTING

Worldwide, creative partnerships among firms and between firms and organizations of the R&D sector have become "weapons of choice" in commercializing new technologies. Such partnerships involve the blending of capital, technology, marketing and raw material resources. These new alliances which emerged in the OECD countries throughout the 1980s have only recently begun to move into the South and to mobilize a new generation of partnerships for economic development.[48]

A combination of trends appears to be leading to the rising importance of new alliances and partnerships. The worldwide trend for removal of trade barriers has opened markets for small and medium-sized companies that were previously only accessible to large companies. SMEs targeting such new markets are more likely to enter partnerships in order to share R&D and other costs.

Of critical importance is the fact that technological development in areas such as information technologies is offering new opportunities. It has enabled - and forced - SMEs more than ever before to use leading-edge technologies; moreover, with the growing knowledge-intensity of production, comparative advantage based solely on the existence of location-specific raw materials or cheap labour is being eroded.[49] Additionally, to take advantage

---

[47]See UNCTAD, Final Report of the Ad Hoc Working Group on the Interrelationship between Investment and Technology Transfer (TD/B/40(2)/17 - TD/B/WG.5/12), 1994.

[48]Sandor L. Boysen, "Biotechnology strategic alliance: a blending of capital, technology, marketing and raw material resources", *ATAS Bulletin*, No. 9, New York, 1992, p. 270.

[49]Lynn Krieger Mytelka, "Rethinking development: A role for innovation networking in the "other two-thirds", *Futures*, August 1993, p.1.

of new science and information-intensive forms of engineering requires more than communications facilities; technical professions and laboratories need access not only to domestic science and engineering information resources but also to the emerging international networks for sharing scientific information and for scientific, computer-based collaboration-at-a-distance. These new developments are not only compelling economic agents to respond rapidly to changes in the market but require an industrial structure of great flexibility, and SMEs specializing in technology for industrial use and occupying specific "niches" are being seen in a novel way as key strategic actors in the economic setting.[50]

The globalization of financial markets along with their deregulation has given SMEs access to capital not previously available. However, this trend has also called for sharing the risks created by huge capital inputs in the light of the long R&D cycles needed to commercialize new products. Alliances appear to respond to the need for flexible responses to global market trends as they add strength without establishing larger entities created by traditional mergers and acquisitions; in this context, partnerships allow countries "to quickly assemble overall innovative capabilities for single projects or for programmes involving multiple projects".[51]

II. FROM TECHNOLOGY TRANSFER TO ALLIANCES AND PARTNERSHIPS: SCOPE AND CONCEPTUAL ASPECTS

Over the past decade, emphasis in the concept of technology transfer has gradually shifted towards a new set of strategies which could all be described as "creative partnerships". A new terminology has accompanied this transition reflecting sometimes overlapping, sometimes differing concepts. The underlying idea has been to find forms of technological cooperation that are no longer "one-way" and that also involve a longer-term mutual benefit beyond short-term financial success.

These new forms of collaboration have been referred to, for example, as strategic alliances;[52] technological cooperation;[53] strategic partnerships;[54] technology partnerships;[55] and strategic technology partnering.[56] The common feature of these new forms lies in the sharing of technological capabilities and in the deliberate cooperative intentions which may or may not include government incentives. C. Freeman and J. Hagedoorn refer to such partnerships "as those firm agreements for which joint R&D and/or other innovative activities are part of the agreement and that can

---

[50]Lewis M. Branscomb, "A summary of global technology trends of possible strategic interest to the People's Republic of China", Springer Verlag, Berlin-Heidelberg, 1990.

[51]Sandor L. Boysen, *op. cit.*, p. 276.

[52] Ibid..

[53]Stephan Schmidheiny, *Changing Course - A Global Perspective on Development and the Environment*, Cambridge, MA, 1992.

[54]Lynn Krieger Mytelka, "Strategic partnership and the developing world", paper presented to the UNCTAD Ad Hoc Working Group on the Interrelationship between Investment and Technology Transfer, second session, December 1993.

[55]Final Report of the Ad Hoc Working Group on the Interrelationship between Investment and Technology Transfer, *op. cit.*, UNCTAD, 1994.

[56]Chris Freeman and John Hagedoorn, "Catching up or falling behind: Patterns in international inter-firm technology partnering", *World Development*, vol. 22, No. 5, 1994.

reasonably be assumed to affect the long-term product market positioning of at least one partner. Joint ventures with shared R&D resources, R&D corporations, joint R&D pacts, cross-licensing agreements, research contracts and second-sourcing agreements build the largest part of this group of cooperative agreements".[57]

Similarly, Boysen describes the highly diverse forms of alliances as including long-term multi-project partnerships that pool the production, research and marketing divisions within a single country or across several countries to accomplish strategic goals, joint ventures between two companies to create a single product or service, or flexible networking mechanisms that promote multi-country research consortia at the pre-competitive and development phases.[58]

Schmidheiny describes technology cooperation as a new form of long-term partnership in the international business world which includes training of employees, improvement of technologies and the introduction of new management systems in the partnering businesses. Technical education, innovation and sustainability are features inherent in such partnerships.

Mytelka defines strategic partnering as a new form of inter-firm collaboration that contributes more directly to structural competitiveness by stimulating innovation and accelerating technology diffusion. Like Schmidheiny, she emphasizes that new forms of cooperation are two-way partnerships focused on joint knowledge production and sharing as opposed to one-way relationships such as the transfer of technology under licensing agreements, production under a traditional sub-contracting agreement, or distribution under a franchise.[59] The partners are thus provided with key complementary assets to ensure the further development, production and marketing of new products. The author also states that an important element of firms' strategic partnerships is their longer-term planning approach rather than an approach favouring short-term financial gains.

Mytelka considers that Governments have a role to play in encouraging the formation of alliances through enabling mechanisms, especially as linkages among firms and between firms and research institutions may not occur spontaneously or if firms are unaccustomed to think strategically or to innovate.[60] Such mechanisms would require access to financial and technological resources. Furthermore, they could include the creation of a legal framework such as the 1986 Federal Technology Transfer Act in the United States which endorsed closer working ties between government laboratories and industry. Singapore's national biotechnology programme, also adopted in 1986, involved a venture capital pool to provide R&D incentives to multinationals and other foreign technology companies. In addition, it has established an Institute of Molecular and Cell Biology which recruits researchers worldwide and attracts the support of a leading multinational. These combined measures have enabled Singapore to fill the gaps in national technological development and to leapfrog into biotechnology R&D.[61]

Mark Dodgson summarizes the current technology cooperation phenomena as follows: "There is a plethora of definitions... including a huge range of activities. They are formed by firms with other firms - suppliers, customers and, occasionally, competitors - and with higher education institutes and

---

[57]*Ibid.*, p. 772.

[58]Boysen, *op.cit.*, p. 270.

[59]Mytelka, "Strategic partnership...", *op. cit.*, pp. 1-2.

[60]*Ibid.*, pp. 7 and 9.

[61]Boysen, *op. cit.*, pp. 275-276.

contract research organizations. Collaboration takes place in the research, development, manufacturing and marketing functions, and takes a wide variety of forms. Vertical collaboration occurs through the chain of production for particular products, from the provision of raw materials, through all the manufacture and assembly of parts, components and systems, to their distribution and servicing. Horizontal collaboration occurs between partners at the same level in the production process....Technological collaborations... are not simple contracts between organizations of once-and-for-all sales of a product, service or licence, but continuing arrangements where partners extend their expertise through sharing skills and personnel. The aims of these linkages may include increased knowledge of technological threats and opportunities and improved capabilities in product development and efficiency in production....".[62] Dodgson also examines motivation aspects of technological cooperation; however, his work does not cover in particular the motivation for cooperating with SMEs from developing countries.

In the view of Dodgson, the aims of technological collaboration include improvements in the innovation process, and various technological objectives of corporate strategy and public policy. In particular, they encompass: (a) improving the development process; (b) enhancing efficiency in the chain of production; (c) merging "previously discrete" technologies and disciplines such as technology collaboration initiatives between mechanical and electronic engineering in the creation of "mechatronics"; (d) learning through information exchange about the potentials of collaboration and of particular partners; (e) corporate strategies, to use, for example, collaboration to improve innovation as described above; and (f) public policies, aimed, among other things, at increasing technological cooperation to strengthen the technological capacity and therefore the performance of firms and national innovation systems.

III. TECHNOLOGY PARTNERSHIPS IN DEVELOPING COUNTRIES

In an initial review of the literature, strategic alliances and technology partnerships still figure largely as phenomena of the OECD countries and of some newly industrializing countries (NICs). So far, the use of these models to affect the innovation capability of countries in the "other two-thirds"[63] has been marginal, and the international distribution of strategic technology alliances involving developing countries, particularly the least developed countries (LDCs), is clearly lacking compared to the dimension which such partnerships have achieved in the "TRIAD" countries (United States, Japan and Europe). Thus, the total percentage of TRIAD/LDC alliances for the period 1980-1989 was 1.5 per cent while intra-TRIAD alliances represented 91.9 per cent.[64]

Freeman and Hagedoorn found that interfirm technology partnering could benefit firms from developing countries by improving their technological capabilities through technology transfer and partnerships with more advanced companies from the developed economies.[65] To accelerate the inclusion of countries hitherto disconnected from such alliances, Mytelka calls for a move away from traditional industrialization strategies based on the mass production model towards a more flexible networked structure for local industry. Donor agencies and international financing institutions could

---

[62]Mark Dodgson, *Technological Collaboration in Industry. Strategy, Policy and Internationalization in Innovation*, Routledge, London and New York, 1993, p.10.

[63]Mytelka, "Rethinking development...", *op.cit.*, p. 18.

[64]Chris Freeman and John Hagedoorn, "Catching up or falling behind: ...", *op. cit.*, p. 774.

[65]*Ibid.*, p. 772.

support such a reorientation similar to the efforts by national Governments to promote R&D-based alliances.[66]

Various examples of the application of the alliance/partnership model in developing countries are provided by Mytelka.[67] In Nigeria, networks of firms are being used to adapt, modify and manufacture quality spare parts for automobiles; this is accompanied by a local apprenticeship programme and in business-financed investment in training and engineering; in the Republic of Korea, a programme was set up to stimulate innovation in the micro-electronics sector through the formation of strategic partnerships among firms and between firms and local R&D institutions; in Costa Rica, a special centre was established to foster innovative behaviour in small and medium-sized enterprises; on the regional level, in Latin America, the Bolívar Programme was created to stimulate strategic partnering activity among companies and between Latin American and foreign firms.

As most developing countries do not have the funds, skills or infrastructure to pursue a technologically based innovation process completely on their own, a mode and level of cooperation that qualitatively differ from traditional technology transfer are needed. Such cooperation involves inter-firm and inter-organizational cooperative programmes and projects, the integration of local technologies and suppliers, and enhancement of the expertise, including engineering, in order to commercialize local and foreign R&D effectively. For the purpose of the Workshop, the term "technology partnership" is used to describe the concept underlying such cooperative programmes which have an inherent capability-building quality and which may represent a "step-up" from the "strategic alliance" model usually applied in the OECD countries.

IV. REVIEW OF SELECTED EXPERIENCES

Practical and particular issues critical to technological partnership include aspects concerning (i) the role of the small firm in the process of technological collaboration, (ii) the motives for such cooperation by participants from the private sector, (iii) specific modalities of technology transfer by SMEs of developed market-economy countries to developing countries, particularly through various forms of technological partnership arrangements, and (iv) the role of diverse actors in facilitating technology and industrial partnerships, in particular between enterprises from developed and developing countries. An important aspect concerning the latter relates to the role of public policy in providing a supportive environment and sustaining enabling policies.

An initial review of existing literature and of practical experiences has indicated, however, that, while a certain number of related elements and cases have been examined, there is a real gap in terms of detailed and comprehensive analyses of the technology partnership phenomena and of its most critical issues. Despite the growing interest—well reflected in the literature—in technological cooperation, the overall profile of the phenomenon needs to be clearly defined, particularly as regards trends, forms and focus of cooperation, technological base and strategic nature. This is particularly so with respect to technology partnerships involving small and medium-sized enterprises from developed and developing countries.

The importance of formulating supportive macroeconomic and sectoral policies and of arrangements to promote technological cooperation among small and medium-sized enterprises has been documented, as has been the fact that in many of the developing countries or groupings such enterprises lack a policy environment as well as sufficient resources for technological

---

[66]Mytelka, "Rethinking development...", *op.cit.*, p. 18.

[67]Mytelka, "Strategic partnership...", *op. cit.*, p. 8.

innovation. In this context, the idea has been advanced of partnership arrangements at the local and inter-country levels which could, at least partly, respond to these shortcomings.[68]

In the 1980s, the UNCTAD secretariat undertook a programme to analyse, on the basis of empirical studies, the role of SMEs from developed market-economy countries in the transfer of technology, mainly to developing countries. The findings reinforced the view that developing countries can benefit from the increased diversification of the sources of their technology imports made possible by SMEs of developed countries. At the same time, evidence obtained from, for example, Kenya showed that, in fact, SMEs and transnational corporations (TNCs) operate in different industries and in different contexts, particularly with respect to the size of the projects in which they are involved. Whereas TNCs' projects were mostly generated in cooperation with the local Government, SMEs' ventures resulted from private, individual initiatives in the host country. Moreover, the Kenyan experience showed that, in contrast to TNCs, SMEs operated in relatively labour-intensive industries such as textiles, metal products and, above all, engineering industries. At that time, these industries were also characterized by the relative simplicity of the technologies employed which made them better suited to the requirements of the small-scale and family-type segments of the industrial sector of developing countries.[69] On the other hand, the reviewed TNCs had an advantage for larger-scale projects, particularly in process industries, where the technology was more advanced. An important policy implication of these observations was that SMEs and TNCs satisfy different types of technological requirements in developing countries and that policies should therefore be sensitive to these differences.[70]

Concerning the motives for collaboration, more recent evidence drawn from Canadian experiences[71] as well as home country evidence obtained by UNCTAD in the examination of SMEs in countries such as France, Germany and Italy, indicate that SMEs are not only defensive (keeping market shares, reacting to protectionist measures) in transferring technology to developing countries but also "aggressive" (attraction of external markets, entry into new markets). The latter attests to the vitality of many SMEs, to the high level of their R&D capability achieved in certain "niche" sectors, and to their enhanced competitive position. Another important factor influencing technology transfer by SMEs (20 per cent of the French sample) is the client relationship they maintain with TNCs in order to penetrate difficult markets on a more durable basis.

With regard to the modalities and forms of technological partnership of SMEs with their clients in developing countries, both the above-mentioned

---

[68]See "Technological cooperation among developing countries: an examination of selected aspects" (UNCTAD/DST/Misc.4-UNCTAD/ECDC/Misc.127), paper presented at the Regional Workshop on R&D Community-Enterprise Cooperation in Technological Research and Commercialization/Application of Results, New Delhi, November 1994.

[69]These matters have to be explored thoroughly in the case of LDCs, for example, which may have specific technology needs, such as productivity enhancement and concerns for trade and production diversification. Also the question of the relative complexity of technologies has to be explored carefully, particularly in the light of the rapid technological changes taking place.

[70]UNCTAD, "Trends in international transfer of technology to developing countries by small and medium-sized enterprises" (TD/B/C.6/138), 1986.

[71]Jorge Niosi and Jacques Rivard, "Canadian technology transfer to developing countries through small and medium-sized enterprises", *World Development*, vol. 18, No. 11, 1990.

Canadian case-study as well as the work of UNCTAD indicate that while TNCs prefer more "internalized" forms of cooperative arrangements in developing countries such as wholly owned subsidiaries, SMEs, in the majority of cases, favour non-equity technology transfer arrangements as, for example, licensing agreements, and in fewer cases deal with equity involvement as joint ventures. The reasons for this, as indicated in the Canadian study, include the high costs of equity participation in terms of capital, personal time of the SMEs' officers, and communications. Local legislation against wholly owned subsidiaries and risk and management difficulties of foreign ventures in developing countries are also reasons for arm's-length transactions.[72]

With respect to the technological effect of SMEs on the recipient country, the analysis of the Kenyan experience[73] shows that the unpackaged and flexible character of SMEs' technology transactions with their recipient partners enabled the latter to acquire technology from a variety of sources. TNCs' affiliates developed most of their production activities through formal contractual links with parent companies (involving integrated technology packages) because of the more sophisticated nature of the technologies involved. The contrast in behaviour may also be due to the fact that, in most of the cases covered, it was the Kenyan partner that took the initiative in the technology transaction with the SME, mainly because of the former's precise knowledge of its technology requirements and the SME's limited capacity for exploration. Moreover, the limited managerial and financial resources of SMEs compared with the TNCs would make it less likely that they would be able to transfer an integrated technology package.

The Canadian experience indicates that in more than half the cases examined of technology transfer arrangements of SMEs in developing countries, the SMEs themselves initiated those arrangements, though in the case of countries with active industrial policies, such as India and the Republic of Korea, the initiative came mainly from host country firms. The Kenyan experience reveals that, in the case of technology suppliers from among developed countries' SMEs, the supply of machinery, technical assistance and know-how were the main subjects of the agreements examined. In the case of Canada, know-how was the most common subject of transaction followed by technical services. In either case, it was relatively rare for patents and trade marks to be the subjects of technology agreements.

The available literature provides examples of the successful pooling efforts of a number of enterprises in developed market-economy countries. These efforts are taking place through cooperative network arrangements with a view to achieving enhanced competitiveness in internal and external markets as a result of economies of scale, sharing of resources, exchange of information and combinations of complementary skills and technologies leading to innovative products and production processes. The evidence of such networking may be found, for example, in Denmark, Germany, Italy and Spain. These cooperative networks are of particular importance to SMEs.[74]

---

[72] *Ibid.*.

[73] See "Impact of technology transfer by foreign small and medium-sized enterprises on technological development in Kenya, report by the UNCTAD secretariat" (UNCTAD/TT/85), 1987.

[74] See, for example, Frank Pyke, *Small Firms, Technical Services and Inter-firm Cooperation*, International Institute for Labour Studies, Geneva, 1994, p. 5.

The example of the Danish Cooperation Network Programme has been considered particularly successful.[75] The basic objective of this programme has been to encourage small firms to join in cooperative networks in order to achieve economic goals that none of them could hope to attain alone. Implicitly, the overall aim is to increase the efficiency, standards and international competitiveness of Danish small-firm industry. A prominent role has been played in this Programme by the Danish Technological Institute. As reported, a particular advantage of cooperation was perceived to be the sharing of sales and marketing costs. But further attractions, according to a respondent from one of the firms interviewed, included the fact that by offering themselves as a group, and combining their different, as well as in some cases similar, machinery, they could provide customers with both a greater range of technical possibilities and a greater quantitative capacity. There are now possibilities for cooperation on other matters, including the achievement of ISO 9000 certification, seen as a particularly heavy investment for one company to make alone. It is likely therefore that a cooperative venture that began purely in terms of marketing will now be extended to production matters.[76]

As in the case of cooperative networks between SMEs within developed countries, the initiation of technology partnership arrangements with developing countries may well be facilitated by promotion measures either by the Governments or specialized institutions of developed countries. There is evidence of successful supportive activities of a similar kind in developed countries. The work of the Swiss non-governmental organization Technology for the People, which assists in the initiation of contacts between enterprises in Switzerland and developing countries and the organization of technology transfer partnerships, could be mentioned in this respect.[77]

[75]See "A focus on the Danish Technological Institute and the Danish Network Cooperation Programme", by Frank Pyke, International Conference on Endogenous Regional Development in a Global Economy (Valencia, 1992), Background paper No. 3.

[76]*Ibid.*.

[77]See *Journal de Genève et Gazette de Lausanne*, 9 February 1995.

SOME REFLECTIONS ON INTERNATIONAL TECHNOLOGY PARTNERSHIPS BETWEEN SMEs

by
Roger W. Short
Projects Director, Small Enterprise and Local Economic Development Association (SELEDA), Songy

INTRODUCTION

In preparing this short reflection on international technology partnerships between small and medium-sized enterprises (SMEs) I have drawn, in particular, on my practical experiences in relation to technology and SMEs. Despite the fact that these included very different experiences in a variety of environments, a number of common key words and concepts occur in most, if not all of them, namely: information; communication; cooperation; finance; sustainability; integrated approach; supporting institutional environment; and real needs. Whilst there may or may not be a consensus on the words chosen, there has been a strong tendency in the past to assume that success in one environment means that a particular model or concept can be packaged and transferred elsewhere. I believe that the time has come to focus on the needs of the target group and as we have come to this Workshop to discuss (a) technological capacity-building in developing countries, this means the institutional framework in those countries, and (b) international partnership between SMEs.

We need to examine why many programmes in these fields appear to have failed. We must also try to avoid being distracted by "buzz words" such as incubators, technoparks, service centres, business communication centres, industrial districts, networks, network brokers, etc., for these are only bricks in the overall fabric of sustainable technological and innovation development in SMEs. What is required is a policy at either national or regional level and an appropriate institutional framework to support that policy. This in turn will facilitate investment and sustainable development. These comments may seem superficial, but it is evident that many SME business and technology support centres in the world do not function because policies in this field at a national, regional or even local level are inadequate or non-existent. Having said this, I am aware that sustainable policies cannot be introduced over night. Therefore, in order to arrive at sustainable policies a number of manageable, realistic and small pilot demonstration projects ought to be considered.

I. ISSUES

A. Structural adjustment

Structural adjustment programmes in both the industrialized and developing countries have resulted in a marked increase in the number of micro, small and medium-sized enterprises. Virtually all governments and international donor agencies appreciate the importance of these enterprises as employment generators. As regards the technological development of these enterprises, and their involvement in transnational partnerships, a number of key issues arise. Structural adjustment and the economic policies of many governments in the past years have not only affected the manufacturing sector but also the sector of industrial technological service providers. Large State or quasi-State organizations, often with correspondingly large overheads, have had their direct and/or indirect subsidies reduced. This has frequently meant increased fees which many micro or SMEs cannot afford. A number of mechanisms have been introduced to overcome this financial problem either by the enterprises or the service providers. Examples of the former are to be found in Emilia Romagna (Italy) where firms have been jointly involved in the establishment and financing of service centres. An example of the latter is the Danish Network Programme. By encouraging companies to work in clusters it is hoped that together they will be able to afford the services of the major technological service providers.

In relation to sustainable technology transfer and technology partnership between SMEs financing problems arise. For example some of the major turnkey contractors in Denmark hire technology transfer specialist institutions (e.g. technical colleges) or enter into consortia with them. However, these are usually in cases where donor agencies make provision for the technology transfer component. Unless SMEs are made aware of the need for effective transfer and the availability of funds they will be reluctant to enter into such arrangements.

Structural adjustment has also had a major impact on the large State-funded industrial and technological R&D institutions in developing countries. Many of these have tended to be inward looking in their research and have only a limited experience of interacting with the market and in particular SMEs. CARIRI, in Trinidad and Tobago, when faced with the problem of reduced government contributions, opened a permanent technology information centre on an industrial estate, where entrepreneurs are able to see the industrial technologies and processes developed by the main CARIRI institute. One success of this initiative was related to the activity of one of the companies using a recipe for a Caribbean sauce developed by CARIRI. Within a few years this company was able to export to Europe and North America. For institutions in industrialized countries accustomed to undertaking contract research on a daily basis, this example may not appear to be of any importance. However, it does illustrate two points: the need to minimize the effort SMEs have to make to obtain useful information, and the volume of resources that can be tapped in the institutions of developing countries that are forced to interact with industry.

B. Information and communication

Access to information is critical in all areas related to SMEs and technological development. The example given concerning CARIRI resulted from a three-month visit to Denmark by two members of the Institute's staff to study the technological service system. The model of technological information centres that existed in Denmark was adapted to suit the needs of the environment in Trinidad. Similarly, the Danish Network Broker programme drew much of its inspiration from the industrial districts of Emilia Romagna but concentrated on inter-firm collaboration rather than on the overall system of the enabling environment.

At the level of information on technological opportunities for enterprises, CARIRI can again be cited as an example. During a visit paid to the exhibition centre in the course of an international seminar in Trinidad, a portable fruit harvesting machine developed by CARIRI was found to be appropriate for use in a number of African countries. In another case an Indian R&D institute was able to provide valuable advice to an institute in the United Republic of Tanzania which enabled the latter to redirect its R & D strategy to ensure that the results of a particular research project would be more economically viable.

During the development of a programme for technology management in Western Siberia, a number of emerging high-tech contract research SMEs were visited. A critical issue in the countries of former Soviet Union is that the client base for R&D has virtually disappeared or has little funding. Information on markets outside the former Soviet Union is extremely limited.

Limited access to information limits institutions' potential for interacting effectively with industry in general, and more specifically with SMEs, and for identifying new production processes and opportunities.

C. Cooperation and ethics

A major problem for companies involved in technology collaboration is overcoming mistrust. The company possessing the technology must be sure that the potential partner will not abuse a business relationship. For example there have been cases in an Asian country, where agreements on production technologies were confined to use in its domestic market. Within a short time the goods produced by the particular process were being exported from that country in contravention of the business agreement between the two companies. Conversely, companies in industrialized countries need to have a better understanding of the ambitions of potential partners in developing countries.

II. POSSIBLE WAYS FORWARD

There is clearly a need for improved communication and collaboration among the various actors if appropriate strategies for technology partnership are to be developed. Through a series of small manageable pilot projects the following need to be examined: (1) policies in different countries; (2) the institutional support structures; (3) financial and commercial aspects; and (4) human resource development requirements.

How can this best be done? One way may be for one or two regions in industrialized countries to collaborate with a region of a developing country. By guiding a number of SMEs through the process of entering and managing pilot technology partnerships, appropriate policies and enabling environment and support structures could be elaborated. Simultaneously, in order to facilitate the cross-fertilization of experiences, Internet might be used as a medium for on-going and cost-effective communication. UNCTAD is linked to Internet, so it would be possible to have electronic conferences relating to, among others, the topics outlined above. Over a period of time the interventions on Internet could be reproduced in hard copy for those unable to be linked electronically in the initial phases. If an inter-regional approach is taken, the industrialized regions might be prepared to support the Internet costs of the developing regions with which they are collaborating.

IMPLICATIONS OF THE GLOBAL INFORMATION HIGHWAY FOR DEVELOPING COUNTRIES: OPPORTUNITIES FOR TRAINING AND TECHNOLOGY TRANSFER

by
Günther Cyranek
Information Technology Assessment, Zurich

The process of globalization, accelerated by computer systems and networks, has created new kinds of markets and new ways to manage activities. The availability of information technologies (ITs) has »shrunk« the world to an extent that was impossible before, and also the required response time in the global community has been dramatically reduced. The implications of this phenomenon could offer new opportunities for developing countries.

The globalization of systems and activities has had a tremendous impact, for instance, on competition, organization and control, and has enabled interorganizational systems and information-enabled alliances to come into being. The new information technologies have facilitated the physical movement of work from areas with high-cost labour to areas where labour pools are both high quality and low cost. In a world where the economy is increasingly service-oriented and with the growing use of information in economic activities worldwide, these trends will accelerate, especially as telecommunications costs drop. Another important factor is that the traditional understanding of informatics, mostly as a technical discipline, is changing, encouraged by a stronger link between system developers and users, e.g. participative design methods, which provide broader access to the needs of the user, are more and more common.

I. POSSIBLE APPLICATIONS IN THE DEVELOPING COUNTRIES

Topics for the analysis of new IT applications in the developing countries should include:

- *human being-computer interaction*: demands for socio-cultural aspects in the design of such interaction;
- *computer and cooperation:* opportunities and risks for new models of labour organization in enterprises; new qualifications for cooperation;
- *computerized networks:* consequences of regional and global computerized networks; methods of computer-mediated communication; demands for design, security aspects, data protection;
- *multimedia systems*: potential for applications of multimedia systems in training.

The use of IT must at least be able to improve management in the economic sector and to increase the efficiency of government administration to enable bureaucracy to be reduced. In the public sector, in particular, the application of IT must be able to enhance the distribution of resources in the provision of electricity, transport and telecommunications.[78] Many of the problems faced by the use of IT exist in Africa, Asia and Latin America - as well as in industrialized countries.

In the context of cooperation for development, the transfer of technology from the industrialized countries to developing countries plays a

[78] Cyranek G. and S. Bathnagar (eds.) (1992): *Technology Transfer for Development: Prospects and Limits of Information Technology in Developing Countries*, New Delhi, Tata McGraw Hill.

key role in strategies for modernization. Information and communication technologies are particularly important in this regard. The developing countries cannot avoid becoming involved in the accelerated computerization of the world. For the purposes of cooperation for development, it is therefore essential that guidelines for successful technology transfer be established. We also have to see what developing countries can learn from models for technology transfer in industrialized countries.[79]

II. THE ROLE OF APPLICATION-ORIENTED TRAINING

If we are interested in the implications of the information highway for developing countries in the near future, we should analyse the experience with computer applications in the last few years. The World Bank's Development Informatics Unit has analysed 76 projects which the Bank funded in Africa during 1983-1990. It was found that Africa's infrastructure in telecommunications is grossly inadequate in terms of unmet demand, low penetration nationwide, and poor quality and reliability of service.

The analysis of projects funded by the World Bank in seven sectors, namely public administration, agriculture, poverty alleviation, rural development, environmental management, infrastructure and education identified the following problems as core factors in IT application: institutional weaknesses such as inadequate planning; shortage of human resources; funding difficulties; local environmental problems such as a lack of physical facilities and vendor representation; and technological and informational changes occurring during the project's life. As a result of the study, the failure of IT applications is being increasingly seen as an organizational problem.[80]

Training is essential for the promotion of IT in developing countries. A stronger focus on training in computer systems that is application oriented and geared to local and national needs seems essential. Up to now, curricula for training in the LDCs have all too often been rigidly modelled on those in the industrialized countries. Contrary to the common practice today, the focus of technology transfer must not be hardware and software in general, but should be oriented to local needs.

III. THE IMPLICATIONS OF GLOBAL NETWORKING

A number of questions need to be explored in this context. What does computerized networking really imply for developing countries? What could be the legal, economic and social implications? What are the appropriate approaches and strategies that would help organizations in developing countries to harness the enourmous potential inherent in IT? Should telecommunications - necessary for globalization - be given priority over other infrastructure development in developing countries? What role would globalization play in the currently less information-intensive economies of the developing world? Are there better opportunities for technology and knowledge transfer to developing countries?

Various activities to improve the accessibility of developing countries to the information highway are taking place, beginning with Internet services. The active role played by **information needs in development** is expressed in a summary description of the activities of Bestnet, outlining and explaining some of the most critical factors in this respect.

---

[79]Cyranek G. (1993): "Technology Transfer between university and enterprise: Institutions in Baden-Württenberg, Germany", University and Enterprise in a New Competitive Setting. Proceedings of the Workshop at the University of Buenos Aires, (UNCTAD/DST/1), Geneva.

[80]Moussa A. and R. Schware (1992): "Informatics in Africa: Lessons from World Bank Experience", *World Development*, 12 (Vol. 20), pp. 1737-1752.

The following 10 categories for information needs in development provide an instrumental tool for analysing new information-oriented service applications, and can assist in the attempt to assess specific training needs for global involvement, including the developing countries.

Effective utilization of existing knowledge. To improve the effective utilization and sharing of existing knowledge and resources at the local, regional and national levels; i.e. to have one's own node in a distributed network.

Local environment. To design and implement information systems and services that are relevant to the local environment: computer conferences and databases.

Data transfer at national and regional levels. To improve sharing and data transfer at the national and regional levels, i.e. to handle multiple standards.

Improvement of indigenous capacity-building. To improve indigenous capacity to plan, develop and implement national and regional information policy: promoting the development of Internet nodes, in cooperation with public data networks. The distribution of nodes leads to technology transfer to those countries and the building of local capacity in both technical and programmatic areas.

Sustainable information programmes. To secure a long-term commitment for sustainable information programmes: local long-term commitments by both the institutions and governments involved.

Promoting South-South cooperation. To stimulate greater use of local technical expertise in information handling by promoting South-South cooperation, including exchanges of educational programmes and collaborative research.

Virtual exchange of students. To build human resources in information sciences through needs-based training at all levels, and particularly the training of managers and trainers. The promotion of the "virtual exchange of students and faculty" among participating institutions includes courses in information sciences, telecommunications and related disciplines.

Agents of change. To improve the capacity of people involved in the provision of information to act as agents of change in conjunction with projects in agriculture, health, education and economic development.

Communication between rural and urban inhabitants. To promote a two-way flow of communication so that rural and urban inhabitants participate in an interactive dialogue on issues affecting them. For both rural and urban sectors, new educational opportunities should be made available in health care, agriculture, pest control, and courses across a range of academic disciplines.

Virtual laboratories. To improve the capacity of local scientists and technologists to obtain relevant information and bring about a more effective transfer of technology at the grass-roots level. The Bestnet project involves the formation of "virtual laboratories" for computer-communications-supported collaborative work.

TECHNOLOGY TRANSFER AND PARTNERING POSSIBILITIES THROUGH THE SOFTWARE APPROACH - THE CASE OF THE RHONE ALPES REGION IN FRANCE: A SUMMARY NOTE

by
François Ullmann
Director of International Projects
Training Unit, Chamber of Commerce and Industry, Grenoble

Developing countries can enhance their assets by being host areas to European enterprises working in the high technology services to further harmonious regional complementarity. This paper briefly examines motivation and forms of partnership possible with firms from the Rhone Alpes Region in France, as well as related information technology aspects.

The Rhône Alpes region ranks among the leading regions in Europe on account of its dynamic role in the computer and related services sector, mainly because it is the home ground of more than 500 specialized enterprises of renown, it is the headquarters of more than 20 prestigious companies that are world leaders (such as Cap, Gemini, Sopra, I.T.M.I., Merlin Gerin, Schneider Group, Hewlett Packard, O.S.F.) it hosts and supports more than fifteen engineering schools, it is backed by several specialized training centres in the field of computer science, it helps this professional network to export its know-how, it participates in the flourishing of research centres that are recognized worldwide and it promotes the establishment of related infrastructure (information highways, high-performance tools, fourth generation languagues - 4GL).

I. MOTIVATION AND FORMS OF PARTNERING WITH ENTERPRISES FROM THE RHONE-ALPES REGION

Most of the companies offering computer services devise and develop specific software or packages of programmes for several hundred applications covering a vast array of professions. The majority of these enterprises export their expertise mainly to the OECD countries and face rather brisk international competition. The presence of these enterprises on the international market is vital for ensuring the continuity of the large investments that such specialization requires. Further expansion into a geographical area that is not already covered represents a massive incentive to take advantage of new potentials.

The African market is a prime target as the continent has immense needs. In order to ensure its development, Africa should be able to rely on modern technology to optimize and reduce the costs that any desire for economic advancement entails. It appears that the specificity of the African market can only be dealt with in a sustainable manner in Africa by Africans, with the assistance of Western cooperation. The main line of cooperation between counterpart enterprises based on a balanced partnership respecting local professional sensibilities will enable the design of projects that responds to the African market.

The economic conditions offered by partnership with enterprises in the developing countries represent an important criterion. Such a partnership may be productive if it is based on a macroeconomic foundation that favours its growth.

A. The enterprise approach

A partnership with enterprises in the developing countries would assume different forms depending on the technical nature of the partnership. For example, some of the possibilities that would lead to technology transfer in developing countries would include: joint contracting, association of groups of enterprises, the creation of an agency for a French enterprise, the creation of a decentralized service by a French company, the creation of a company held jointly by the French and African partners, delocalization of a computer service by a French enterprise, the concept of multi-enterprises.

We shall leave it up to the partner enterprises to negotiate among themselves the best status that would facilitate the implementation of their joint project. Let us point out, for the sake of information, that the possibility of creating a private or a public company, as done in France, is perfectly realistic. Indeed, Francophone African business law is largely inspired by French business law. The partner enterprises will therefore increase their prospects in this administrative challenge to be able to create the wisest set-up, both from the point of view of technical problems to be overcome as well as of the legal and administrative aspects to be settled.

B. The product approach

Some of the French service companies would wish to adapt their product to African needs because, to date, customization is still minor by comparison with the potential volume of business involved. In fact, the professional software solutions are often devised to be finalized in relation to the markets or particular regions. In this scenario, the adaptation cost and additional revenue ratio is preponderant in defining the policy to be pursued.

It is evident that the targeting of products merits advance study. For example, there are applications in fields such as: equipment maintenance C.A.M., C.A.D., C.A.I.; the management of services linked to international trade; the development of communications software (to simplify the transmission of data from terminals in a local network to the telephone network, a software that allows each of the terminals of this local network, using Windows, to share a single modem, "numéris" (digital) adapter or X25 card to communicate with the outside world. Another example of this may be illustrated with software that allows terminals to access SNA servers with X25 cards.

C. The services approach

The consequence of this type of product is that the services derived from them can be related to each other. For example: "facilities management"; "l'info-gérance" (outsourcing) through telecommunications.

D. The market/product partnership

The relationship between the identifiable needs of the market and the solutions offered by these products to be customized would make it possible to envisage, for example, the following symbioses on a given territory in the region: the appropriate management of an installed base of materials and, thus, through its maintenance, the achievement of considerable savings to the beneficiaries; the optimization of production (agricultural or otherwise) while furthering export promotion; the streamlining of professional resources as a result of the processing of commercial or technical data, therefore providing all enterprises with access to technology.

II. POSSIBLE CONTRIBUTION OF ENTERPRISE PARTNERSHIP BETWEEN TWO REGIONS: INTEREST OF THE PARTIES AND RELATED TRAINING ASPECTS

Enterprises from the Rhône-Alpes Region make their growth in computer science available in developing countries through their assistance, which should take place on the ground, in the following fields: localization/translation (project philosophy and formulation); integration of packages; adaptation to local uses; personalization of software according to professional "customs"; interfacing according to the possible existing applications; updating of versions and current procedures; software maintenance of equipped sites; training linked to the evolution of the users' needs; small specific developments.

A. Interest for the parties concerned

Without the complementarity of the enterprises in the two regions involved in a common project, the strengthening of software services would be problematic to implement. Being able to "associate" with locally recognized professionals and to keep abreast of changing needs are essential elements for the project's viability. In this way, the African users can progressively benefit from a modern computing tool adapted to their own needs at lower cost. Developing countries in Africa are the preferred base for this type of professional partnership because the conditions necessary for both the economic and technological aspects are unique on the continent. Existing infrastructure combined with the international opening up of the region to receive this springboard to technological access, makes it commercially viable to match development needs and the research findings of the business community.

B. Training accompanying this type of partnership

Several categories of training action and involvement are necessary to implement this phase of a project.

1. Training for information systems involves: their design by the users through bread-boarding and prototyping tools; their implementation in open or proprietary systems; and their administration; then later on, their evolution in to projects which are centralized or spread out over different geographic sites in customer/server technology.

These different points raised will allow the use of the latest, the fastest, the most profitable techniques covering the various facets of the subject while conserving material and human investments.

2. Training in operating systems

This includes training in: the OS, DOS, Windows, Windows NT systems outfitting microcomputers; the IBM, DEC, H.P., BULL proprietary systems on small or large-scale electronics; UNIX running on material platforms by different manufacturers;

Also study adapted to the following is required: local telecommunications networks; and resource servers and application servers, meet current needs of enterprises more exactly (various sizes and geographic locations mixed together).

3. Training in software application (for programming or adaptation)

Training in this area requires the following to be studied: third generation languages, the most famous of which is COBOL; the 4GL (fourth generation languages); and fifth generation languages (the name is more commercial than technical) specifying the use of class techniques and "object-oriented" programmes ("OO") guaranteeing enrichment through the heritage of objects, programmes and structures developed (the enrichment of an element is extended to the family of the object of which these elements form a part).

4. Training for software maintenance and computing services:

Training would include: top-down analytical methods; methods of analysis by example, through bread-boarding and prototyping; and the use of CASE tools which embrace all the stages of the life of a computer application that primes the feasibility study, goes through problem specifications, design, conclusion, implementation, maintenance and re-engineering that mainly authorizes the retrofitting of older applications with today's technologies.

TECHNOLOGY TRANSFER, COOPERATION AND CAPACITY DEVELOPMENT

by
the OECD Secretariat

INTRODUCTION

Over the past several years, the OECD and its Member countries have given growing attention to technology cooperation with and technological capacity development in developing countries. While the private sector is the major source of technological innovation and the main agent of technology diffusion and implementation, OECD Member country Governments recognize that they can play a significant role in influencing how technology transfer and cooperation take place, i.e., through national policies and programmes that facilitate private sector action, their bilateral assistance programmes and their active participation in international organizations dealing with technology transfer, cooperation and capacity development issues.

This paper briefly presents some major elements of OECD work on technology cooperation and capacity development in two of the Organization's Committees: the Environment Policy Committee (EPOC) and the Development Assistance Committee (DAC). It then summarizes the major results of the recent OECD Workshop on Development Assistance and Technology Cooperation for Cleaner Industrial Production in Developing Countries. The paper concludes with a brief survey of OECD Member countries' activities aimed at promoting technology cooperation and capacity development in developing countries.

I. OECD WORK ON TECHNOLOGY TRANSFER, COOPERATION AND CAPACITY DEVELOPMENT

The Environment Policy Committee (EPOC) provides a forum for Member countries to work together on assessment and development of policies, strategies and measures for environmental protection. In particular the Committee seeks to promote effective integration of environmental and economic policies and related technological innovation and diffusion. Its Pollution Prevention and Control Group conducted a three-year programme on Technology and Environment, which focused on technological innovation and diffusion to reduce the pollution burden and prevent pollution. Through a series of case studies and workshops, the programme explored: (1) government policies necessary to stimulate the development, dissemination and use of cleaner production technologies; (2) specific sectoral issues for energy, transport, industry and agriculture; (3) information and technology transfer outside the OECD area; and (4) education and life-cycle analysis as tools to promote cleaner production.

The OECD Development Assistance Committee (DAC) is the principal international forum where bilateral aid donors, together with some multilateral donors, discuss their development cooperation programmes and strategies. Through its Working Party on Development Assistance and Environment, DAC Members endeavour to strengthen the contributions of aid policies and programmes to environmental sustainability and improved natural resources management.

With regard to technology cooperation and capacity development, the Working Party focuses on identifying opportunities for and barriers to cooperation on cleaner technologies through development assistance programmes. Its work also includes the identification of effective policies and actions by aid agencies to encourage the demand for cleaner technologies, reduce the transfer of environmentally damaging technologies and promote technological capacity development in developing countries. The Working Party is currently considering drawing up a set of good practices for donors in the area of technology cooperation, with special attention given to initiating and supporting technological partnership arrangements between small and medium-sized enterprises (SMEs) in developed and developing countries.

II. THE HANOVER WORKSHOP ON CLEANER INDUSTRIAL PRODUCTION IN DEVELOPING COUNTRIES

As part of OECD's follow-up activities to UNCED and Agenda 21, the Development Cooperation and Environment Directorates jointly organized a Workshop on Development Assistance and Technology Co-operation for Cleaner Industrial Production in Developing Countries, held in September 1994 in Hanover, Germany. Participants were drawn from OECD Member states and developing countries, and represented government, the private sector, international organizations, non-governmental organizations and the academic and research communities.

Areas identified for priority attention included increased emphasis on capacity development, better access to timely and accurate information, improved access to and use of existing financial resources and closer interaction with the private sector, particularly SMEs. More specifically, some of the major conclusions were as follows:

The private sector is the major source of technological innovation and the main agent of technology diffusion and implementation. To date, however, business has not been sufficiently involved by aid agencies and recipient countries. While the private sector is the principal developer and user of technology, governments must take a leadership role in creating a policy framework conducive to increasing the demand for cleaner products and technologies.

Developing countries are faced with three fundamental constraints in facilitating a more rapid diffusion and implementation of environmentally sound technologies, namely, a lack of institutional and managerial capacities to manage technological change; little access to timely and accurate information on available technology options and limited capacity to assess the information in a specific context; and a lack of financial resources and appropriate finance mechanisms, particularly in the case of SMEs.

In order to be effective, technology cooperation should focus on strengthening indigenous capacities and thereby bringing about changes conducive to environmentally sound management. This calls for closer interactions with the relevant actors — government at all levels, private sector associations, plant operators, consultants and the research community. Aid agencies, both bilateral and multilateral, need to incorporate pollution prevention approaches into their existing strategies and programmes. Such approaches can range from low-cost "good housekeeping" measures to capital-intensive hardware investments. Donors must improve their own capacity in environmentally sound management in order to become better equipped to shift from pollution control to a pollution prevention approach.

Technology cooperation and capacity development efforts can significantly benefit from increased coordination among bilateral bodies as well as between bilateral and multilateral agencies, including international financial institutions. Greater policy coherence within both donor and recipient countries is also necessary. This concerns primarily the development, environment, trade and industry agencies and associations.

III. OECD MEMBER COUNTRIES' ACTIVITIES IN SUPPORT OF TECHNOLOGY COOPERATION AND CAPACITY DEVELOPMENT

A. Development assistance

Given the objective of the present Workshop, it seems useful to present a brief survey of selected OECD Member countries' activities in support of technology cooperation between developed and developing countries. This survey, which does not claim to be exhaustive, draws on country reports submitted to the Hanover Workshop.

1. The United Kingdom is increasingly focusing its technology cooperation policy on private sector operators. The Technology Partnership Initiative (TPI), in particular, promotes direct access by enterprises in developing countries and newly industrializing economies to information on environmentally sound technologies available in the United Kingdom and on the firms that can supply such technologies there. Moreover, the United Kingdom has taken steps to increase such firms' awareness of the growing market for ESTs in developing countries. There is evidence that these efforts have already facilitated EST links.

2. Denmark, through its Danish International Development Assistance agency (DANIDA), provides assistance in promoting the use of ESTs in developing countries, including R&D support. One example is DANIDA's cooperation with the Government of Nicaragua in promoting low-cost ESTs. Moreover, the Industry Foundation for Development Aid (IFU) has sponsored a number of cleaner technology projects. IFU is a sister organization of DANIDA, and offers partnerships for joint ventures, loans and guarantees. Project areas, for example, have included Poland, India, China and several countries in Africa and Latin America.

3. Canada, via the Canadian International Development Agency (CIDA), assists Canadian firms in forming joint ventures with developing country partners, and also provides financial incentives. The ventures are aimed at testing, adapting and demonstrating ESTs for possible transfer. Under the Industrial Co-operation Programme, CIDA, as part of its training activities also provides funding to participants from developing countries to attend technology transfer conferences. Other Canadian federal departments and institutions, such as Industry Canada, Environment Canada and Natural Resources Canada disseminate information on cleaner technologies through participation in international meetings as well as specialized training sessions on issues of concern to developing countries. The International Development Research Centre (IDRC), one of Canada's development assistance agencies, has placed particular emphasis on R&D problems faced by SMEs in developing countries; it formulates specific ESTs and has a number of policy and promotional initiatives directed towards SMEs.

4. The Netherlands has a programme of grants to investment projects in the industrial sector with a positive environmental impact. These projects must be innovative in nature, concerning existing or new technologies. They may involve end-of-pipe solutions as well as cleaner production options, including the use of renewable inputs, and act as a catalyst for similar actions in various industrial sectors. Examples to date include wind generators, solar home energy systems and organic waste management facilities.

5. Australia designated the Australian Agency for International Development (AusAID) to promote sustainable development in developing countries. AusAID gives preference to industrial projects that meet local needs, create employment and involve appropriate technologies and local skills. It believes that successful cooperation on ESTs requires partnership with government, and with scientific, business, industrial and community groups. Examples of on-going projects are a five-year project in Indonesia to strengthen the capacity of the government environmental protection agency including deployment of ESTs; and the use of ESTs in East Java to help pollution prevention actions. Australia is developing a database and information network to assist other countries in readily accessing EST information relevant to their needs. Within Australia, cleaner production through EST use is a major programme, and an Australia Centre for Cleaner Production is being set up to provide information and expertise.

6. Germany sponsors the German Investment and Development Agency (DEG), which promotes private investment and technology transfer between private sector companies in Germany and in developing countries. Among other activities, the DEG is engaged in the initiation of business cooperation in the field of industrial environmental protection. Specific examples include DEG's co-operation with India and Thailand. The initiatives usually consist

of three phases. In the first, specific fields of collaboration with a market potential for long-term engagements are identified, and publicized in Germany and the prospective host country. In the second phase, potential host country partners are identified and visited by consultants with the objective of assessing cooperation needs and capabilities. The outcomes of this phase are also made public. Finally, potential cooperation partners in Germany are selectively approached and proposals are submitted to companies looking for a developing country partner. Both sides can avail themselves of the advisory services and know-how of the project staff in Germany and in the developing country.

7. Norway finances technology cooperation and capacity development programmes on waste minimization and EST strategies in a number of countries, with a special focus on economies in transition. Some of the programmes, managed by the Norwegian Society of Chartered Engineers, aim at increasing industrial productivity through ESTs, e.g. lower material spillage, water use, energy consumption, etc., with significant profitability for companies. Such programmes combine outside and on-the-job advice and training, including the training of trainers, group work and data search in international databases. They are regarded by both donors and recipients as a very cost-effective way of transferring ESTs know-how and reducing environmental hazards.

8. Japan is active in technical cooperation and capacity development by, among other things, establishing centres such as the Environment Research and Training Centre in Thailand. Broadly speaking, this approach consists of a team of technology and environment experts who live and work in a developing country for a time in order to learn about capacity, infrastructure and the cultural setting for technology cooperation. Assistance is provided for the development of appropriate local capacity and infrastructure to use various types of technology efficiently and in an environmentally sound manner. Finally, a technology centre within the developing country is created to transfer information about environmental protection, environmental risks, efficient energy and resource use, etc. Japan also provides advice and follow-up on the transfer of appropriate pollution prevention technologies.

9. The United States, through its Environmental Pollution Prevention (EP3) project administered by the United States Agency for International Development (USAID), aims to create and support locally sustainable pollution prevention programmes in both urban and industrial sectors of developing countries, and provide access to the relevant information and expertise available in the United States through a clearing-house set up under the project. Country programmes have been established in Chile, Ecuador, Egypt, Indonesia and Tunisia. Capacity development, including information transfer, is promoted through training programmes in the United States and in developing countries. Trainees are informed on how to assess pollution prevention, how to measure process inputs and outputs and how to evaluate options and quantify costs and benefits of implementing ESTs. In addition, a vendor database is being developed through which EP3 countries can access information about United States firms that offer ESTs and services.

B. Export promotion and technology cooperation

OECD Governments can also contribute to increased technology cooperation through export promotion programmes. On the supply side, export promotion is one of the principal possibilities available to governments to influence the volume and types of goods and services exported from their area of jurisdiction. It is difficult to determine at present to what degree environmental goods and services benefit from general export promotion activities, as most government export promotion agencies do not keep records of the businesses that make use of their services. However, several OECD Governments have tailored portions of their export promotion programmes to serve the interests of the environmental industry more effectively, although some newer initiatives are also promoting cleaner technologies. For example, the United States Overseas Private Investment Corporation (OPIC), a government agency that provides medium- to long-term financing and insurance for United States business ventures in developing countries, has set up a privately owned and managed Environmental Investment Fund, to identify, invest in, and support new or expanding business enterprises in developing countries and Eastern Europe that contribute to sustainable natural resources development and practise sound environmental management. The priority areas targeted by the Fund are sustainable agriculture, forestry management, ecotourism and pollution prevention. The Nordic Environmental Financing Company (NEFCO), a publicly supported venture that provides financing for firms from Nordic countries to export environmental technology to Central and Eastern European countries is a similar concept that could be applied to promote the transfer of cleaner production technologies.

A number of policy alternatives concerning the developmental and environmental dimension of export promotion and export credit activities might be considered by OECD Governments to promote technology cooperation. For example, it could be useful for governments to keep better data, wherever possible, on the volume and type of exports of environmental technologies that benefit from export promotion programmes. This information would assist governments in identifying those technologies that are not currently receiving support and cases where discrepancies appear between the priority assigned by governments to environmental technology transfer and the contribution of export promotion activities to the achievement of this objective. Governments might also investigate ways in which their existing activities and programmes could be redesigned in order to serve the specific needs of environmental technology exporters more effectively.

OECD countries might also consider conducting environmental reviews of their export credit and export promotion activities to determine whether the exports in question are beneficial or detrimental to the environment of foreign countries and/or to the global commons. General methodologies and procedures could be developed for screening such exports to ensure that they are environmentally-friendly, that they are not inappropriate for the purchasing countries, and that they include capacity development effects to the extent possible.

A study of the relationship between development assistance programmes and technological capacity development could be instructive for those involved in export promotion and export credit activities. This is particularly true for environmental review and assessment procedures, which are developed in foreign aid agencies. The experience of aid agencies in implementing these procedures, as well as the effectiveness of OECD efforts to harmonize environmental assessments of development assistance, would provide valuable information for trade policy officials. A better knowledge of the ways in which aid agencies are engaged in technology cooperation projects, and of the kinds of technologies transferred through development assistance, could help governments to design export promotion activities that more effectively complement the efforts of their aid agencies to foster the transfer of environmental technologies.

TECHNOLOGICAL CAPACITY-BUILDING AND SOCIAL CONDITIONS: THE CASE OF THE EMILIA ROMAGNA REGION, ITALY, AND POSSIBLE INTERNATIONAL COOPERATION

by
Valeria Bandini
European and International Projects Department
Emilia Romagna Technological Development Agency
(Agenzia per lo sviluppo tecnologico dell'Emilia Romagna - ASTER), Bologna

INTRODUCTION

Economic and technological development depends on the presence of a number of "critical elements" that create a system capable of auto-evolving, i.e. able to determine endogenous growth. For example, the development of human resources makes increasing technology productivity through innovation and technological development; at the same time, higher development rates help to enhance the human capital accumulation process.

Technological capacity-building is fundamental for developing countries, not only from a strictly economic point of view, because high technological capacity improve the quality and quantity of overall production, but also from a more general "social" viewpoint, because it forms part of the non-material assets of skills and knowledge that contribute to the social and cultural wealth of a country.

The level of technological development of a region is related directly to the equipment of firms and the competence of the human resources they employ. Equipment is usually acquired on the market (in the case of developing countries often from abroad), while human skills improvement is less related to market forces, but indirectly affects the capacity for "internal" technological development and innovation (particularly incremental innovation). However, technological development depends also on other conditions as well, for example: a favourable environment for innovation and technical knowledge, a modern and efficient training system, a stable relation between firms and universities, a generalized ability on the part of entrepreneurs to manage technological change effectively, the presence of service centres, etc. Social, institutional and economic conditions must therefore be considered together.

The Emilia Romagna experience is an example of an economic system where social and private business networks, together with public policies have determined the conditions for high technological capacity-building and for innovation. The combined action of the three elements (social, private and public) was particularly effective in the case of technological development through incremental innovation, whereas stronger public intervention appeared to be necessary when changes occurred in the technological trajectory, for example, in the transition from mechanical to electronic technologies.

Two major components of the economic environment should be identified: one refers to network goods, and the other is represented by elements that we define as "relational goods".

Example of network goods are telephone lines, water pipelines, electric grids, railways, roads, etc. The presence of these elements is necessary to attain economic development. The crucial problem is how to design policies for the development of the networks that are essential to achieve selected growth objectives. Depending on those objectives, certain network goods will be more strategic than others. In the light of characteristics of a region and economic specialization, it will be possible to identify the most important network goods that need to be established in order to maximize positive "externalities". These externalities can significantly influence the trend of industrial development. In fact, network externalities represent an important element in determining the number of firms operating in a selected region. However, network goods are not sufficient to guarantee economic growth. Once the structure of such goods has been created, it is necessary to develop "relational goods" that will utilize the network goods already existing or to be created. Examples of "relational goods" are an attitude of cooperation, entrepreneurial culture, the capacity to enter into partnerships and to join the relevant clubs and professional associations.

Labour specialization among firms localized in the same region may be a strategy that SMEs could pursue to compete successfully with large corporations. The division of labour among small firms allows for higher flexibility, a reduction of production costs, more opportunities for firms, and more frequent incremental innovations, etc. In order to achieve this goal, important intangible factors to maximize efficiency and effectiveness among SMEs must be considered, such as friendly relations, cooperation, the same historical culture, and the capacity to build on past experience.

For a long time, technology transfer was considered to be the transfer of a single technology according to a top-down process essentially the simple introduction of a new technology into a well-structured firm. This mechanism describes what happens in large companies or in the relations between large firms and their "satellites"; it does not take into account "environmental" conditions. But empirical analysis shows that the situation for small and medium-sized enterprises is quite different and that the local social and economic context is very relevant where such firms operate. The top-down concept does not throw light on the technology accumulation process of SME systems, nor is it able to orient actions to support the technological upgrading of SMEs.

The situation becomes more complex when the relations between companies operating in the local production system of a developed country are analysed, and all the more so when the relationship between small firms of a developing country are concerned. Moreover, the top-down approach can be considered in only one type of business relations between developed and developing countries, and would certainly not be exhaustive in the case of the desirable business links and cooperation that could fruitfully develop between SMEs.

The adoption of this approach implies, to some extent, not taking into consideration the desirable cooperation that could be developed by establishing relationships between SMEs of different countries. However, this undoubtedly requires a certain degree of support by public or institutional bodies (information services, networking, guarantees, etc.).

I. THE EXPERIENCE OF EMILIA ROMAGNA

Emilia Romagna represents in Italy an area where political, social and economic actors have been able to create a positive environment based on the networking of private, social and public elements. They should be considered as dynamic factors, because their evolution and integration with other elements, that are part of the model, contributed to the positive nature of the experience.

The region is known for its rapid economic development, strongly supported by exports, and based on the existence of many small enterprises concentrated in delimited territorial zones. These small enterprises often specialize in single stages of production and are integrated in a production cycle, which assumes the form of a local production system or a true industrial district, with a high technological level.

The lines of this development model, now known as the "Emilian Mode", originate in the convergence of economic, social and institutional factors that have allowed the market to operate without the creation of particular imbalances. A strong entrepreneurial tendency and the presence of local institutions oriented towards participation have led to a form of economic and social integration that is regulated by a mixture of competition and cooperation. These economic and social factors have obviously a long history. Yet they have been extremely effective in activating a development process owing to a combination of industrial and employment policies and social policies for the local community.

Very briefly, the Emilian model is characterized by: (1) a dense network of SMEs in a subcontracting relationship; (2) a local specialization of sectors in industrial districts; (3) a form of development centred around human beings and medium-sized towns; (4) the active presence of entrepreneurial associations; (5) the development of a cooperative movement; and (6) active local and regional governmental business support centres.

Therefore, in order to understand the development of the Emilia Romagna model, the following networks have to be taken into consideration: A. private business network; B. social network; C. public network.

A. Private business network

Private business networks, including private firms and their associations, are a very relevant factor for economic development. In order to be effective, such networks require a high degree of coordination and exchange of information. The existence of cooperation and competition and a low degree of opportunistic behaviour are at the basis of networking and the growth of firms.

According to a recent survey, firms with fewer than 50 employees represent more than 95 per cent of all the firms operating in the region. Yet despite their small size on average, the region has enjoyed growth rates that are higher than those of the Italian economy as a whole, even though the main regional industries are in competition with Italian and international industries in sectors dominated by large firms.

The strong points of private business networks can be summarized as follows: (a) a strong-minded attitude to business risk (probably deriving from the characteristics of agricultural activity at the beginning of the century); (b) technical skills that are widely diffused; (c) social cohesion and an environment favouring social mobility; (d) specialization in industry that has a low capital intensity.

In an environment where SMEs assume a major role, inter-firm networks acquire great importance. At the regional level, various entrepreneurial associations have contributed through different proactive actions: supplying firms with basic services (accounting, legal matters, etc.), attending to firms' demands for more complex services, and participating in the definition of public industrial policies. Moreover, entrepreneurial associations belong to the boards of directors of the regional service centres (see C. below).

B. Social network

Social networks play an important role in economic development as they create the culture needed to reach that goal. Friendship, a cooperative attitude, the readiness to share know-how and solve problems together with other actors are all necessary to create a "positive" competitive environment in which SMEs are able to develop and compete successfully with large corporations.

Social policies have played an important part in strengthening the dimensions of the community by promoting a more direct relationship between families and local institutions. In this, the creation of a welfare and health services network, involving the following elements, was particularly important: (a) establishment of schools for toddlers, and the creation of day nurseries which also favour the entry of women into the job market by reducing their domestic workload; (b) support and integration of handicapped youngsters; (c) provision of health care for women and children; (d) creation of general medical services and services for mental health care; (e) definition of human resource policies in providing support to: technical institutions, professional schools, centres for the vocational training of trade unions, and for professional training of entrepreneurial associations and other related groups; (f) environmental protection; (g) involvement in trade union negotiations and the monitoring of relevant local government regulations.

Thus, the role of the local authorities was to promote a more widespread participation, which proved crucial for the mobilization of economic, social and cultural resources.

C. Public network

The public network is made up of local government policies and public agencies. Their role is to create a macroenvironment defining industrial policies clearly and offering public goods and services efficiently. In particular, the Emilia Romagna region has pioneered a rather innovative development policy in Europe, with the emphasis on supplying information rather than conventional financial assistance.

The following aspects of policy innovation should be mentioned:

1. Networking: one of the distinctive features of regional policy is that regional authorities, partly by the need to tap private sources of finance, try to involve a wide constituency in the design and delivery of policy. Networking extends to the economic level between firms themselves and intermediate institutions, such as trade associations and service centres, thus enabling the parties to keep abreast of technological innovation and market fashions;

2. Informational competence: the capacity to generate and utilize information on policies and activities within and beyond the region is of critical importance in regional development. Examples are international databases to provide SMEs with access to a wide array of commercial and technical information;

3. Decentralized delivery: the success of regional development in Emilia Romagna derives to no small extent from the fact that it is based upon a decentralized service delivery system. Services are delivered by locally based agencies, which have an intimate knowledge of their clients' sectors of activity.

Emilia Romagna industrial policies were characterized by four types of intervention, which developed temporarily in the following sequence:

1. The first involved the creation of "craft villages" or "equipped areas", providing enterprises with the land required for their development. The local authorities aimed to offer craftsmen and owners of small enterprises an area equipped with the necessary infrastructures and services.

2. The second improved the conditions for credit access by favouring the development of guarantee cooperatives. These cooperatives undertake to guarantee the credit obtained by the partners (craftsmen and owners of small enterprises) from credit institutions. In so doing, they endow the individual partners with a negotiating power in obtaining credit that they probably would not have had otherwise.

3. The third refers to human resource qualification - one of the main field of activity for technological development interventions. Public policies devoted to the enhancement of technical institutions and the perfecting of action for professional and vocational training have led to a significant influx into the job market of technically trained personnel (specialized workers and technicians), and favoured the rapid spread of technical skills.

4. The fourth is that of "real services centres". These centres aim at providing entrepreneurial ventures with technical services and assistance through information concerning, for example, new technology and market trends. Some of these centres have transversal functions which involve all sectors, and specific functions oriented towards individual departments or sectors.

D. Real services

It is important to understand the concept of "real services". In the present context real services are to be distinguished from financial services (grants, loans, tax breaks, etc.) and cover a wide range of services, principally concerned with information, R&D, market research, technical consultancy, professional training, and quality control techniques, among others. Although the services are not always given free of charge, the fees are below the prevailing market rates.

The real services are supplied by ERVET, the regional development agency established in 1974, either directly or through its wider support network, which consists primarily of the service centres system. One of ERVET's distinctive features is its shareholding structure, which integrates the potentials of the public and private sectors, credit and finance institutions, entrepreneurial associations and chambers of commerce.

The real services not supplied directly by ERVET are supplied through two types of centres: sectorally-focused district centres, geared to the specific requirements of firms in a particular sector, and horizontal centres, geared to economy-wide issues like technology transfer, quality insurance, subcontracting and export promotion. Each of these centres is supported by ERVET, with the participation of the entrepreneurial associations and, in some cases, of local authorities and chambers of commerce.

II. CONCLUSIONS: POSSIBLE INTERNATIONAL COOPERATION

The Emilia Romagna region is equipped by its regional and international experience to be active in the field of international cooperation and to contribute in promoting technological capacity-building in developing countries. Its intervention would be based on the following lines of action: (A) Collaboration at the institutional level; (B) Technical assistance for economic-productive development; (C) Inter-enterprise collaboration.

A. Collaboration at the institutional level

This provides for the support and assistance of institutional structures in the definition, implementation and management of activities carried out by the public administration, the public services and the structures operating in the social sector (e.g. NGOs). Such assistance is to be provided by regional public institutions and by other organizations in the following areas: social welfare; initiatives for the training and requalification of the population, with particular attention to the more disadvantaged categories; development of the health and welfare system, in terms of organization, management and structures; development of the infrastructure system.

B. Technical assistance for economic-productive development

This refers to the definition of projects aimed at revitalizing the local economy and promoting small and medium-sized enterprises as a fundamental factor in economic development. Projects should be local, delimited at territorial level, and focused on priority sectors. The promotion of local entrepreneurship must take into account the social fabric in such a way as to favour endogenous growth and must involve the activation of permanent service structures for enterprises, based on the experience of the Emilia Romagna region.

C. Inter-enterprise collaboration

This provides for the promotion of partnerships at the commercial, production, financial and technological levels, between Emilia Romagna and developing country entrepreneurs. The partnerships would aim at creating investment possibilities for operators in the Emilia Romagna region and at supporting business initiatives at the local level in developing countries.

SUPPORTING TECHNOLOGY TRANSFER AND INNOVATION OF SMEs - A SUMMARY NOTE ON THE ASTER EXPERIENCE

by
Paolo Bonaretti
Director, Emilia Romagna Technological Development Agency
(Agenzia per lo sviluppo tecnologico dell'Emilia Romagna - ASTER), Bologna

The present summary note refers to the experience of Emilia Romagna region and particularly to that of ASTER, the Emilia Romagna Development Agency, which is active in the field of technology transfer and pays particular attention to the situation of small and medium-sized enterprises (SMEs) and their specific needs.

I. THE ROLE OF ASTER AS A REGIONAL AGENCY FOR SMEs

Clearly, the role played and the activities carried out by an agency like ASTER in supporting SMEs technology transfer mechanisms and their innovation process is among the important experiences to be considered when analysing the different aspects of technological capacity-building. The relation that can be established between a supporting organization and enterprises, particularly small and medium-sized companies, is of crucial importance.

The first point to be underlined is the capacity to understand the needs of SMEs and the ability to work directly with them in order to improve their capacity to assess their own strengths and weaknesses in facing a technology transfer process. Their consciousness of the problems will give them a better understanding of the proposed solutions and help them to contribute actively in the implementation process. The supporting institution must also be aware of the relevance of cooperation and imitation mechanisms and stimulate them. In so doing, they aim at the common upgrading of groups of companies interconnected by client-supplier linkages or other kinds of relations existing between the companies and the different entities (research centres, universities, technological experts, trainers, etc.) operating in a certain territorial area and contributing to technological upgrading. Obviously, any experience must be considered in its spatial and temporal dimensions, and each experience has something to teach.

The first point to take up deals with what exactly a SME is considered to be. This is not a trivial question because a number of different definitions exist, depending on the specific context to which the definition applies. For example, the definition according to State aid programmes is not the same as the definition laid down for the Research and Technological Development programmes funded by the European Commission. Moreover, definitions may differ depending on the parameter considered, such as the number of employees, turnover, fixed assets, etc. However, if the criterion is the work force, firms are usually considered to be of small or medium size if the number of employees is <u>less than 500</u>, and large if the number of employees is <u>more than 500</u>. The data contained in the last document published by the European Observatory on SMEs show that more than 98 per cent of the firms in Europe have fewer than 500 employees. In this document there is also a very interesting sub-classification of companies, which group them into micro, small, medium and large firms. In the light of this sub-classification, a firm would be considered a small or medium-sized enterprise if it employs <u>from 10 to 500</u> persons.

With regard to the mechanisms of innovation, the ASTER experience shows that the behaviour of small firms resembles that of micro firms rather than medium-sized ones. To pursue this hypothesis, more interesting results could probably be obtained by dividing enterprises into three classes: micro and small enterprises (MSEs), medium-sized and large firms. An analysis of this typology shows that, if the dimension of the firms increases, the innovation moves from "incremental" to "radical". In other words, in the micro firms, innovation is considered to be **market pulled**, i.e. mainly a consequence of market needs. The market is, of course, always requesting new products or better services, and a micro firm is obliged to adapt itself and its process/organization to the new needs. The only possibility of pursuing this goal without expensive modifications is to change gradually, using a tested technology/methodology. In these firms the limitation of financial means and available skills is balanced by a high rate of productive flexibility. In large industries, on the contrary, innovation is **technology pushed**, that is, mainly as a result of research and development activities, which can be undertaken inside the firm or outside it. Large firms usually have the capacity (i.e. skills and finance) to keep up with information, to select a solution and to implement it. Innovation for such firms can be radical, with big investments in plants and people. In this context, technology transfer is a mechanism able to generate a new solution for an old problem, or a new solution for a new problem, using methods/techniques/tools that are already well established. While R&D is fundamental for large firms, it is also important for SMEs.

Of course, technology transfer cannot be considered an absolute concept. A solution that can be innovative in one company will not necessarily be so in another. Moreover, an innovative solution can be effective in one case and not in another case, because of the different contextual situations, e.g. organization, people, market situation.

II. SPECIFIC FUNCTIONS

An organization supporting innovation in SMEs should approach its tasks in various ways.

A. Contact with the enterprises

The first "contact" with SMEs is very important for an organization in charge of technology transfer. Using the "on site" visit technique, the initial contact can improve the organization's knowledge of the company and its relationship with it. This is a good way to become informed of the opportunities for the firm and to perceive its difficulties. Moreover, a visit to the firm allows for a check on the existence of a context and of capacities for taking full advantage of technology transfer.

B. Needs analysis

People working in this area tend to agree that SMEs usually do not know what problems they have, but have an approximate idea of their objectives (for example, increasing productivity or production control). Without the supporting organization, a firm will often try to solve its problems through its habitual suppliers. The result is that if the supplier sells computers, he will advocate a new computer as the best solution. If, on the other hand, the supplier is a trainer, he will press for a set of training courses for the firm's employees as the optimal solution. In both cases the solution will be partial and, if the firm is unlucky, it will be ineffective. Needs analysis is a method of analysing the firm in order to identify the "real" problems, in order to work not only on their effects but also on their causes. Evaluation of the context enables a feasibility plan to be formulated for the innovation process. This plan will then be compatible with the existing situation and will be more credible if the people suggesting it are not the direct vendors of the solution. The tools used to analyse the needs of a company include technological audits. A technical report follows the audit, and usually contains a structured description of the company, and a comparison between the actual and the projected situation (that is before and after the expected innovation). The aim of the comparison is to identify the differences, and the task is to move from one situation to another. The technical report also contains a summary description of the timing and costs of the innovation process. The analysis and the feasibility plan have to be discussed with the client, in order to increase their efficiency and to exert immediate quality control.

C. The diffusion of information

The main purpose of providing SMEs with information on innovations is to transmit to them the results of R&D activities. The provision of information can be improved by merging the sector/activity/interest with the information. We have found that printing big catalogues containing all the results of research obtained in a given laboratory or programme is ineffective. On the contrary, small documents presenting information on a particular topic/product are quite efficient. It must also be taken into consideration that information based on case studies, that is, on results obtained in specific situations, is very constructive because it stimulates the mechanism of imitation. This mechanism is frequently used in the innovation process of SMEs. The tools used in the tasks of information/diffusion are well known: the organization of events and seminars, and the printing of newsletters. It is important to remember however, that, when SMEs are targeted, all these initiatives have to consider specific aspects and have a clearly focused content.

D. Support in planning and implementing projects

SMEs seldom have the necessary skills and experience to plan and submit projects in either the framework of national or of international programmes for innovation. Furthermore, they need support in identifying the financial sources (regional, national or international programmes) and in selecting the technology providers.

When requested, they need to be helped in the search for suitable partners to form consortia. For example, in 1990, 50 SMEs were contacted by ASTER in Emilia Romagna in order to understand their contexts and their needs. The Advanced Manufacturing Technology area was identified as critical to these firms. As a consequence, 17 SMEs were audited in the area of AMT, and, in 1991, ASTER, together with nine of them, submitted a specific project proposal for EC funding. During the definition phase, a consortium with six intermediaries and 11 SMEs from Italy, France and Spain was set up and the specific project proposed was accepted and funded, by the European Commission. Its main purpose was the development of a suitable mechanism to support SMEs in the selecting off-the-shelf products in Advanced Manufacturing Technology, concentrating on production planning software and CAD/CAM integration with information systems. A "check-list" methodology was set up and used to match SMEs' needs with technical solutions. The selected solutions were implemented and tested in the pilot firms, and the results were publicized in several seminars and events. In 1994, the project was extended to other countries and topics in order to improve the diffusion of the results. A new consortium with five intermediaries and six end-users from Italy, Ireland and the United Kingdom was established. The project is now in progress.

Another example of ASTER's activity is its participation in the project on "Managing Integration of New Technologies" (MINT). ASTER is one of the 21 main contractors of the project throughout Europe, and is responsible for the coordination and realization of 100 diagnoses in five Italian regions. The basic idea of ASTER's MINT activity was to find a "regional way" to implement the project, taking into consideration all regional/national situations. ASTER has organized and managed a consortium with five regional agencies, giving them the possibility, in the framework of a common methodology, to be flexible with respect to the needs of their firms. The areas of intervention of the MINT project were: Advanced Manufacturing Technology (AMT); quality; process innovation and control; product innovation; and strategy.

III. FINAL REMARKS

The following conclusions may be drawn: the importance of programmes addressing SMEs' specific needs should be emphasized; regional organizations such as ASTER can improve the efficiency of innovation programmes for SMEs through their daily contacts with them; stimulation of the "imitation" factor through a reliable diffusion of information is also important, as well as close collaboration with well-established international networks in order to keep technologically up to date. Of great importance is the social and economic environment favouring enterprises at the regional level, and consequently, also the linkages between an organization such as ASTER, entrepreneurial associations and other institutions supporting SMEs. All these elements will contribute to the international character of the innovation programmes of SMEs.

DANISH PROGRAMME SUPPORT TO TECHNOLOGY TRANSFER

by
Poul Brath
Manager, Focal Point for Technology for Developing Countries (FpTDc),
Danish Technological Institute, Taastrup

INTRODUCTION

This submission deals with Danish initiatives to establish economic and technology partnerships with institutions and private enterprises in the developing countries. For two reasons, it will concentrate on the state of the art for these programmes rather than try to evaluate the local outcome from investment or business-to-business projects. First, except for the investment programme (promotion of joint ventures), the technology partnership programmes have only existed for a couple of years and no final conclusions can yet be drawn concerning them because of the long-term perspective of technology. Secondly, the full mastery of the technology, and of assimilation and incremental innovation activities takes a long time to develop in a third world setting.

I. THE FOCAL POINT FOR TECHNOLOGY FOR DEVELOPING COUNTRIES

A. Background

The Focal Point for Technology for Developing Countries (FpTDc) has existed since January 1991. It was originally established on a three-year trial basis with financing by the Danish International Development Assistance Agency (Danida). The grant has now been secured until the end of 1996. Many new activities have been added to since the start of the Focal Point, and the staff has been increased correspondingly to the present five consultants. Furthermore, the growth of activity has meant an increase in the use of external consultants to assess, in particular, sector-specific and technical issues in connection with the companies' transfer of technology that is especially suited to the conditions in specific developing countries.

The physical location of the Focal Point has always been at the Danish Technological Institute in Taastrup, near Copenhagen, because of the Institute's close relationship to the Danish SME sector. Owing to the long tradition of incremental innovation in the big SME sector and a Danish industrialization process largely based on this sector, it was obvious that this entrepreneurial craftsmanship tradition should be linked to technology upgrading in locally owned enterprises in the developing countries.

B. Activities

The Focal Point is currently active in four ways, all of which overlap in practice. These are: (1) to assist Danish companies in all matters concerning technology transfer to developing countries. The aim of the Focal Point's consultancy assistance is to ensure that the technology provided by Danish companies can function - on both a short-term and a long-term basis - in the technical, social and economic conditions of the developing countries; (2) to inform companies about problems and possibilities in the aid market and the commercial markets of the developing countries; (3) to administer a subsidy scheme from which Danish companies can obtain financial to develop products suitable for conditions in the developing countries. In this connection, the Focal Point offers assistance in the planning of the development projects; (4) to publish the newsletter 'Nyt fra Kontaktpunktet', and the series 'Information' and to organize conferences and seminars. By these means relevant information on technology transfer is communicated to Danish companies, donor organizations and others engaged in technology transfer to developing countries.

In 1994, the Focal Point participated in 93 assignments with Danish companies. The distribution among sub-sectors was widespread.

C. The subsidy scheme

After many years of using Western technology in aid projects, it has often been found that existing technology is not directly suitable for applicable in developing countries. In view of the insufficient technical and organizational adjustment and development of appropriate technology, a subsidy scheme was established with the Focal Point in January 1994.

The aim of the subsidy scheme is twofold: (1) to ensure the development and use of suitable technology that can contribute positively to technological development in the developing countries, and (2) to strengthen the Danish business community's potential and relevance as supplier to the developing countries.

In order for a Danish company to obtain support through the scheme, it must meet two conditions: that the product does not already exist on the Danish market, and that the Danish company has a specific purchaser for the new product in a developing country. A qualified applicant can obtain coverage for 50 per cent of the development costs, to a maximum of DKK 1.5 million, so the Danish company must finance part of the costs itself. In addition to subsidizing the technical product development, the scheme can also cover expenses for preliminary studies and the local partner's visit to Denmark. In 1994, 10 projects were initiated under the subsidy scheme. It is believed by the Focal Point that transferred technology becomes more applicable locally as well as commercially more viable if the user of the technology is involved in the development work instead of being a passive recipient of the end product. Besides helping to finance the technical development in Denmark, the subsidy scheme also supports efforts to improve communication between the technology producer and user. For that reason consultants from the Focal Point or local developing country consultants participate in the technology assessment carried out at the local company and then closely follow the implementation and use of the technology to assure the process of capacity-building in the developing country.

D. The overall development objectives of the Focal Point

Through practical 'educational' work with Danish companies and a thorough knowledge of the preconditions of technological change and innovation in developing countries, the Focal Point hopes to support a process of technological capacity-building, and, in so doing, to avoid technology transfer that may turn out to be useless, as has sometimes happened in the course of aid-supported technology transfer over the last 30 years; to promote more suitable technology for the developing countries in question by consultancy and financial support to Danish companies; to ensure that the technology transfer and specific product and/or process development derives from or is carried out in close collaboration with the developing country recipient. Apart from aiding capacity-building itself, this procedure will prepare the way for a long-term learning and incremental innovation process based on suitable technology and a better understanding in the developing country recipients of the different components of the technology concerned. Lastly, the Focal Point hopes to contribute to sustainable economy and technology development in developing countries, based on mutual and equal benefits between economically independent partners in the North and the South.

E. How to secure capability-building through technology transfer

The Focal Point has often found that Danish companies with little or no experience of the needs and conditions of developing countries have difficulty in freeing themselves from traditional Danish conceptions of product design and of standards for material specifications and operator qualifications when working in a different social environment. The Focal Point has therefore published guidelines for the investigation of general business conditions in the developing countries in order to make it possible to include the most relevant requirements at the design phase in Denmark. It is emphasized that Danish companies concerned must also have a thorough knowledge of cultural, market and social conditions in the recipient countries. Practical experience of exporting to developing countries and cooperation with partners there has shown that the incorporation of the local technological production conditions is a precondition for a successful long-term engagement in the commercial market as well as in the international aid market.

F. Assessment of the Focal Point's achievements so far

Until now it has been difficult to measure the achievements of the Focal Point largely because the Focal Point never sees the results of most of the consultancy work. The following conclusions can nevertheless be drawn: (1) Danish SMEs have shown that they are able to provide useful process and product technology. However, there is still a long way to go before technology, and especially human resources, are automatically developed, adjusted or just reconsidered before trade, licensing or joint venture programmes are established; (2) under the new Minister for Danish International Development Assistance it has finally been agreed to spend a small part of the aid budget on upgrading the Danish resource base, including the Danish private sector, in order to avoid some of the failures of the past; (3) design and maintenance is still a major problem for Danish companies, but the Focal Point foresees that the biggest challenges in future will emerge in the cultural and organizational aspects of managing and transforming technology; (4) until now the Focal Point has mostly concentrated on the Danish companies concerned and their operations in Denmark. It will now be required by the subsidy scheme to place more emphasis on the developing country enterprises, the matching of technology partnerships and the ongoing assimilation of Danish technology; (5) at both national and international levels greater collaboration is needed among institutions prepared to support technology capacity-building in one way or another.

II. OTHER DANISH TECHNOLOGY PARTNERSHIP PROGRAMMES

All the Danish programmes active in technology transfer and described below are complementary with the Focal Point.

A. Danish Association for Small and Medium-sized Enterprises

This was the first to carry out a Danida-financed pilot project with the purpose of establishing technology partnerships with medium-sized enterprises in Zimbabwe. The pilot project was carried out over a three-year period from 1990. The fundamental purpose of the project was to act as a facilitator for direct business-to-business collaboration. The support budget was low - DKK 12 million - and mainly covered travel expenses, training and machinery. Process-oriented training was delivered by the Danish company. Only small product developments appropriate to the local environment in Zimbabwe were undertaken. Thanks to a flexible and non-bureaucratic administration the Association managed to establish 15 technology partnerships, 50 per cent of which were successful in terms of local capacity-building. Assimilation into the local production system also seemed to proceed satisfactorily.

At the end of the pilot project, Danida had built up its own Private Sector Development (PSD) Programme (see B. below) and the former programme was therefore discontinued. Instead, a 'starting' programme for the PSD programme was initiated in closer cooperation with Danida, mainly to support the transfer of technical know-how from Danish companies. At present there is no mutual interest in developing long-term commercial technological partnerships, but it is expected that cooperation with Danish companies will develop further under the PSD programme.

B. Danida's Private Sector Development Programme

Starting in 1993 the programme covers India, Ghana and Zimbabwe. If the results are good, it will be expanded to the other 17 countries selected by Danida for aid assistance. The objectives of the programme are to contribute to the positive development of the private sector in the recipient countries on conditions that are close to market terms. The programme has three components weighted differently from country to country: (1) to support the establishment of long-term collaboration between Danish business enterprises and business enterprises in developing countries; (2) to support the improvement of the enabling environment; and (3) to support the commercialization and privatization of State-owned industrial enterprises aiming at the potential establishment of business-to-business collaboration.

The facilities available for business-to-business cooperation, on a grant basis, cover: start-up activities, initial visits, required studies, etc.; improvement of occupational health and of the impact on the external environment; export promotion; technical assistance, training and education. Through a swap and/or a loan facility it is possible to support the following: imports of capital goods, raw materials, components, etc.; payment of license fees, royalties, etc., and additional export promotion, training and education not covered under the above grant financing for individual business cooperation. On a three-year trial basis DKK 150 million has been earmarked for this programme.

C. Industrialization Fund for Developing Countries (IFU)

This covers a wide range of well-known support activities aimed at establishing joint ventures in developing countries. IFU has been created to promote investments in these countries in collaboration with Danish trades and industries. Since 1978 IFU has been self-financing. Its preferred mode of operation is to follow the Danish and the foreign company from the initial negotiations and, once the joint venture is established, to remain as an active partner during the early years of operation. Its project activities are generally more supply-driven than demand-driven compared with similar European programmes, as, for example, the German Investitions- und Entwicklungsgesellschaft mbH (DEG). IFU has regional offices in both Africa, Asia and Latin America. It provides support with share capital, loans or guarantees and is also willing to find the cheapest sources of supplementary finance. Financially IFU can support partner visits, feasibility studies and training activities with grants. Like the Focal Point, IFU does not operate in the least developed countries only, but follows the World Bank's 'Group IV limit', which currently is US$ 4,865 per capita or less.

D. Danish Cooperation for Environment and Development (DANCED)

This is a fairly new dimension in Danish aid assistance to developing countries. As one of the first countries to follow up on the International Conference on Environment and Development, Denmark decided in 1992 to provide an additional 0.5 per cent of GDP, increasing up to the year 2002. The money earmarked for this programme is divided between the Foreign Ministry (Danida) and DANCED. DANCED has largely devoted its resources to building a strategy for cooperation among private enterprises, organizations and research institutions in Denmark and developing countries. In contrast to Danida, DANCED works in the middle income group of countries, and most of its activities are now in the East Asian countries.

In its work, it draws upon Danish expertise, experience and technology in the field of environmental protection equipment and know-how. Both institutions and private companies play a crucial role in this transfer of technology. DANCED believes that environmental problems have such far reaching dimensions that there is no possibility of solving them over the long term by traditional Danish actions but only by strengthening local capacity. In both Thailand and Malaysia, DANCED supports the creation of centres for cleaner process technology, which are intended to act as a link to the Danish industrial sector. Channels for collaboration have been established between DANCED and the Focal Point, but more emphasis should be laid on coordination, collaboration and awareness of the suitability of transferred technology.

III. SUMMING UP

From a brief review of the Danish programmes it is difficult, at present, to judge which kind of support would be preferable for technology transfer with a view to capacity-building in the developing countries. Investments and grants for studies and training naturally play a crucial role in attracting private companies and to promoting the learning process in developing countries. But in the Focal Point's view it is even more important for sustainable resource-building to determine whether a Danish company concerned in a proposed project has the ability to work in a developing country market, and to ensure that a thorough assessment of the technology has been carried out before the project goes any further. A flexible and holistic approach to technology partnership programmes, comprising all the instruments available, is therefore advocated for a better understanding of capacity-building in developing countries.

A DANISH TECHNOLOGY PARTNERSHIP PROGRAMME: THE EXPERIENCE IN ZIMBABWE[81]

by
Jens Kvorning
Danish Federation of Small and Medium-sized Enterprises, Copenhagen

DANIDA's pilot programme to test a new "business-to-business" partnership concept was launched in 1990 through a grant to the Danish Federation of Small and Medium-Sized Enterprises (DFSME). The Federation is the main organization for small and medium-sized Danish firms operating on a small scale in industry, construction and in the trade and services sectors. That same year, a programme was developed and introduced in Zimbabwe. The present note briefly describes the main lessons drawn from this experience.

I. THE PROGRAMME'S OBJECTIVES

The overall objective of the pilot programme was the creation of contacts between small and medium-sized enterprises in Denmark and similar business ventures in the developing countries which need technological support and assistance. The latter may take the form of assistance in the reorganization of the enterprise for making production more efficient, improving the quality of one or more of the product lines, adding a new product to the existing range, or introducing a new technology. The goal, in essence, is to make the enterprise more competitive internationally.

It is the view of the Federation that smaller enterprises operate under different conditions from those governing major companies. Consequently, the business-to-business programme was designed for smaller ventures on both sides, since it was believed that that would offer a better chance of understanding each other's problems and of benefiting from each other's experience. In carrying out the programme, the DFSME emphasized the fact that the business-to-business collaboration should be based on a sound commercial proposition. Both partners should have a clear economic interest in the project, as a driving force behind their agreement, and what made it unique compared to other development aid programmes launched before.[82]

II. THE PROGRAMME'S OVERALL PROCEDURES

The Federation places great emphasis on the fact that the programme should be down to earth and as smooth as possible. The fundamental point is that the foreign firm and the Danish firm are able to reach agreement on a sensible form of collaboration. The procedure is briefly outlined below.

Foreign firms that are interested in the business-to-business collaboration programme approach the Federation. After further information and visits, the Federation finds a potential Danish partner, and a visit to the foreign company is arranged. A member of the Federation's staff takes part in the visit. If the partners can agree on the basis of a partnership, a Letter of Intent (LOFI) is written immediately. This describes the purpose of the collaboration as well as the materials and the length of time necessary to carry out the programme. The Federation is pleased to offer assistance in the formulation of the LOFI. The LOFI forms the basis of the final contract between the two parties, which must be approved by the Federation. When this

---

[81]The present note draws upon a recent article published in *Development Today*, Oslo, 25 January 1995.

[82]The Swedish International Development Agency (SIDA) funded an industry programme in 1978 which, while following the same basic idea, did not incorporate this particular element.

procedure has been completed, work can begin. Generally, it takes about 2-3 months from when the firms meet for the first time until the project can be initiated.

The two firms themselves jointly plan and control the process of the project, but may involve the Federation to the extent they find necessary. In the course of the collaboration, 1-2 progress reports are delivered, and when the project is completed the firms deliver a final report as well as the accounts for the programme.

Concerning financing, participation in the business-to-business programme is not expensive for the firms. The programme is almost entirely financed by the Danish State as part of the Danish development assistance or the assistance to Eastern Europe. Basically, the technology and know-how of Danish small and medium-sized firms cover a wide field, and the Federation is likely to be able to find suitable partners within all areas of industry.

III. LESSONS FROM THE EXPERIENCE IN ZIMBABWE

During the pilot programme's four years of operation, 19 business-to-business agreements were signed and 14 of these were implemented, while five were given up before or soon after the start of the projects. The main reasons for cancelling signed agreements was the Zimbabwean partners' financial problems caused by the severe economic crisis in Zimbabwe in 1992. Another reason was the initial tests of the technology offered turned out to be unsuitable to conditions in Zimbabwe.

Two of the 14 projects have developed into joint ventures and six have developed into prosperous partnerships running on a purely commercial basis. Four Zimbabwean companies continue to use the technology gained from the cooperation but with little or no involvement from the Danish partner. The last two projects have failed and no concrete positive results can be registered.

A closer look at the successes and failures resulting from this business-to-business pilot project reveals a number of interesting patterns. In the selection of projects, emphasis was placed on testing the concept in several branches of industry, with various kinds of business as long as the enterprise was of limited size, in different regions of Zimbabwe, and with black as well as white ownership.

Except for the ownership pattern where only two of the 14 projects were owned by non-Europeans, this "broad entry" has resulted in the needed diversity, and it serves to illustrate the concept's potential in a broad context.

As regards the capacity of Danish SMEs to perform in developing countries, firstly, it appeared that Danish SMEs have skills and technology which are often relevant and useful in a developing country like Zimbabwe. It has also been verified that Danish SMEs that possess the right skills and technology can normally be persuaded to enter into an agreement even though it implies a considerable commitment.

Secondly, the pilot programme has shown that Danish SMEs are in most cases capable of trasferring their technology to a partner if an *adequate supportive framework* is established. Inadequate language skills have not been an obstacle of any significance either during the planning or during the implementation of the projects. Their ability to cope with the intercultural barriers has in most cases proved to be excellent. this problem has in fact been a challenge which the Danish companies have counted as one of their benfits from participating in the projects.

The supportive framework established to bring the partners together and to provide them with all the services they needed to perform well has proved to be necessary and adequate. The companies participating in the pilot project have all stressed that, without this support, they would never have entered into or gone through with the partnerships. On the other hand, it has been surprising to find that in most cases the need for support and monitoring was limited once the agreements were concluded and implementation could begin. Support during the implementation phase has been important in only five projects.

Thirdly, small family-owned businesses on both sides seem to produce far more successful and stable partnerships than those involving big conglomerates or their subsidiaries with corporate ownership and employed management. An agreement depends mainly on the commitment of those persons who developed the idea and negotiated the terms. It is therefore very unfortunate if one of the two key persons leaves the partnership, especially if this occurs during the initial process of transferring the technology when goals have not yet been reached.

Of the nine family-owned and managed Zimbabwean companies that implemented their projects, none changed their management during the test period. By contrast, all the employed managers in the five subsidiaries of conglomerates changed their management during the test period. The partnership has continued in only one of these cases and the two failed projects are both in this last group.

A fourth lesson is that it is possible to make the administration of a business-to-business partnership scheme simple, flexible and fast enough to meet the needs of SMEs. If owner-managed, SMEs are characterized by quick decision-making, and they expect the same from their counterparts. A good project idea is often very dependent on quick action. It has therefore been one of the pilot programme's highest priorities to reduce the time elapsing the first meeting between the partners to the approval of their "letters of agreement" to a minimum. In fact, it was brought down to 6-8 weeks.

A fifth lesson is that SMEs can be committed to a partnership for a longer period even at very great distances physically and psychologically as long as they find the right partner. They are prepared to wait for the commercial benefits if the right "chemistry" has been established and they trust each other's intentions.

A sixth and final lesson is that "increasing returns to scale" can be achieved even in small business-to-business projects. Several of the participating companies both in Denmark and in Zimbabwe have become involved successfully in more than one project. Their involvement in new projects only needs very limited administrative support.

IV. CONCLUSIONS

The experience outlined above would seem to indicate clearly that small enterprises in developed countries can play an important role in technology cooperation and assistance to developing countries, particularly, if provided with some basic support. The lessons drawn from the above experience show that the business-to-business cooperation could become a fruitful tool in Danida's Private Sector Development Programme (PSD), both for the creation of commercially viable small partnerships and for maturing partnerships that have the potential to grow into bigger projects with the support of the other PSD facilities. Additionally, it would appear that, on account of its thorough knowledge of the working of smaller enterprises, the Federation is well suited to undertake the role of "match-maker" between the companies in Denmark and the companies abroad. The experience derived from the project in Zimbabwe can be useful in solving the firms' practical problems and helping them through their teething troubles. This type of support could prove invaluable in promoting effective technology partnership between SMEs from a developed country and enterprises in the developing regions.

ENVIRONMENTAL TECHNOLOGY COOPERATION - BACKGROUND TO THE SETTING UP OF THE TECHNOLOGY PARTNERSHIP INITIATIVE

by
Stella K. Blacklaws
Deputy Head, Technology Partnership Initiative
Department of Trade and Industry, London

I. THE POSITION REACHED AT THE RIO CONFERENCE

A. Issues

At Rio, developing countries argued for the transfer of technology to take place under "non-commercial" or "preferential" terms. They laid much emphasis on the transfer of "leading edge" technologies, fearing that they would otherwise be offered out-dated solutions. There was initially a strong focus on mechanisms to acquire hardware (e.g. through compulsory purchase), with less attention paid to essential back-up in the form of expertise and training. Intellectual property rights (IPR) were often presented as an impediment to the process of sustainable development; and technology in the public domain tended to be viewed as if it were owned by the public sector.

The United Kingdom acknowledged that international technology transfer was important to achieving the goal of sustainable development. But it argued that transferring leading edge technology was not necessarily as high a priority as transferring "appropriate" technology and supporting know-how and that, while aid programmes had a role, technology transfer on the scale required would not take place unless normal commercial channels were fully exploited. This position was supported by three studies[83] on technology transfer commissioned by the UK to inform the negotiations. They revealed that there were many mechanisms for successful technology transfer although no single mechanism was the key for all. Commercial transactions were shown to be the single most effective means to transfer technology. (OECD reports indicate that some 93 per cent of technology transfer occurs as part of the normal flow of commercial transactions between and within businesses). Technology transfer was considered more likely to be effective if both parties had an interest in its success.

The studies also reinforced the view that "hard" technology should be accompanied by the provision of technical and managerial skills and other back-up (the so-called "soft" technologies) if it is to be absorbed, maintained, adapted, used and diffused in the recipient countries. The concept of "technology cooperation" was developed to cover technology transfer in this broader sense. In so far as this involves the transfer of know-how it also raised IPR and financing issues. In this context, the studies concluded that respect for commercial mechanisms and incentives, including an effective IPR system, was important to the successful transfer of technologies.

There are three main strands to the UK's effort to promote technology cooperation: the aid programme; conventional export promotion; and special initiatives focusing on environment and the needs of developing countries.

---

[83]Global Climate Change: the role of technology transfer. Conservation of Biological Diversity: the role of technology transfer. Technology Cooperation: Britain's experience.

B. Aid programme

The overall aim is to promote economic and social development in other countries, and the welfare of their people. A large part of the bilateral aid programme consists of technical cooperation - the transfer of knowledge and expertise to developing countries through consultancies and training - as well as the provision, where appropriate, of capital goods and equipment for mutually agreed development purposes. The experience of the Overseas Development Administration (ODA) has shown that "hard" technology, while superficially attractive to developing countries, often falls quickly into disuse because of shortages of experienced local engineers and spare parts, and recurrent local costs. Such technology transfer has not proved a cost-effective use of UK aid funds, and is therefore a diminishing component of ODA's programme.

C. Export programme

The United Kingdom's export promotion programme in effect promotes technology transfer through commercial channels. DTI's support for United Kingdom exporters was reorganized during 1993. Export promotion was separated from trade relations and given additional resources, including 100 secondees from British industry - export promoters - to provide specialist market knowledge and advice to UK companies. There is now a greater emphasis on encouraging UK companies to move away from sales-based exporting towards partnerships, joint ventures and investments.

D. Technology Partnership Initiative

Discussions in the run up to Rio highlighted the need for developing countries to be better informed about the enormous range of expertise and best practice and technology options available to them through commercial channels. It was to address this need that the Prime Minister of the United Kingdom announced the Technology Partnership Initiative (TPI) at the UNCED.

The Initiative was launched at the Global Technology Partnership Conference in March 1993. It focuses on the environment-related needs of developing countries most likely to benefit from business-to-business cooperation. A network of national and international multipliers in touch with the business communities in these countries is used as a channel of information and advice on best practice and UK expertise and technology. All multipliers have received a "Guide to UK Environmental Technology and Services" which signposts UK suppliers and national and international organizations able to facilitate technology cooperation. The network also receives Newsletters containing case studies, news of relevant initiatives and special features on particular environmental issues highlighting the UK expertise and technology available to deal with them. In response to feed back from the launch Conference, the first two features covered environmental management and training and sources of finance. The Initiative is also underpinned by DTI's Hands-on Training Scheme (HOTs) which provides subsidized training for decision-makers in the use of UK technologies and techniques.

The Initiative has sponsored seminars on environmental management and training in Argentina, India, Taiwan, China and Uruguay. The Initiative is also supporting production of a second volume of UNEP's Cleaner Production Worldwide Booklet (containing cleaner production case studies) and the present UNCTAD Workshop on technology cooperation with developing countries, including least developed countries. UK companies prepared to part-finance training places under HOTs have been identified and suitable developing country candidates are being sought. The network of multipliers has expanded to accommodate new members from developing countries; and at least 12 Newsletters are planned over the first three years of the Initiative.

In the United Kingdom, export promoters draw on the Initiative as necessary in their regular contacts with business. In particular, they alert businesses to the special circumstances that exist in the developing countries where very often the best way to do business is through joint ventures, etc. This message and the activities of the TPI have been promoted at recent UK seminars covering investment finance, services available from the Commonwealth Development Corporation, and the EC Investment Partners scheme which supports joint ventures between European and developing country businesses.

APCTT'S EXPERIENCES IN STRENGTHENING REGIONAL COOPERATION IN TECHNOLOGICAL CAPACITY-BUILDING - WITH EMPHASIS ON SMALL AND MEDIUM-SIZED ENTERPRISES AND TRANSFER OF ENVIRONMENT-FRIENDLY TECHNOLOGIES

by
Jürgen Bischoff
Director, Asian and Pacific Centre for Transfer of Technology of the United Nations Economic and Social Commission for Asia and the Pacific, New Delhi

INTRODUCTION

There is now widespread recognition that technology is an important strategic factor in the development process in order to achieve economic and social standards. However, the developing countries have to adopt different approaches to develop capabilities for the utilization of science and technology as well as to ensure sustainable economic development. This involves commitment from the highest levels of government in policy formulation and implementation, institution-building, human resources development as well as creation of right type of technology climate for promotion of investment-related technology transfer. Technical developments are also now altering the pattern of trade and technology transfer, thereby creating new opportunities and challenges for countries. This is influencing intraregional technology flows, trade in capital goods, foreign direct investment and the supply of technical and consultancy services. Therefore, the question of technological capacity-building in developing countries encompasses the status of the efforts made by national governments to restructure trade and industrial policies, create necessary infrastructure and supporting institutions, strengthen linkages and promote information flows at various levels.

Many newly industrializing countries have been able to attract considerable foreign investment and expand their local technological capacity as they had adequate domestic resources. However, there are a number of developing and least developed countries of the region that have been left out of the mainstream of economic and technological development. There is considerable scope for assisting such countries to enhance their capabilities through regional and interregional cooperation. Most of the least developed countries are placing emphasis on the development of small and medium-sized enterprises (SMEs), as these tend to cater to the needs of the rural population and provide employment for people living near them. In this context, the role of the private sector is crucial but the sector faces problems due to the lack of effective institutional support arrangements. Mechanisms do not exist for systematic identification, development and dissemination of relevant technologies. APCTT as a regional institution is actively involved in evolving suitable technology transfer mechanisms with a view to accelerating the process and increasing their technological capabilities.

This paper will cover some of the initiatives taken by APCTT in this direction by strengthening regional cooperation in technological capability-building with emphasis on SMEs and transfer of environment-friendly technologies.

I. THE IMPORTANCE OF TECHNOLOGICAL INFORMATION

Easy access to technology information is an important prerequisite for technology transfer. Efficient national information services and networks are essential. Enterprises are not only interested in technology sources but are keen to know the techno-economic details of specific technologies available for transfer. In order to ensure proper absorption of the information, it is necessary to enhance the national capabilities and institutional mechanisms. With this in view, APCTT is implementing the "Mechanism for Exchange of

Technology Information" (METI) programmes with the active participation of 12 member countries in the region. There is also a definite need to create awareness of the need for such information and to strengthen networking at the enterprise level, especially among promotional agencies, small-scale industries and financial institutions. In order to bridge the existing gaps, APCTT has evolved an "International Network for Transfer of Environment-Friendly Technologies" (INTET), and is also testing an experimental scheme together with the Small Industries Development Bank of India (SIDBI) to assist small-scale industries (SSIs) in technology-transfer-related problems. APCTT's INTET, for the exchange of technology information on environment-friendly technologies deals with technologies available worldwide.

II. PROMOTION OF TECHNOLOGY EXCHANGE

The catalytic role played by APCTT in promoting flows of technologies and facilitating access to them on favourable terms needs to be further strengthened. There is also a definite need to enhance national capacities in the evaluation and assessment of new and clean technologies. The ability of developing countries to receive, transfer, adopt and develop new technologies and to a large extent manage them successfully depends on the development of endogenous technological capacity.

APCTT is now issuing a bimonthly publication "Value Added Technology Information Service" (VATIS) with updated information on priority sectors such as: food processing; waste management; sources of non-conventional energy; ozone layer protection and biotechnology. It is proposed to cover more sectors and areas depending on the needs of the member countries. The APCTT also organizes business meetings and promotes technology market forums such as "Techmarts" to bring together buyers and sellers of technology in specialized and high-tech areas. In addition, it disseminates information on technology offers and requests, and on available consultants through its bimonthly publication "Asia-Pacific Tech Monitor" and through exhibitions and workshops.

III. TECHNOLOGY MANAGEMENT PROGRAMMES

To facilitate the formulation of dynamic national policies aimed at the promotion of technology transfer, APCTT initially implemented the "Technology Atlas" project and brought out specific reports for the benefit of developing countries of the region. Currently, the Centre is concentrating on certain practical aspects of technology management. It is organizing specific capacity-building programmes that include awareness creation, technology demonstration and the organization of national and international workshops and training programmes to promote R&D and enterprise cooperation in general, as well as in specialized fields such as technology monitoring, evaluation, pricing, assessment, etc. The main focus is on the development of human resources and of mechanisms for technology transfer and absorption, for the modernization and technology upgrading of SMEs as well for the acquisition of venture capital. It also places emphasis on the promotion of women in entrepreneurial positions.

Regional and interregional cooperation aimed at facilitating the transfer of technology from more developed and industrializing developing countries could give an impetus to technology transfer to other developing and least developed countries. In this context, the promotion of technical cooperation among developing countries (TCDC), through, among other things, investment-related technology transfer, is extremely promising. APCTT provides advisory services and promotes consultancy assistance to SMEs through the exchange of experts. Engineering and management consultancy services are important technical support tools in encouraging technology flows. There is a need to develop these capabilities further in developing and least developed countries. APCTT is also assisting member countries of the region by promoting TCDC in order to ensure better utilization of local consultants, especially in the evaluation and assessment of relevant technologies.

IV. CONCLUSIONS

The least developed countries in the region face many developmental problems. The capital goods sector is almost non-existent, and their inadequate human, financial and technical resources have been found to be major constraints on their efforts to industrialize rapidly. The results of ongoing industrial restructuring policies and programmes have been mixed. New avenues and opportunities are being sought to strengthen and improve their technological and industrial competitiveness. The widespread diffusion of new and emerging technologies appears as a critical determinant in promoting competitiveness. Managing technological change in the coming years will pose several challenges to developing countries of the region. It is consequently essential for technology transfer and promotional agencies working at national, regional and international levels unite their forces in sharing and disseminating information, as well as in implementing relevant programmes in areas relating to technology development, transfer and utilization. This would ensure the effective use of scarce resources in delivering the desired output and encourage increased donor support.

ANNEX

Summary experiences of Bangladesh and Nepal

APCTT has initiated a study on "Technology management experiences of selected countries in the Asian region", based on information extracted from the country reports presented by participants in workshops and seminars. Some of the aspects relate to technology transfer and utilization in developing and least developed countries of the region. In this context it has been thought useful to give some information on technological issues in Bangladesh and Nepal in this annex.

Bangladesh

Though the importance of S&T in the national development process is fully recognized, the explicit role of technology in industrial development is not well focused in the laws of the country. The Bangladesh Council of Scientific and Industrial Research (BCSIR) has at present six laboratories working in areas such as food processing, nutrition, energy, biotechnology, herbal medicine, chemicals, leather, polymers, etc. However, commercialization of technologies by BCSIR has suffered due to lack of a perceived need for technologies, small market size, incomplete development of technology and availability of alternative technologies from abroad.

There is as yet no centralized technology agency in Bangladesh for coordinating technology activities at the national level. These activities are initiated and implemented in a fragmented manner by different departments and institutions. The Department of Science and Industry and the National Council of Science and Technology (NCST) do not have any operational units for implementing certain activities. Research projects undertaken in R&D laboratories are not subjected to any formal techno-economic evaluation. Nor is there any demand for indigenously developed technologies from national laboratories. However, successful efforts to commercialize and diffuse some of the agricultural technologies have been made. Bangladesh also encourages the inflow of foreign capital and technology in many industrial sectors. Nevertheless, there is no fiscal incentive for R&D investment, which is crucial for technology development. A comprehensive tax structure or differential tariff rate as instruments for encouraging and promoting technology development and transfer have also yet to be evolved.

With regard to imported technology, there is now a defined mechanism for technology acquisition as well as for the assimilation and adoption of such technology. Since the current emphasis is on the development of small and cottage industries, there is also a need for concerted efforts to improve the productivity, diffusion of new technology and upgrading of technological development in the SSI sector. In this context, Bangladesh should evolve a technology policy that is supported by an adequate institutional framework including legal and fiscal measures. The human resources development programmes should receive the highest priority and mechanisms for setting up pilot plants and for the evaluation and assessment of foreign technologies should be further strengthened.

Nepal

Nepal has a limited number of science and technology (S&T) institutions engaged in technology development. However, many private R&D institutions and NGOs are emerging of late. Major R&D activities are centred around agriculture, forestry, medicine, metrology and irrigation. The National Council for Science and Technology (NCST) is the highest-level body set up to formulate S&T policies and programmes. Subsequently the Regional Centre for Applied Science and Technology (RECAST) was established under the Tribhuvan University to undertake R&D activities in specific areas. The coordination and linkages between R&D organizations and user agencies are not satisfactory. Investment in R&D is only about 0.13 per cent of GNP, which is the lowest even among the South Asian Association for Regional Cooperation (SAARC) countries. A skilled workforce is lacking in most of the government-funded laboratories. With regard to human resources development, Nepal is mainly assisted by foreign countries in training its people in advanced fields of science and engineering technology.

At present there is no organized mechanism for technology transfer or for supporting indigenous technology development and utilization. Technologies developed by R&D institutions are mostly in the social services sector, and hence do not evolve much interest among entrepreneurs. In the industrial sector, as indigenous technologies need to be tested on a pilot scale and there are no financial arrangements for acquiring risk capital, the tendency is again to look for proven technology from abroad. RECAST is now playing an active role in strengthening linkages between the generator of technology and its users.

Technical and management consultancy organizations are not well developed and SMEs therefore have to depend largely on their own channels for marketing arrangements. Since 1992, a new industrial policy was adopted in Nepal. Its main purpose is to de-license major industrial activities, except in a few critical sectors. The Government is now implementing reforms with the emphasis on small-scale and export promotion industries. However, clear-cut priorities have yet to be established for the allocation of resources in specific areas.

EXPERIENCES WITH PARTNERSHIP AND CAPACITY-BUILDING

by
John H. Skinner
Senior Advisor, UNEP Industry and Environment Centre, Paris

I. PARTNERSHIPS AT UNEP IE

The UNEP Industry and Environment Centre (UNEP IE) was established in 1975 to bring industry, governments and non-governmental organizations together to work towards environmentally sound forms of industrial development. UNEP IE was active in UNCED's preparation and participated in the various industry forums. Following UNCED, UNEP IE reviewed its strategy and with the help of an Advisory Group formed by its partners in industry, government and NGOs, reoriented its activities to support the initiatives of Agenda 21. Some major activities with an emphasis on international partnerships are described below:

Cleaner Production. UNEP IE launched its Cleaner Production Programme in 1990. This concept is strongly supported in Agenda 21. It now includes: national cleaner production workshops, a publications series translated into several languages, ICPIC – the International Cleaner Production Clearinghouse, Cleaner Production Centres established in cooperation with UNIDO and a series of cleaner production demonstrations in China and Africa. The programme networks with experts and transfers information to a broad audience.

APELL. The APELL Programme (Awareness and Preparedness for Emergencies at Local Level), which promotes the prevention of, and response to, industrial accidents, was developed in 1988 and was also acknowledged in Agenda 21. This is a good example of an international partnership actively developed by UNEP IE, the chemical industry (the International Council of Chemical Associations), and governments to prepare the APELL Handbook, which is now available in 14 languages. Furthermore, APELL recommends national and local partnerships to prevent accidents and prepare for emergency response, and 20 APELL seminars and workshops have been held over the past five years reaching decision-makers from industry, government, local authorities, and communities. Over 70 national governments now have APELL focal points for disseminating APELL information.

OzonAction. UNEP IE is also responsible for the clearinghouse function envisaged in the Montreal Protocol on Substances that Deplete the Ozone Layer. The OzonAction Information Clearinghouse transfers information on ozone-depleting substances and covers: policy and technical options, descriptions of alternative technologies, an international directory of experts, document abstracts and news bulletins. Workshops, conferences and training activities are held and country programmes have been established to provide practical assistance to industry and governments in phasing out ozone-depleting substances.

Tourism and Transport. Agenda 21 cites the importance of tourism, one of the world's largest and fastest-growing industries, in promoting sustainable development. The UNEP IE tourism programme, launched in 1991, involves partnerships with international organizations, particularly UNESCO and the World Tourism Organization, and has developed links with tourism industry associations. The programme involves publications, training, technical assistance, networking and the preparation of guidelines on tourism and the environment. Transport is another area highlighted by UNCED and in 1993, UNEP IE devoted an issue of the Industry and the Environment Review to this subject and is evaluating work in this field in order to develop future programmes.

EnTA. In 1993, UNEP IE launched a new programme on Environmental Technology Assessment (EnTA). The goal of EnTA is to encourage the use of technology assessment as a tool to support the development and application of environmentally sound technologies that are consistent with sustainable development. Two specific aims are to encourage cleaner production and to discourage the export and use of technologies that pose potential environmental hazards, especially in developing countries. To guide this effort, an international advisory group has been established, and the first issue of the EnTA Newsletter was issued. Future activities will include work on guidelines on the environmental information that technology importers can and should provide to importing countries.

Sectoral Activities and Information Transfer. UNEP IE sectoral activities provide comprehensive guidance to specific industry sectors to encourage improved environmental performance. Environmental management tools and technologies such as waste and energy audits are addressed. A series of technical guides have been prepared jointly with industry, and over 15 industrial sectors have been covered to date. A technical guide on the environmental impact on oil exploration will be published soon. The response to the guides in other sectors shows the demand for such technical guidance. The Industry and Environment Review is issued quarterly and is distributed to over 10,000 persons worldwide including government, industry and educational organizations.

Consultations with Industry, Government and NGOs. UNEP IE is in continuous consultation with its various partners in carrying out its programmes and responsibilities pursuant to Agenda 21. In response to UNCED, in 1993 UNEP IE held specific consultations on two subjects: voluntary codes of conduct and sustainable consumption patterns. At a meeting with representatives of 30 international and national industry associations, voluntary environmental reporting was extensively discussed as a precondition for implementation of industry's voluntary codes of conduct on environment and sustainable development, such as the Business Charter for Sustainable Development formulated by the International Chamber of Commerce. More than 100 corporate reports on the environment, as well as some first guidelines on environmental reporting, were discussed. UNEP IE also began its contribution to implementing Agenda 21's chapter on changing consumption patterns at another meeting with various stakeholders on this subject. There is a need for more understanding of the relationship between industry and consumers in determining the level and sustainability of consumption patterns and several organizations identified follow-up actions to further identify problems and solutions.

II. SOME GOALS FOR PARTNERSHIPS

Partnerships should enhance compliance with environmental laws and standards. They should be viewed as complementary to environmental control and enforcement programmes and not substitutes for them. Partnerships can furnish technical and managerial assistance, provide forums for consensus building and help to develop institutions within government and industry to improve voluntary compliance with environmental standards. In order to assist governments in building an institutional capability to carry out environmental programmes, UNEP IE published a report in 1992 entitled "From Regulations to Industry Compliance: Building Institutional Capabilities." In April 1994, UNEP IE joined with the environmental agencies of the Netherlands, Mexico and the United States, and the World Wildlife Foundation, to sponsor the Third International Conference on Environmental Enforcement in Oaxaca, Mexico. In November, a regional workshop on environmental compliance and enforcement in countries in Asia with rapidly advancing economies was held in Beijing and Beihai, China.

Partnerships should also encourage cleaner production and other preventive approaches as the strategies of choice for dealing with environmental problems. The traditional approach to environmental protection has been an end-of-pipe solution; a cleaner production or preventive strategy is different, it means not creating pollution in the first place. This can be accomplished by substituting less toxic materials in product designs, recycling within industrial processes or increasing process efficiencies, and extending product lifetimes. Cleaner production usually entails cost savings in terms of reductions in waste treatment and disposal costs, reduced liability for environmental damages, lower raw material costs and process efficiencies.

Partnerships should support public information and environmental education. They can improve the information flow to stakeholders and decision makers and educate the public on the nature of environmental problems and what can be done about them. They may also involve research into the social and economic aspects of environmental protection in order to better understand and design economic incentives and information and education programmes.

TECHNOLOGY TRANSFER FROM THE PERSPECTIVE OF AN ENVIRONMENTAL CONSULTANCY

by
Geoffrey S. Prosser
Managing Director, W.S. Atkins (Environment), Epsom

INTRODUCTION

This paper will begin by making some general comments on capacity building. It will then deal with particular importance of the environmental dimension and performance, and, lastly will refer to some environmental projects as an example of a generalized approach to economic evaluation of expenditure.

I. GENERAL COMMENTS ON CAPACITY-BUILDING

While it is now accepted that technology is vital for economic development, acquiring technology is not an easy process. It entails inputs such as skills, information and services. It also requires more intangible inputs such as interaction between the main actors involved in the process, and a favourable economic, institutional and legal environment, and transfer of technology and managerial skills mechanisms for the purposes of technology partnership.

It is now generally accepted that those countries that have fallen behind, for whatever reason, in the race for industrialization, face a far more difficult task than those fortunate enough to have qualified as an industrialized country in earlier times when competition was less intense. Most developed countries recognize that they must play a part in assisting the less fortunate to develop their economies, which are heavily handicapped by the competition they face from mature and sophisticated industrial nations. Moreover, the constraints imposed by environmental concerns limit what can be done and usually add to the costs. Thus the concept of capacity-building by technology transfer has come into being. Invariably, however, resources are limited and it is just not possible to do everything that may be desirable within the limits of the funding available. It is essential therefore to find some means of deciding what projects and programmes are to be favoured. How is this to be done, and why is the environmental dimension so important?

II. THE ENVIRONMENTAL DIMENSION

It is unfortunate for the newly industrializing countries that the planet simply cannot tolerate the uncontrolled industrial development that was the foundation of wealth in the mature industrialized countries. We now realize that much of the early development of industry and technology was harmful to the environment and improvements have gradually taken place over the years, partly due to economic advantage gained from more efficient processes and partly to legislation. In the United Kingdom, legislation began with the Alkali Act of 1863, and the most recent law has been the comprehensive Environmental Protection Act in 1990, the effects of which are coming into force about now.

A useful approach is to consider and benefit from the experience of developed countries that have already gone through the process of introducing the environmental dimension into the economy. There is no need to reinvent the wheel. Industrialization must now be accompanied by improved environmental performance, and funding is unlikely to be available for projects with harmful environmental effects. This clearly affects industrial processes in the main but the concerns are wider than this. Tourism, for example, has come under scrutiny in recent times because of its harmful effect on the environment in certain parts of the world.

The United Kingdom is pledged to share the benefits of its technology and experience through partnerships with British companies.

III. AN ENVIRONMENTAL IMPROVEMENT PROGRAMME AS A CASE STUDY

Although the programme referred to in the heading concerns environmental issues, the principles could be applied to other areas of technology equally well. The central problem is usually lack of resources to tackle all the problems at once. It is necessary therefore to prioritize the expenditure of resources in such a way as to gain the maximum benefit for any given level of expenditure. In the case of an environmental improvement programme, the benefit could be measured as the effects on human health and preservation of the environment generally. The establishment of short-term sectoral expenditure priorities for environmental improvement is therefore the first question to be tackled.

Atkins' experience is mainly within Europe. Countries in general seldom suffer from widespread pollution problems. It is usually local problems caused by specific industries or the use of low-grade fuel in industrial and domestic situations that are the main concern.

One approach has been to develop local and regional environmental management plans. This may, however, result in marginal improvements in some areas while much greater benefit could be obtained elsewhere for the same level of expenditure. A preferable approach, where resources are limited, is to determine, on a sectoral basis, where affordable projects can offer significant benefits, can be implemented rapidly and can be replicated.

The short-term priorities are to: (a) reduce on-going environmental damage from existing operations, (b) mitigate the effects of past damage, and (c) avoid new sources of damage. While the case for mitigating the effects, or potential effects, of past pollution must not be overlooked, such problems are less widespread and vary significantly in nature and extent from site to site. Avoiding new sources of environmental damage is mainly a problem for the supplier of technology to address. The priority for countries that are industrializing rapidly is therefore to upgrade existing operations and the task is to ensure that limited resources are spent with maximum benefit. While the methodology discussed for this assessment is of a general nature, it should be borne in mind that it can be translated to other areas of investment equally well.

Because, in practice, resources are usually committed at the project level, the cost and benefits of expenditure proposals can be most conveniently discussed in connection with project appraisals. The analysis, therefore, focuses on the project level and is concerned with identifying criteria for deciding how investments should take place so as to allocate resources efficiently. Financial costs and benefits are relatively easy to estimate. More dffficulty arises in assessing the wider implications for resource utilization and the direct and indirect effects on the environment. The basic assumption is that a project is acceptable if the total discounted benefits are greater than the total discounted costs, that is, the net present value (NPV) of the project is positive. We seek to maximize the NPV for any project by assessing the change in NPV with the scale of project expenditure. This is shown on Figure A.1. At any point on this curve, the marginal cost and benefit can be determined. There are, of course, practical difficulties associated with uncertainties about project costs, ignorance of environmental effects, problems in valuing some of the effects and so on, but the methodology does, at least, provide a framework for prioritizing projects.

To take another example concerning quantification of the effects of reducing pollution levels, Figure A.2 illustrates a typical situation when low levels of pollution are tolerable and cause little damage. As levels rise above a threshold level, the extent of the damage caused rises more or less in proportion until no further damage can be caused. We can see that the reduction in pollution level required to obtain a given gain will be the same starting from points A and B, but much greater starting from point C where diminishing returns have set in. There are, of course, many difficulties in practice, particularly with assigning costs to inherently unquantifiable variables such as improvements to human health. Political factors will often intervene as well. However, some kind of methodical approach along these lines will generally provide guidance as to where investment is likely to provide the maximum benefit. It must be remembered that the provision of this methodology and experience in its use is in itself technology transfer.

Figure A.1

Project scale with and without funding constraints

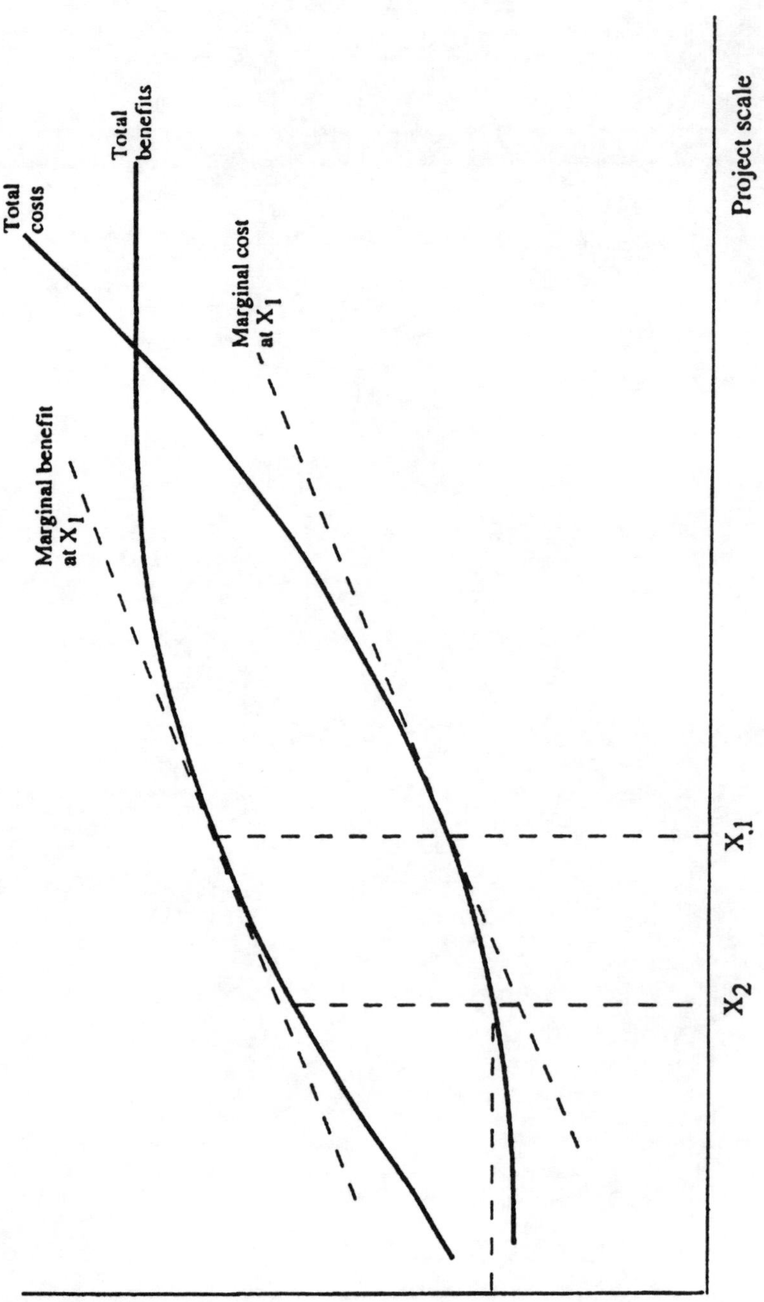

Figure A.2

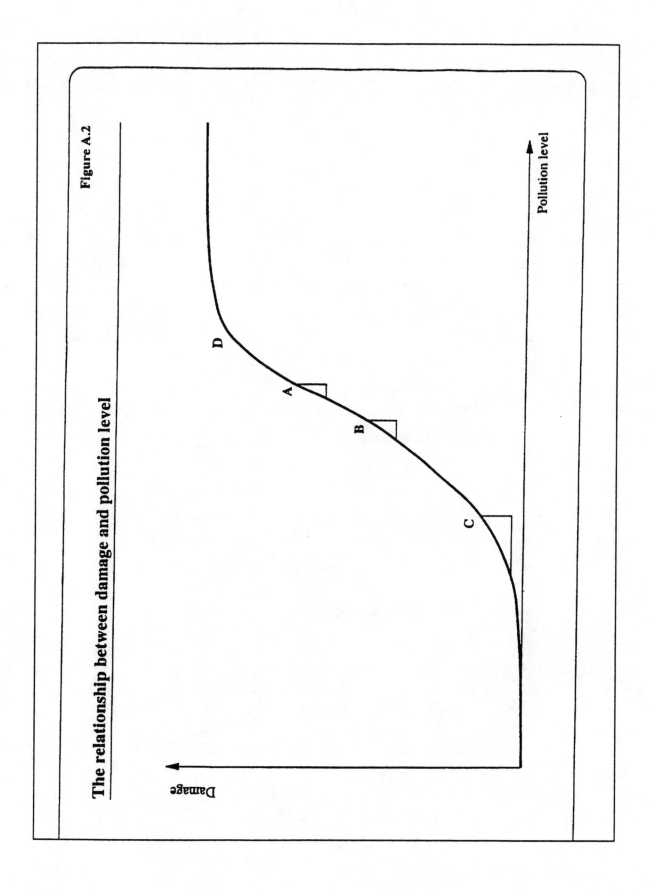

The relationship between damage and pollution level

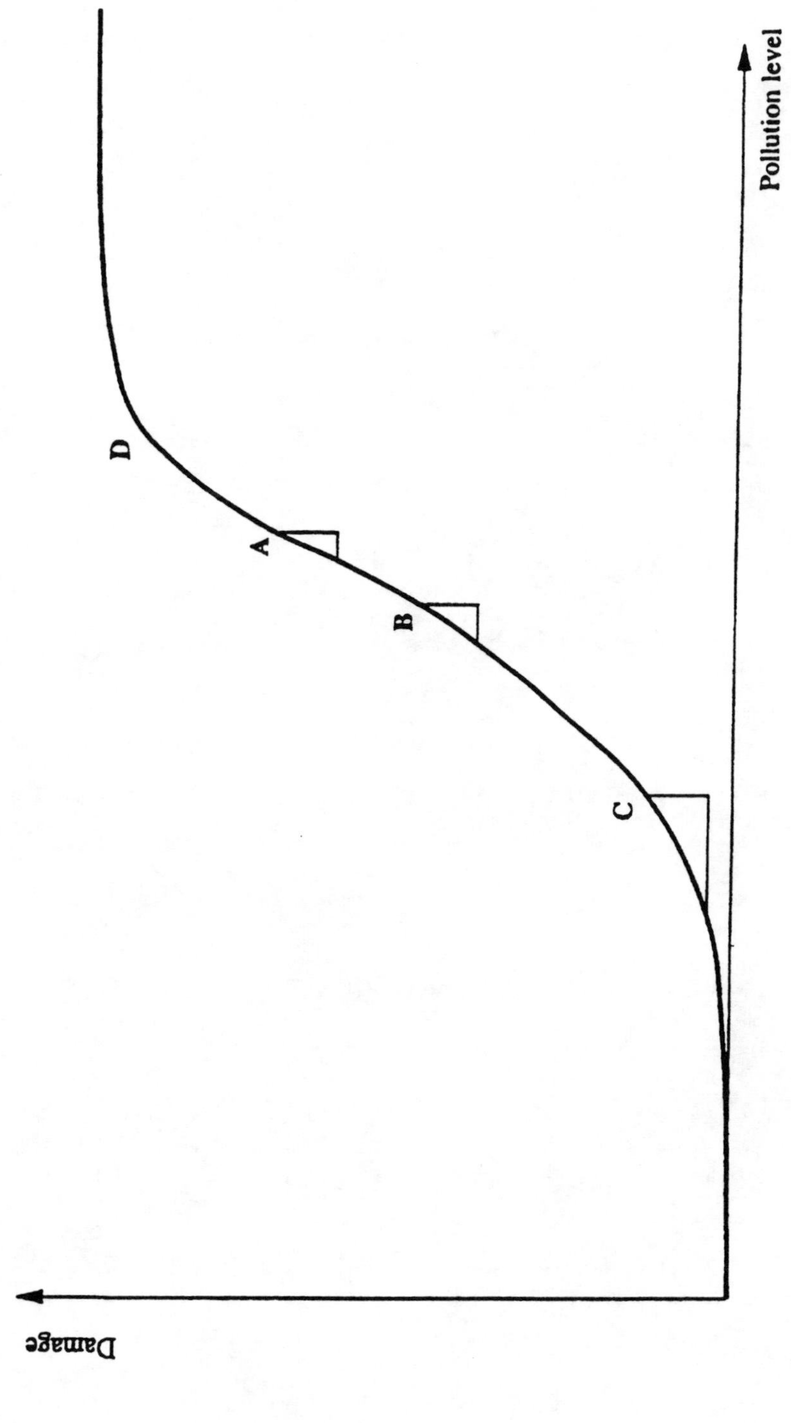

SURVEY OF THE QUALITY AND USEFULNESS OF UNCTAD PUBLICATIONS AND OF THEIR END-USERS

The UNCTAD secretariat, in the context of its programme evaluation activities and in response to intergovernmental requests, is seeking the opinions of end-users in order to have basic data for assessing the quality, usefulness and effectiveness of *inter alia* its research reports and publications. As the success of such an exercise is critically dependent on an adequate rate of response we should appreciate it if you would take time to answer the questions below and submit any other comments that you may have concerning the current document.

1. Title or symbol number of document . . . .

2. When did you receive the document? . . . .

3. How did you receive the document? *(tick one or more boxes)*

Through Permanent Mission to United Nations ( )
From ministry or government office ( )
Directly from UNCTAD secretariat ( )
By participating in an UN/UNCTAD intergovernmental meeting ( )
By participating in an UN/UNCTAD sponsored training course or seminar ( )
From UN bookshop ( )
From university libraries ( )
Own request ( )
UNCTAD initiative ( )
Other (please specify) . . . .
. . . .
. . . .

4. For what main purposes do you use the document? *(tick one or more boxes)*

Policy formulation ( )
Analysis and research ( )
Legislation ( )
Background information ( )
Education and training ( )
Management ( )
Other (please specify) . . . .
. . . .

5. How do you rate the document as regards:

Its usefulness to your work *(tick one box)*

Extremely useful ( ); Very useful ( ); Useful ( ); Marginally useful ( ); Not at all ( ).

Its quality, in terms of the following aspects *(tick one box in each case)*:

	Outstanding	*Excellent*	*Good*	*Adequate*	*Poor*
Presentation and readability	( )	( )	( )	( )	( )
Originality of ideas	( )	( )	( )	( )	( )
Wealth of information	( )	( )	( )	( )	( )
Up-to-date information	( )	( )	( )	( )	( )
Technical accuracy	( )	( )	( )	( )	( )
Quality of analysis, including objectivity	( )	( )	( )	( )	( )
Validity of conclusions	( )	( )	( )	( )	( )
Clarity of recommendations	( )	( )	( )	( )	( )
Comprehensiveness of coverage	( )	( )	( )	( )	( )

6. Other observations *(if any)* . . . .

. . . .

. . . .

. . . .

Finally, we would appreciate it if you could provide the following information about yourself:

Name . . . . Occupation/Functional title . . . .

Address . . . .

Your answers are for internal use and will be kept confidential. Thank you for your co-operation.

Please forward the questionnaire to : PROGRAMME CO-ORDINATION AND EVALUATION UNIT
EXECUTIVE DIRECTION AND MANAGEMENT
UNITED NATIONS CONFERENCE ON TRADE AND DEVELOPMENT
PALAIS DES NATIONS – CH-1211 GENEVA 10